The Refugee Convention at Fifty

A View from Forced Migration Studies

Edited by
Joanne van Selm, Khoti Kamanga,
John Morrison, Aninia Nadig,
Sanja Špoljar-Vržina, and Loes van Willigen

*This publication was made possible
by a grant from the Andrew W. Mellon Foundation*

International Association
for the Study of
Forced Migration

LEXINGTON BOOKS
Lanham • Boulder • New York • Oxford

LEXINGTON BOOKS

Published in the United States of America
by Lexington Books
A Member of the Rowman & Littlefield Publishing Group
4501 Forbes Boulevard, Suite 200, Lanham, Maryland 20706
www.rowmanlittlefield.com

PO Box 317
Oxford
OX2 9RU, UK

British Library Cataloguing in Publication Information Available

Library of Congress Cataloging-in-Publication Data

The Refugee Convention at fifty : a view from forced migration studies /
edited by Joanne van Selm . . . [et al.].
    p. cm.
    Includes bibliographical references.
    ISBN 0-7391-0565-5 (cloth : alk. paper) — ISBN 0-7391-0566-3 (pbk. : alk. paper)
    1. Refugees—Legal status, laws, etc.—Congresses. 2. Convention Relating to the
Status of Refugees (1951)—Congresses. 3. Forced migration—Congresses.
4. Population transfers—Congresses. I. Selm, Joanne van.
    K3230.R45R438 2003
    325'.21'090511—dc21   2002156561

Printed in the United States of America

♾™ The paper used in this publication meets the minimum requirements of
American National Standard for Information Sciences—Permanence of Paper
for Printed Library Materials, ANSI/NISO Z39.48-1992.

Contents

1 Introduction   1
   Joanne van Selm, Khoti Kamanga, John Morrison,
   Aninia Nadig, Sanja Špoljar-Vržina, and Loes van Willigen

2 Opening Keynote Address: The Refugee Convention at Fifty   9
   Gilbert Jaeger

3 Global Solidarity: Report of a Plenary Session   23
   Compiled by Joanne van Selm

4 Regional Approaches to Forced Migration   31
   George Okoth-Obbo, on Africa;
   Courtney Mireille O'Connor, on Latin America;
   Morten Kjaerum, on Europe; and
   Supang Chantavanich, on Asia

5 The Refugee Convention Applied: Moral, Medical, Ethical,
   and Judicial Questions and Limitations   47
   Geoffrey Care, Edvard Hauff, Annemiek Richters, and
   Loes van Willigen

6 Refugees: Whose Term Is It Anyway? *Emic* and *Etic*
   Constructions of "Refugees" in Modern Greek   65
   Eftihia Voutira

7   Insisting on the *Jus Cogens* Nature of *Non-Refoulement*   81
    Jean Allain

8   Turkey, UNHCR, and the 1951 Convention Relating to the
    Status of Refugees: Problems and Prospects of Cooperation   97
    Kemal Kirişçi

9   Whither the Accountability Theory: Second-Class Status
    for Third-Party Refugees as a Threat to International
    Refugee Protection   113
    Jennifer Moore

10 The Geneva Convention and the European Union:
    A Fraught Relationship   129
    Carl Levy

11 Roma Asylum Applications in the United Kingdom:
    "Scroungers" or "Scapegoats"?   145
    Dallal Stevens

12 Human Smuggling and Refugee Protection in the European
    Union: Myths and Realities   161
    Aninia Nadig and John Morrison

13 The Fight against Migrant Smuggling: Migration Containment
    over Refugee Protection   173
    François Crépeau

14 Medical Anthropology in the Service of Forcefully
    Migrating Populations: Current Boundaries, Future Horizons,
    and Possible Delusions   187
    Sanja Špoljar-Vržina

15 The Refugee Convention and Practice in South Asia: A
    Marriage of Inconvenience?   203
    Sumit Sen

16 Closing Keynote Address   219
    Jeff Crisp

Appendix: Convention Relating to the Status of Refugees, Adopted
          on 28 July 1951 by the United Nations Conference of
          Plenipotentiaries on the Status of Refugees and Stateless
          Persons, Convened under General Assembly Resolution
          429(V) of 14 December 1950   231

About the Editors and Contributors   249

1

Introduction

Joanne van Selm, Khoti Kamanga, John Morrison,
Aninia Nadig, Sanja Špoljar-Vržina, and
Loes van Willigen

THE GENESIS OF THIS VOLUME

This book contains a selection of papers presented at the seventh conference organized by the International Association for the Study of Forced Migration (IASFM) in January 2001, in Midrand, South Africa.

The IASFM brings together academics, practitioners, and policymakers working in the field of forced migration. The major activity of the association is the organizing of a conference every two years. The next conference will be held in 2003 in Chiang Mai, Thailand.

In 1999, as preparations for the seventh conference got underway, it was not difficult to come up with a theme for the 2001 meeting. July 28, 2001 marked the fiftieth anniversary of the signing of the Convention Relating to the Status of Refugees. While our conference would be held some six months before that date, it seemed more than appropriate for an association devoted to the study of refugee and related issues to focus its attention on the key legal text that impacts not only the law, but also the politics and sociology of forced migration.

The conference brought together scholars from a wide range of disciplines, nongovernmental organization (NGO) staff, international organization professionals, and national-level policymakers to discuss the impact of this legal document on forced migrants, the states they migrate to and

1

from, and the societies they join and leave behind. Three particular angles were broadly covered as subthemes: the scope for solidarity between states in ensuring that legal and political commitments are upheld; regional approaches to refugee protection and displacement generally; the human and social consequences of forced migration for those covered by, or excluded from, refugee protection.

This book includes the keynote speeches presented to the conference by Gilbert Jaeger and Jeff Crisp. The three plenary sessions covering the subthemes set out above are summarized in three papers. Further, a selection of papers from the conference has been made. Making this selection was difficult: the editorial group sought to ensure a geographic and disciplinary spread, which reflects the participation in the conference, while also bringing a high academic standard to the subject, and innovative thinking to the world of policymaking and implementation in our field.

The chapters selected come from anthropology, law, political science, and sociology. The chapters are written by academics, practitioners, and policymakers. They also reflect the content of the conference, and while the discussion of the papers is not included, they are sure to spark discussion among the readers, which will surely mean they have a life beyond the 2001 conference.

A CHANGING WORLD: A LASTING CONVENTION?

As the seventh biennial conference of the IASFM was being planned, it was clear we lived in a world that treated the refugee question (among others) very differently from the world in the context of which the 1951 Convention Relating to the Status of Refugees was drafted. Five decades saw the Cold War and all the related conflicts, crises, and forced migration heat up and cool down, and ultimately end, with large population flows being part of the whole process. The last of those five decades saw a whole new context to convention protection (or the denial thereof) emerging.

The first four decades of the 1951 convention's existence and implementation saw major events that challenged its foundations and its usefulness. The Hungarian uprising of 1956; the Prague Spring of 1968; and the Polish movements of the early 1980s were all the type of movements and migrations that fit the mold of the east–west convention split, even if the convention was not always used for managing the status of the individuals involved in the large-scale migrations. The Vietnam "boat-people" crisis was not the type of displacement situation that the convention could truly handle: resettlement became the key to ensuring protection for many, if not all, and to solidarity between states in the southeast Asia region and the developed world. Policymakers focused on the post–World War II Europe, who even initially wrote a geographical limitation into the convention, did not envisage forced displacements in Africa, Latin America, Asia, and from those continents to North America and western Europe. In 1968, a Protocol to the convention Relating to the Status of Refugees was drafted and signed to make the convention universally applicable. In addition, regional initiatives including new declarations and conventions, as well as policy changes, meant that refugee protection, while becoming a universally applicable phenomenon, took on regionalized tints and forms. The natural extension of regional approaches in the developing world was perhaps always going to be a regional approach in part of the developed world. The process of European integration meant that ultimately, European Union (EU) member states would move towards a discussion of the common management of migration within the European context—and their efforts in this direction gained momentum in the 1990s, just as the Cold War was ending, and just as a different type of largely ethnically and religiously based conflict was emerging on all continents. As the 1951 convention reached its fiftieth anniversary, it looked likely that at least a small number of states, chiefly in the developed world, and not only in Europe, might seek to move away from this basis that had served both states and refugees remarkably well over the years.

Testing the validity and potential for continued existence of the convention was therefore one aim of this conference.

As the conference was underway, the Office of the United Nations High Commissioner for Refugees (UNHCR) was developing its plans for a year of anniversary commemoration. It would be inappropriate to "celebrate" the convention's longevity: the necessity for an international agreement on how the status of refugees is determined and the place they take in states offering them protection inherently signifies the continuation of displacements, wars, hardships, and suffering. The main commemorative channel in UNHCR was to become the Global Consultations, a three-tracked process leading to the first gathering of the states parties, and their reaffirmation of the fifty-year-old document and its contents. The three tracks dealt with those issues that are generally recognized as core matters, discussed over the years within the Executive Committee framework; those issues which are not dealt with in the convention, but on which there is some emerging sign of consensus and finally, those issues which have emerged over the last few years, but on which there is little or no consensus, and which in general are very controversial. This eighteen-month-long process of commemoration and discussion did indeed lead, almost one year after the IASFM conference, to a reaffirmation of the convention by all the states parties at a meeting in Geneva, Switzerland.

Prior to that December 2001 meeting, the context in which we all, including refugees, live, had again, seemingly changed. The impact of the horrifying events of 11 September 2001 was naturally most immediately felt in New York, in the area around Arlington, Virginia, and Washington, D.C., and in Pittsburgh, Pennsylvania, as well as in the homes and hearts of all those people around the world who lost loved ones in the attacks. Among those people hardest hit by the rapid secondary reactions were refugees. Thousands of refugees had already been selected for resettlement to the United States, but were stranded in countries of first asylum that, as their very selection as candidates for resettlement indicated, were not necessarily safe for them. Many thousands more were impacted by the near shutdown of the resettlement program for almost a year, as only twenty thousand of the seventy thousand ceiling figure for the fiscal year of 2002 had been resettled by the three-quarter mark of that period. Hundreds of thousands of people who had been granted asylum or were waiting for asylum were impacted in countries around the world. If they happened to be Muslim, of Arab origin, or from Afghanistan or Pakistan, for example, there was some change at least in the reactions both of authorities and many members of the general public towards them as individuals going about their now normal lives. For millions of Afghans, the months following September 11 and the ouster of the Taliban brought about the possibility for return—one grasped quickly by more than a million Afghans in Iran and Pakistan, and more hesitantly by the hundreds of thousands who over the previous two decades had sought protection farther away from home. However, even the possibility for return—the idea it could be less dangerous and more feasible to remake a life in Afghanistan—would change the perspective for these refugees.

While September 11 had an impact on refugees' lives and prospects in various ways, it also had an impact on the thinking about the 1951 convention. During its fiftieth year, proof came once again that the drafters had been broad enough in their thinking to create a tool that could even stand the test of unthinkable challenges. As pundits cried out that surely terrorists would seek to enter "enemy" territories as refugees, taking the route left open by the softhearted, defenders of refugee rights were able to point to Article 1F, which clearly excludes from refugee status those guilty of crimes against humanity and acts against the principles of the United Nations (see appendix). The convention, as a written document, contained just the right words. Whether states could implement this provision in a useful way was another matter.

No juridical, politically charged document, with wide ranging social impact could possibly be perfect. It is quite amazing that the 1951 convention has withstood the test of fifty years. Even on the day after its signing, the *Times* opined that:[1]

> From time to time, whenever an international effort is concerted to deal with a refugee problem, the attempt at definition is made; the resultant form of words may serve its immediate purpose, but it is likely to be useless for any other. . . . For victims of future upheavals or future persecutions—displaced perhaps by a seizure of power in a country now relatively free—the convention will have to be extended or a new convention made. . . . [T]he convention, though it does

not go far, will be valuable to the limited extent to which it gives him [the refugee] the freedom to rehabilitate himself.

The convention has gone a long way, looking often like it might be time for a change—not only because the nature of the victimization that causes refugeehood had changed, but also because the way states manipulate even a general definitional term to limit responsibilities has seemed to pose its own challenges. The chapters in this volume demonstrate some of those challenges—all coming prior to the latest of September 11.

THE CHAPTERS IN BRIEF

In opening the conference, Gilbert Jaeger drew on his own fifty years of experience with the field of refugee protection to give an overview of the drafting of the 1951 convention and its bumpy ride to the half-century mark. In many ways, Jaeger's contribution is the substantive introduction both to this volume and to the conference at which it was presented—mapping the field in which the convention remains the core juridical text.

Three plenary sessions, bringing together speakers from policy, practitioner, and academic backgrounds opened each day of the conference, and summaries of those sessions are the contents of chapters 3, 4, and 5. In discussing global solidarity, Peter van Wulffte-Palthe, Irene Khan, and Jens Vedsted-Henson trod on the shaky ground of many decades of controversy. The summary, compiled by Joanne van Selm poses the key questions that arose: What does "global solidarity" mean? Is it the same as burden or responsibility sharing? How is solidarity put into words, and how does it find development in action? From the global level of thinking about refugee protection, the second plenary (and chapter 4 in this volume) turned to the regions. Looking at four major regions, Africa, Latin America, Europe, and southeast Asia, speakers George Okoth-Obbo, Courtney Mirreille O'Connor, Morten Kjaerum, and Supang Chantavanich charted the way in which geographical entities made up of neighboring states have chartered a course bringing some collective form of action to the implementation of the universal convention and its protocol. That action has not always been positive, nor coherent: the nation-state certainly still holds sway in all the regions considered, and in those not considered and for which time was sadly lacking in discussion (especially the Middle East). Chapter 5 in this volume turns to the very interesting discourse between legal and medical practitioners on the ethical and judicial questions and limitations posed by the application of the convention in refugee status determination. Geoffrey Care, Edvard Hauff, Annemiek Richters, and Loes van Willigen explore the minefield of misunderstandings and confusion, which brings not only two disciplines together, but also puts the fate of an individual on the line.

The following ten chapters in this volume represent individual paper presentations made at the conference. The order of these chapters is quite arbitrary, although together they build a picture of both the state of refugee and forced migration studies at the turn of the century, and the situation in which the convention was viewed at the turn of its half-century.

Eftihia Voutira questions the way in which the term "refugee" has been appropriated by various actors who play some type of role in the field of forced migration practice or research. Asking rhetorically "whose term is it anyway," Voutira undertakes an anthropological journey to understand why it is important to understand the different ways in which the term "refugee" is understood and applied in the international context.

Having explored a nonjuridical angle on the question of the definitional clause of the convention (which is much more often undertaken as a legal and political discussion), we turn in this volume to a legal exploration of what has perhaps become the most vital clause of the convention as a whole: the principle and obligation of *non-refoulement* or the nonreturn of individuals to situations in which they may be in danger. Jean Allain argues that after fifty years, legal practice and thinking has brought us so far that the *jus cogens* nature of *non-refoulement* is something we can insist upon.

One aspect to the convention which is little studied, but can have major implications not only for individuals but also for international relations, is the fact that states have the right to limit the application of the contents to those fleeing displacement situations within Europe. Few states maintain this limitation: Turkey is one of the few. Kemal Kirişçi examines the implications of the geographic limitation in Turkey for its cooperation with the global refugee agency, UNHCR. Kirişçi sees ways in which the export of the EU norms for status determination and protection, as well as for border control and other restrictions, will potentially alter the situation in Turkey as it seeks membership of the EU.

Remaining with the European context and the shaping of new norms of decision making and sharing responsibility, Jennifer Moore examines the situation of those refugees whose cases become footballs kicked about between states that find various means and mechanisms to avoid the adjudication of the status of some who arrive in their borders. Focusing on the matter of accountability, and state and nonstate actors, Moore casts light on the high court decisions in the United Kingdom which brought questions of EU integration to light, as individuals claimed not to be able to find adequate safety in France and Germany when their persecution claim was based on the actions of persons not representing the state.

Carl Levy draws our attention more generally to the EU's collective relationship with the 1951 convention. Tracing the history of European integration on asylum issues, and the ways in which the convention has been discussed and manipulated by EU-level actors, he explores the nature of the "fraught" relationship between these fifteen states and the convention that they have all signed and cited with unremitting frequency for five decades.

Dallal Stevens addresses the issue of Roma asylum-seekers in the United Kingdom. The Roma, or gypsies, are a group for whom the protection afforded by the 1951 convention, when they are forced to flee, has proved limited over the last fifty years. Stevens assesses British legal, political, and social reactions to the arrival of groups of asylum-seeking Roma from the Czech and Slovak Republics at the end of the 1990s, and the application of the convention to those people.

Two chapters deal with the issues raised by the smuggling of asylum-seekers. Human or migrant smuggling is a big business that has received increasing attention over the past decade. Aninia Nadig and John Morrison summarize four papers on the governmental approaches to tackling refugee smuggling and trafficking in Europe and how this compares to European commitments to uphold the 1951 convention. The conundrums and contradictions run right to the center of policymaking itself and there are important lessons for researchers as well as practitioners in how to better understand the phenomena. On the evidence available already, many existing approaches to trafficking and smuggling are seen as challenging key aspects of the 1951 convention. François Crépeau looks at the legal issues raised both internationally, through the UN protocols on smuggling and trafficking, and in the Canadian context specifically, by political attempts to contain migration. In his analysis, the migration containment strategies employed all too often have the effect of denying protection to refugees in genuine need.

A chapter on medical anthropology and forcefully migrating populations presents an extension of the discourse of anthropological thought within forced migration studies towards the ongoing synthesis between anthropology and natural sciences. Faced with myriad studies of ethnicity, social suffering, and body-oriented theories (to mention only a few of the most prominent) there needs to be a pause for reflecting upon what a certain population benefits from being a subject of such studies. Špoljar-Vržina questions the ways in which (medical) anthropology has or has not become a useful medium of articulating the problems of forced migrants.

The final chapter drawn from the conference's individual papers brings us back to the legal and political aspects of the convention. This chapter, by Sumit Sen, deals with south Asia with a focus on Tibetan and Bihari refugees in India. The application of the 1951 convention in south Asian states and indeed the turn these states give to refugee protection generally, is something of a "marriage of inconvenience" Sen argues. Many states in the region have not ratified the convention, and the relations with UNHCR have often been problematic. As such, this final chapter in the selection of conference papers brings us full circle in the discussion of the convention.

The concluding chapter presents the final keynote speech of the conference. Jeff Crisp summarizes his views of the four-day meeting, and his
thoughts on the situation of forced migration studies and practice as the convention turned fifty. This succinct and insightful overview formed a resounding and thought-provoking finale to this meeting of scholars, practitioners,
and policymakers. As a chapter, it forms an equally thought-provoking conclusion to this volume.

NOTES

This chapter has been drafted by the editors. The editors would like to thank Khalid
Koser for his assistance in the language editing of some of the chapters in this volume.
   1. *Times*, (31 July 1951), p. 7.

2

Opening Keynote Address: The Refugee Convention at Fifty

Gilbert Jaeger

THE PERIOD 1945–1950

At the beginning of the twenty-first century, the problem of refugees is not always perceived correctly, partly because other population movements submerge it, for example, economic and social migrants, and internally displaced persons. A somewhat similar situation existed in the period 1945–1950 in Europe when major attention was not focused on refugees but on the displaced persons whose number far exceeded them.

Institutions

As regards institutions: the Office of the High Commissioner of the League of Nations continued to exist until 31 December 1946, the formal end of the League. It had practically merged with the Inter-Governmental Committee for Refugees (IGC) created at Evian in 1938 and which operated until 30 June 1951. On 9 November 1943 the forty-four wartime "united nations" had established the United Nations Relief and Rehabilitation Administration (UNRRA) mainly to repatriate some 7,000,000 "displaced persons" from Central Europe and other areas to their home countries. In the spring of 1946 there were still some 850,000 "nonrepatriable" displaced persons. UNRRA ceased to exist on 30 June 1947.

The refugee agency of that period was the International Refugee Organization (IRO) established on 15 December 1946 by Resolution 62(1) of the UN General Assembly. It worked as the Preparatory Commission for the IRO (PCIRO) from July 1947 to August 1948 and fully as the IRO from August 1948 to an ultimate cessation date of 28 February 1952. The major activity of the IRO was the resettlement of 1,049,000 refugees and displaced persons, mainly to the United States, Australia, western Europe, Israel, Canada, and Latin America. A "hard core" of some 150,000 persons still needed to be taken care of after the IRO had ceased its activities.

In Palestine the period 1945–1950 was marked by the emergence of the independent state of Israel on 14 May 1948. With regard to Palestine refugees, the UN General Assembly created on 19 November 1948 the United Nations Relief for Palestine Refugees, and by Resolution 302(IV) of 8 December 1949 the UN Relief and Works Agency for Palestine Refugees in the Near East (UN-RWAPNE, now UNRWA).

It should be noted that no UN agency was specifically in charge of the score of millions of refugees, quasi-refugees, internally and externally displaced persons in China and Korea, not to mention the fifteen million Indians and Pakistani who crossed borders before or after the 1947 partition.

International Legal Instruments

The international legal instruments of the League of Nations period comprised five Arrangements made between 1922 and 1935, concerning Russian, Armenian, and other refugees; the Agreement of 1928–1929 between Belgium and France; the Convention Relating to the International Status of Refugees of 1933; the Convention of 1938 concerning the Status of Refugees coming from Germany, and the related protocol, as well as the Evian Resolution of 14 July 1938.

All of these legal instruments were still valid at the end of the World War II. However, they concerned only specific categories of refugees, defined by origin or nationality. They were not relevant for refugees during or after World War II.

Immediately following World War II, there was a *vacuum juris* regarding travel documents for refugees. At the initiative of the IGC an international conference was held in London and delegates signed the Agreement of 15 October 1946 relating to the issue of a travel document to refugees who are the concern of the Inter-Governmental Committee on Refugees. This London Travel Document was widely resorted to until states could issue the Convention Travel Document.

The legal instrument conceived to deal with the refugees and displaced persons of World War II was the IRO Constitution and particularly its Annex

I. This instrument would not last longer than the IRO, which originally was not supposed to exist beyond 30 June 1950 (although as noted above, it ultimately continued to function until February 1952).

A Study of Statelessness

The international community was well aware of the relative absence of international legal instruments. On 1–2 March 1948 the Economic and Social Council requested the Secretary-General inter alia, and following a resolution of the Commission on Human Rights, "to undertake a study of national legislation and international agreements and conventions relevant to statelessness and to submit recommendations to the Council as to the desirability of concluding a further convention on this subject."

The Commission on Human Rights was concerned with "the legal status of persons who do not enjoy the protection of any government." Hence the title *A Study of Statelessness* and also the emphasis placed in the Study on refugee problems. The study was in fact the birth process of the 1951 convention. It shows very clearly the link between the conventions of 1933 and 1938 and the new convention of 1951. Rather than separate conventions for each category of persons, it recommended a *lex generalis.*

For many years the 1951 convention was referred to in connection with territorial asylum. In this respect it may be noted that the draft convention envisaged in the study would have included provisions concerning:

(a) The following subjects:
  1. Personal status;
  2. Rights formerly acquired;
  3. Property rights;
  10. Taxation;
  11. Military service;
(b) A travel document taking the place of a passport;
(c) The procurement of documents enabling stateless persons to perform various acts of civil and administrative life;
(d) Entry, sojourn, expulsion, and reconduction [*sic*].

Clearly, the problem of asylum was not the major preoccupation of the international community in the period 1948–1949. The convention itself would be more positive.

The General Assembly Resolution 429(V)

In its Resolution 319(XI)B of 11 and 16 August 1950 the Economic and Social Council was inclined to follow the recommendation of the study leading to a convention approved by the General Assembly. Eventually, by its Resolution 429(V) of 14 December 1950 the General Assembly:

1. *Decides* to convene in Geneva a conference of plenipotentiaries to complete the drafting of and to sign both the Convention Relating to the Status of Refugees and the Protocol Relating to the Status of Stateless Persons;
2. *Recommends* to governments participating in the conference to take into consideration the draft convention submitted by the Economic and Social Council and, in particular, the text of the definition of the term "refugee" as set forth in the annex hereto;
3. *Calls upon* the United Nations High Commissioner for Refugees, in accordance with the provisions of the Statute of his Office, to participate in the work of the conference.

JULY 1951–JANUARY 1967

The Conference of Plenipotentiaries

The conference met in Geneva from 2 to 25 July 1951. Including the two observers, the twenty-eight plenipotentiaries represented seventeen States from Europe, six from the Americas, four from Asia, one from Africa, and one from Oceania. Obviously, the decolonization process had not yet started. Four intergovernmental and twenty-nine NGOs also participated in the conference.

The 1951 Convention Relating to the Status of Refugees was opened for signature on 28 July 1951 and would remain open for signature until 31 December 1952.

A Brief Global Analysis of the 1951 Convention

The 1951 convention:

— defines the term "refugee,"
— defines the legal status of the refugee,
— takes into account the interests of contracting states,
— provides for cooperation between contracting states and UNHCR,
— settles the relation between the convention and previous treaties,
— contains the usual final clauses.

Relations between the Convention and UNHCR

The 1951 convention is a treaty between states. It is not, as some less informed people believe, the main legal instrument of UNHCR whose terms of reference is the Statute of UNHCR adopted by the UN General Assembly on

14 December 1950. However, the prominent role of the high commissioner is recognized in the preamble to the convention, while article 35 sets out the modalities of cooperation of contracting states with UNHCR.[1] During the first fifty years this cooperation has gone through ups and downs because of both administrative and political weaknesses in governmental systems and of weaknesses in the UNHCR itself. Much more attention is being given to this cooperation in recent years.

The 1967 Protocol

Article 1 of the 1951 convention deals with the definition of the term "refugee." The "inclusion clauses" are contained in section A.[2] The definition refers to "events occurring before January 1951." As time went by this reference became obsolete and was increasingly less relevant to refugees (or, refugee protection) of the postwar period. Furthermore, article 1, section B, required an optional declaration from contracting states:

(a) "events occurring in Europe before 1 January 1951," or
(b) "events occurring in Europe or elsewhere before 1 January 1951."

With the emergence of refugee situations in other continents, particularly in Africa, the restrictive declarations to "events occurring in Europe" became increasingly embarrassing for coherent international action.

Following a request from his Executive Committee, the high commissioner called, in 1965, a colloquium at Bellagio, which drafted a protocol to the convention. After having been revised and amended the protocol was approved by the Economic and Social Council, taken note of by the General Assembly, signed by the president of the UN General Assembly and the secretary-general on 31 January 1967 and opened to the accession of states.

The 1967 Protocol Relating to the Status of Refugees:

— provides that state parties undertake to apply all articles of the convention (articles 2 to 34), which relate to the status of refugees,
— suppresses, in the definition of the term "refugee," the time limit of 1 January 1951,
— does not provide for a geographic limitation, but enables contracting state that has opted for this limitation when acceding to the convention, to maintain that option,
— is open for accession by all states, whether parties to the convention or not (article V).

This article V has enabled the United States and three other states[3] to accede only to the protocol. The other states parties to the protocol have acceded when they were already contracting states of the convention or have acceded simultaneously to both treaties.

ESSENTIAL ASPECTS OF THE CONVENTION AND PROTOCOL

The Definition of the Term "Refugee"

In front of this assembly of scholars I shall refrain from explaining article 1 of the 1951 convention. Many aspects of the definition will be referred to as a matter of course in the various discussions of the following days. At the end of this introductory speech I may refer to the present adequacy of the definition.

The Status of Refugees

As we have noted, at the preliminary stage of *A Study on Statelessness* the main purpose of the convention was to provide an adequate status for refugees (i.e., for refugees recognized as such and authorized to reside on the territory of the contracting state). In 1951 refugees were given a status distinctly more favorable than the status of aliens in general. This has considerably improved the position of refugees in those contracting states that have effectively implemented the provisions of the convention. However, during the fifty years of the convention the legal status of aliens has considerably improved thanks to new international treaties relating to human rights, to migration, and to their repercussions on municipal law. The difference between the status of aliens and the status of nationals is distinctly smaller now than half a century ago.

Resident refugees have benefited in particular from the recent international treaties on human rights. But their position compared with that of aliens generally is less privileged than before. This lessening is especially obvious in unions of states—we think particularly of the EU—where citizens of one member state enjoy practically the status of nationals in the other states. Be this as it may, even at present the status of refugees provided for by the convention and protocol is a considerable improvement in those contracting states that are less integrated in the system of international human rights treaties.

The Status of Asylum-Seekers

The overwhelming majority of refugees arrive at present in the country where they propose to settle or at least to transit through, as asylum-seekers. The question legitimately arises whether they enjoy any kind of convention status during the provisional asylum period in contracting states, before they are formally recognized as refugees (or before they are compelled to leave the territory of the contracting state).

A number of articles of the convention[4] do not refer to conditions of residence and according to the very nature of the provisions, doctrinal research and the actual practice of states, they are relevant also to asylum-seekers.

In addition to whatever rights may derive from the convention and protocol, asylum-seekers also fall within the purview of the international treaties on human rights. The development of both international and municipal law has improved the legal status of asylum-seekers in their capacity as aliens provided rights are not subject to requirements of residence

Asylum

Through a process of transfer that should be familiar to the scholars in this assembly, the 1951 convention, initially a treaty mainly on the legal position of the refugee, is now considered by many as a treaty on asylum. When a government or an intergovernmental entity takes measures on—or against—asylum, it starts by assuring parliament or the public at large that the convention and protocol will be fully respected.

The 1951 convention is not a treaty on asylum inasmuch as it does not oblige contracting states to grant durable asylum to refugees. However, asylum and the right of asylum are mentioned in recommendation D of the Final Act of the Conference of Plenipotentiaries and in the preamble to the convention. Furthermore, the status of refugees is itself largely a description of the contents of durable asylum.

While admission to the territory of states is also mentioned in article 11 on refugee seamen, the main provisions on admission to the territory and, therefore, on the granting of asylum are contained in articles 31 and 33.

While many articles refer to "refugees lawfully in their territory," article 31 concerns "refugees unlawfully in the country of refuge." There is no doubt that by virtue of article 31 the contacting state agrees to grant temporary or provisional asylum to the refugee who satisfies the conditions spelled out in the article. The possibility of durable asylum is mentioned in article 31.2.

State practice is another matter. While a number of states apply article 31 in a fair manner, in other contracting states the interpretation of the provisions is too narrow and results too often in unacceptable conditions of detention.

In connection with asylum the provisions most referred to are certainly those of article 33: "Prohibition of expulsion or return (*'refoulement'*)." It should be mentioned that this negative approach to asylum, the prohibition of return, is from a doctrinal point of view effectively considered as a modality of asylum.

For many years it was an open question whether the prohibition of *re-foulement* included the refusal to admit a refugee at the border of the requested state. Taking into account more recent international legal instruments, the practice of a number of contracting states and doctrinal research, it is now generally accepted that article 33.1 prohibits *refoulement* also at the border. It is also contended that the principle of *non-refoulement* belongs to *jus cogens*. However, there are still too many infringements of the principle, not only by states and parties to the convention and protocol but also by contracting states.

Another danger has appeared in recent years—the safe country principle. This "principle" is nothing more than a method devised by industrialized states to diminish the number of asylum-seekers arriving at their borders. It infringes the provision on nondiscrimination of article 3 of the convention,[5] one of the few articles to which contracting states may not make reservations, and should, therefore, be rejected outright. Meanwhile, the safe country principle is applied by a number of contracting states and may lead—directly or indirectly—to *refoulement*.

Fully aware of dangers and limitations, I continue to adhere to the interpretation that through the combined effect of articles 31 and 33 the convention and protocol provide at least provisional asylum to the refugee or asylum-seeker. The grant of durable asylum should be assumed if the asylum-seeker is formally determined to be a refugee.

Lacunae in the Convention and Protocol

While later developments of human rights are naturally not reflected in the convention, some contracting states have been embarrassed over the years by two lacunae concerning the reception of asylum-seekers and the determination of refugee status. The first one may be explained by the fact that many states participating in the Conference of Plenipotentiaries already had considerable experience with the reception of asylum-seekers, sometimes in large numbers, and that reception used to be essentially a material process with no or only marginal legal aspects. In fact, the reception of asylum-seekers has become a problem in industrialized countries only since the late 1970s due to their increasing numbers and to delays in the determination process. In the meantime the systems of public relief had expanded and become more costly. Also, more generally, the requirements regarding accommodation and other reception facilities had become more demanding.

Individual states have developed their reception facilities. But at a later stage, to discourage asylum-seekers, they have negatively adapted their municipal laws that have often become unwieldy. On occasion the UNHCR Executive Committee has adopted conclusions on the matter. The best example is conclusion no. 22(XXXII), protection of asylum-seekers in situations of large-scale influx and particularly section II.B, treatment of asylum-seekers who have been temporarily admitted to a country pending arrangements for a durable solution.

I do not propose to expand on reception facilities, which is a subject in its own right. It has very different aspects, in industrialized countries, in the rural parts of Africa, or on the shores of the South China Sea. Conclusion no. 22(XXXII) referred to the latter region.

A more important lacuna of the 1951 convention is that it does not provide contracting states with any guidance on the determination of refugee status. The explanation is again of a historical nature. In the League of Nations period satisfactory solutions for the determination of refugee status had been found in the European states with a significant refugee population through cooperation between the government and refugee voluntary societies, sometimes with the support of the League of Nations. The determination of refugee status was in those days a much simpler process. Many of the governmental delegates to the 1951 Conference of Plenipotentiaries had worked in the League of Nations period and did not feel the need to include provisions on this matter in the convention.

Here again the conclusions on international protection adopted by the Executive Committee showed their usefulness. Reference should be made to conclusions no. 8(XXVIII), 28(XXXIII), and 30(XXXIV). At its twenty-eighth session the Executive Committee requested the Office of the High Commissioner "to consider the possibility of issuing—for the guidance of governments—a handbook relating to procedures and criteria for determining refugee status." The handbook on procedures and criteria for determining refugee status under the 1951 convention and the 1967 Protocol Relating to the Status of Refugees was published in September 1979 and has been used worldwide ever since.

THE PERIOD 1967–2001

Geographical Extension of the Convention and Protocol

While the convention and protocol have over the years been the objects of considerable criticism, the number of states acceding to these instruments has continued to increase. As of 22 November 2000 the number of states and parties to the convention and protocol had reached 140. Only four smaller states were party only to the convention and, therefore would not apply the protocol.

The 140 included the majority of significant states, irrespective of political inclination. Eventually, neither India nor Pakistan are parties to the convention and protocol. Nevertheless, the convention and protocol may legitimately be considered instruments of universal purport.

Regional Instruments

To these universal instruments have been added during the fifty years under review a few treaties and other instruments of a regional nature. The main one is certainly the OAU Convention Governing the Specific Aspects of Refugee Problems in Africa, concluded on 10 September 1969 in Addis Ababa, which has been conceived as "the effective regional complement in Africa of the 1951 United Nations Convention on the Status of Refugees." The provision mostly referred to, in Europe and other regions outside Africa, is the complementary definition of the term refugee in article 1.2. Mention should also be made of the very positive approach to asylum in article II.

Another significant regional instrument is the Cartagena Declaration on Refugees adopted on 22 November 1984 in Cartagena de Indias by the colloquium on the international protection of refugees in Central America, Mexico, and Panama. The Cartagena declaration recommends "for use in the region" a complementary "definition or concept of a refugee," which is similar to the complementary definition of the OAU convention.

But the most important regional development is undoubtedly the interest taken in refugee problems from the 1980s by the Commission of the European Communities and later by the EU. I shall not list here the various resolutions, conclusions, proposals, decisions, and other documents or (soft law) instruments adopted or to be adopted within the framework of the Treaty on the European Union or the Treaty of Amsterdam. While reference is made in many, if not all, EU documents to the convention and protocol, this European policy of harmonization is not necessarily a continuation of the protection policy developed in the initial years of the 1951 convention. The European policy includes the safe country principle to which we objected earlier. Those who adhere to traditional principles are naturally diffident. The policy of the EU is a different approach that, if added to the new so-called proactive protection recommended and sometimes practiced by UNHCR, provides new (better?) perspectives for refugee protection in future years and may require corresponding legal instruments that would differ from the convention and protocol.

The Asylum Crisis

The asylum crisis developed initially in western Europe in the early 1980s but spread in later years to nonindustrialized countries, especially in Africa and Asia. The asylum crisis is fundamentally a numerical problem compounded by migration pressure. Most states can manage a limited number of asylum-seekers of whatever origin or legitimacy. Beyond the manageable number all states adopt negative attitudes and resort to negative measures.

But it is not only numbers that are significant. In some areas the "ethnic" element is the main dissuading factor. In Iran and Pakistan millions of ethnically related Afghan refugees were received after 1979 while at the same time very small groups of Indo-Chinese refugees were rejected onto the high seas in neighboring states, largely for ethnic reasons. Even in the industrialized countries of western Europe the ethnic factor plays a role in the rejection process.

The negative attitudes adopted and negative measures taken by states are directly related to the implementation of the convention and protocol. This is obvious when the definition in article 1 is interpreted in a narrow, even illegitimate manner. I refer to the narrow interpretation of the reasons of persecution (race, religion, etc.) and to the position that the agent of persecution must be a state authority. The implementation of article 31 may be distorted by the illicit theory of "safe countries" or by illegitimate and excessive practice of detention, as we already mentioned. And the criminal act of *refoulement* (e.g., the rejection of refugee ships onto the high seas), is the most obvious infringement of the convention and protocol or, as the case may be, of a *jus cogens* principle.

The asylum crisis is by no means a thing of the past. In recent years it has reached a climax in central and west Africa. More recently it has materialized with a new—but admittedly less tragic—intensity in western Europe, which is at present the target of emigrants (including a few refugees) from various Commonwealth of Independent States (CIS) republics. As long as states are unable to deal with the asylum crisis, it will remain a real threat to the fair implementation of the convention and protocol.

I do not intend to propose remedies to the asylum crisis. This should be a separate subject.

Executive Committee Conclusions

Contrary to human rights treaties concluded in the 1960s and later years, there is no supervisory committee for the 1951 convention or the 1967 protocol. The duty of supervising the application of the provisions of this convention is vested, by article 35, in the high commissioner. There have been several attempts by UNHCR to systematize this supervision but they have not really materialized. There is, however, the Executive Committee of the High Commissioner's Program, the successor of the Advisory Committee mentioned in paragraph 4 of the UNHCR statute and even earlier, of the Advisory Commission in the League of Nations period. The Executive Committee performs executive duties relating to the assistance programs of UNHCR but has retained advisory functions in matters of protection.

I have mentioned twice already the very useful complementary role of the conclusions on the international protection of refugees. These conclusions are approved by the Executive Committee on the basis of drafts submitted by the Subcommittee of the Whole on International Protection with the active participation of the UNHCR Division of Protection. As a legal instrument, a soft law instrument, the conclusions are therefore available to contracting states but also to the high commissioner, to fill lacunae in the convention and protocol and to update the manner in which the convention and protocol may be implemented, without for that matter formally amending the convention.

THE PRESENT ADEQUACY OF THE CONVENTION AND PROTOCOL

During the last twenty or thirty years one has heard frequently in official and less official fora and circles that the convention and protocol are treaties of the past, that they belong to the Cold War period, that their definition does not apply to new categories of refugees such as those fleeing from general violence, from civil war, and from ecological disasters. Those espousing this view say a new convention is needed.

A few misunderstandings must be pointed out. In the period 1948–1951 when the convention was conceived, drafted, and finally concluded, there were other significant population movements, particularly considerable numbers of economic and social migrants. However, the 1951 convention was concluded only and solely on behalf of people fearing persecution.

Even in 1951, the restrictive nature of the definition was obvious. This explains inter alia recommendation IV.E of the final act. Several European states have resorted to some kind of alternative status: B status, asylee, and so on. African states have adopted a complementary definition in the OAU convention and a similar complementary definition has been adopted in the declaration of Cartagena.

Some persons or organizations—particularly NGOs concerned with human rights—would like a wider definition that would compel states to admit categories that they are not willing to admit. Many states, however, do not wish a wider universal definition and would not ratify a treaty or protocol containing such a definition. The restrictive policy of the EU shows the prevailing trend.

However, no door is closed forever. UNHCR has recently launched global consultations that may open up new perspectives.[6]

Meanwhile, we may conclude that after fifty years the convention and protocol remain valid instruments for the protection of refugees who fear persecution. The number of contracting states is greater than ever before.

NOTES

1. For the text of the articles, see the convention in the annex.

2. Ibid.

3. Cape Verde, Ukraine, and Venezuela. (Editor's Note: Ukraine signed in April 2002, at the time of the presentation it was the United States and two other states that were party only to the Protocol).

4. Articles 2, 3, 4, 7.1, 8, 9, 11, 16.1, 31, and 33.

5. See text in the annex.

6. Global Consultations documentation and information concerning the outcomes, including the reaffirmation of the convention can be found at www. unhcr.ch/cgi-bin/texis/vtx/global-consultations

3

Global Solidarity: Report of a Plenary Session

Compiled by Joanne van Selm

Perhaps the first and key question to be raised when considering the subject of "global solidarity" with regard to refugee protection is what exactly does it mean? In the case of this particular topic, that question is likely to remain either unanswered, or with competing answers. Meanwhile, whether any of the visions responding to the question of the meaning of the concept are achievable, or even in all cases desirable, adds another layer to discussion. This chapter sets out some thoughts on the vocabulary of "solidarity," before looking at how words are put into action—or how they might be put into action, and then turning to a discussion of the advantages and disadvantages of regional approaches if one speaks indeed of global solidarity. The visions presented are multiple: the speakers contributing to the conference's plenary session on this subject came from academia, government, and international organizations. The intent of the session was to probe the issue from those three angles, and so at least three voices emerge throughout this chapter.

Global solidarity could be said to be both the expression of an ideal in terms of refugee protection, and simply the latest trend in the vocabulary concerning the idea that all states should work together in the refugee protection regime. Ideally, we would be better off in a world with no wars, no persecution, no refugees, and as a result of these absences, no convention and no need for solidarity. However, we are not in such a position. Rather, we have a system of states which both produces refugees and seeks to protect them, and which both sets up each state as sovereign in managing its affairs, and as a player in international relations. In this system there is likely to be a call to supportive action between states for people. The question is where the call comes from and how it is framed.

Often cast as a discussion about the protection of refugees, solidarity could in fact be a matter of what states owe to their fellow states in the international system. Any benefit that the refugee may accrue from such a "deal" is more indirect in nature. Furthermore, while the discussion about solidarity is cast as being one about protection, it could be recast as a discussion about migration more broadly. Hence, the sections of this chapter will address the wider migration chain as well as the refugee protection issue.

PUTTING SOLIDARITY INTO WORDS

As trends in vocabulary go, solidarity is the latest (or making a revival) following from the consecutive use of the terms "burden sharing" and "responsibility sharing." To some the terms are interchangeable—to others they convey clearly distinct meanings. The term "burden sharing" implies, in a negative regard, that refugees are a burden, a drain, on the receiving state. The form the "burden" or load takes differs—one state may see the presence of refugees as costly in financial terms, another might see their presence as problematic in societal terms. The trend over the past decade has been to reconceptualize burden sharing as responsibility sharing. The term burden has clearly negative connotations. As the then high commissioner, Madame Ogata called for RESPECT as the central theme to the commemoration of the fiftieth anniversary of the 1951 convention as the year marking the event got underway, "burden" would hardly be an appropriate term. Use of the word "responsibility" returns thoughts and discussion back to the central subject of the protection of refugees: the responsibility of states to protect individuals, including those who do not enjoy the protection of their state of origin. Burden also leads us to think not only of sharing, but of shifting: any state that has signed and ratified the 1951 convention cannot shift its responsibilities—it can only share them while living up to them.

Astri Suhrke has set out to explain why burden sharing (as she calls it) has worked in some cases historically, but not in others.[1] It could be argued that in no case has a sense of global solidarity brought states to a position from which they share either the burden or responsibility of refugee protection. At best, solidarity could be imputed to the regional level of sharing refugee protection obligations. However, national interest has generally played the strongest role. So in considering the choice of vocabulary, the question of interest is central. If we distinguish burden sharing (as something between developed and developing states) from responsibility sharing (as something between states in a given region who all acknowledge that they do have a responsibility to protect refugees) then those examples of responsibility sharing that have worked are chiefly those where strong states have been involved. The harmonization of reception standards in the EU is underway in order to stop refugees from shifting around at will, and indeed it could be a basis to sharing the burden of sorts.

Another key question that needs to be asked when considering the trends in vocabulary and indeed discussion of this subject is that of why solidarity or sharing of either the burden or responsibility of protection has become a cutting edge debate in the world of refugee protection. Why the prominence today if the scale of refugee movements has not really changed enormously through the 1980s and 1990s? At least two reasons can be suggested. Firstly, the strategic value of asylum has been reduced with the end of the Cold War. The granting of asylum is no longer a relatively pure foreign policy issue— protecting the enemies of one's enemy. Thus, there are no clear-cut decisions to protect people fleeing a particular regime, and the mass of the world's refugees has become a blurred mass, although a need to pick and choose is still perceived. Secondly, the issue of burden sharing has become as much a natural issue for the rich as for the poor. Where less developed states are in a position of asking the richer states to assist them, richer states are, due to domestic political concerns, increasingly in a position of needing to ask developing states to actually shelter the refugees: there is an almost quid pro quo sense to the discussions—and may be the emergence of a common interest in bargaining about the location of protection. Although there are different approaches to the subject in different regions, the answers to the demands of various states could be met. Where global solidarity is concerned at least, the European and other developed states shy away from the protection of high numbers of refugees. The states of the south are often more concerned about the burden in terms of the financial and environmental impact of protection, although when population balances may shift, numbers do become an issue there too, and solidarity in the form of resettlement is sought. Meanwhile, within Europe, the burden of refugee protection is quantified in terms of the presence of certain numbers of refugees and there is a search for an even distribution of refugees: a regional form of resettlement.

PUTTING SOLIDARITY INTO ACTION

In spite of worldwide discussions on the subject, interchangeably, of burden sharing, responsibility sharing, and solidarity, the unevenness in distribution of responsibilities, costs, and indeed the burden on protection has, if anything, become more pronounced since World War II. Those states which one could argue *should* shoulder more of the costs of refugee protection (e.g., Europe) face their own forms of refugee problems, as populations appear to resent the presence of refugees and asylum-seekers in numbers few developing countries would find significant.

One disturbing, if sometimes understandable, trend among states is to make the fulfillment of their international obligation to guarantee the protection of *non-refoulement* to refugees dependent on the receipt of burden sharing from other states. This has been seen in a range of cases, from Indochina to Kosovo: cases that might also be defined as those which have seen the most successful burden-sharing programs. As such, while being the state recipient of the benefits of solidarity *should not* be a prerequisite to realizing protection obligations, in reality it often is: and for that reason, attention must be paid to solidarity as an element of the broader protection strategy worldwide—and seen as something other than solidarity, pure and simple.

There have been a number of proposals regarding solidarity, from states, international organizations, and people engaged in thinking about refugee protection. In the major "reformulation" project run by Professor James Hathaway, burden sharing formed a core element.[2] In summary, the burden-sharing model in the context of that project was a very well-managed exchange of resources and openings in terms of places for refugees to remain in safety for the duration of the risk to them in their country of origin. This raises the question of whether only a flexible, ad hoc model of solidarity can be effective, such as those models that have been put into practice in the real world, or whether it is possible to create a systematic model of formalized burden sharing. The academic model proposed in that reformulation project might be theoretically attractive but is it also practicable? In thinking about the type of model that might be workable, one must always bear in mind that responsibility in connection with the obligation to protect refugees takes different forms and exists on different levels. If a formal system operates on different levels (with different requirements for different states), some perceive a danger inherent in regional burden sharing—which could create regional blocks and prevent global solidarity. However, others question whether there is necessarily a contradiction between regional commitments and global solidarity?

While some see solidarity as a phenomenon unique to refugee protection (perhaps because there is somehow a notion of refugees as passive actors in the "game" which determines their active futures?) others see it as a wider approach. At its broadest, solidarity could involve, these policy thinkers suggest, a chain approach: the development of an integrated policy that takes into account every step of migration, from the moment a migrant leaves his or her home to the moment he or she is either integrated into a new community or returns. Such a chain, involving both voluntary and forced migration can only operate when applied in a framework of solidarity: when states, and even businesses and civil society share responsibility. This holds true, governmental figures suggest, not only in the field of movement of persons (easier entrance versus easier return, internal aid versus reception in region of origin, etc.), but also in the interaction of migration with, for instance, security issues, economic issues, and development cooperation (drugs, terrorism, trade agreements, etc.)

WHERE AND HOW DOES SOLIDARITY FIT?

Many in government feel that, on the global level, solidarity is simply not operational, in spite of references to this phenomenon and its desirability in a range of international instruments and documents (from the 1951 convention, through the Declaration on Territorial Asylum to a range of Exective Committee [EXCOM] conclusions over the last decades and UNHCR's papers presented to EXCOM meetings). We need rather to look to the subglobal level (i.e., to the regional level), which is where states have more of a tendency to appreciate that they have shared interests and mutual responsibilities.

In the region where solidarity has been most broadly discussed, the EU, there is not even the start of an agreement on the modalities of regional solidarity. The discussions have been going on since the conflicts in and refugee movements from former Yugoslavia and Bosnia, in particular. There have been a wide range of proposals, and some mechanisms such as the distribution of financial resources linked to protection via the European Refugee Fund and the notion of "double voluntarism" in the 2001 Temporary Protection Directive. However, in considering quotas for Kosovar evacuees in 1999, some states even started to include the costs of participating in the NATO bombings in Kosovo, for example, and their past protection of Bosnians, as part of their share of their burden-sharing contribution.[3] While the Dublin Convention meant EU states started out from a distribution mechanism and then worked towards harmonization of their policies, in effect, burden sharing has to be the last piece of the puzzle of a common approach to asylum. The member states must first work on a harmonized asylum system, then on reception conditions, and finally on burden sharing. This should, by then, not really be an issue for the EU member states, but rather an issue of discussion between them and their neighbors—focusing, in other words, on the countries on their borders that would end up, in fact, shouldering more of the burden than the EU states. The need for burden sharing in the EU is dead until the point at which a single asylum system has been established.

Also in the area of broader solidarity, spanning the whole field of migration, closer regional cooperation and coordination could form a first step in the development of a worldwide network for migration management. However, the EU's only semblance of a common policy in this area, as in the area of asylum-seeking immigration, is in seeking to prevent immigrants from arriving in their countries. Asylum-seekers have the benefit, if they prove to be genuine refugees, of being people who Europeans traditionally wish to assist and can tolerate. Economic immigrants are generally, however, perceived as mouths to feed—as drains on the welfare purse. These categories have started to blur, to the detriment of asylum-seekers. However, certain developments may mean that a more rational approach can be taken when both asylum and economic migration are considered as parts of a wider spectrum. The EU member states could find a means of coordinating and cooperating to manage both issues if one considers that the challenge to them is a geographically split one: States of northern Europe generally perceive immigration as an asylum-related problem, and states of southern Europe generally see illegal immigration as their biggest problem. There is increasing awareness of the fact that differences in policies between member states are one source of the problem in both cases, and that common discussion of definitions and modes of action are necessary. A number of studies (albeit disputed studies) have demonstrated that the EU states in fact will need immigration if they are to sustain growth levels and be prosperous enough to finance commitments made through existing welfare schemes related to pensions, healthcare, and other social benefits. If the EU member states are to deal both with the immigration supply (which they actually need) and with the demand they will place on immigrants, then they will need a coordinated and comprehensive system, which should benefit themselves, immigrants, and refugees.

In addressing these issues, the EU member states have, in the 1997 Treaty of Amsterdam, set the goal of establishing a common EU asylum and migration policy by 2004. By then, member states will have to comply with common minimum standards in their asylum policies and with harmonized immigration rules on entry and residence. In 1998 member states adopted a detailed timetable for the implementation of the treaty called the Vienna Action Plan.

THOUGHTS IN CONCLUSION

It might be said that there has been a paradigm shift. The understanding of the term solidarity has been reduced to the issues of money and numbers. This reduction moves the issue away from any idealist understanding of interstate solidarity. It also, in practical terms, moves the issue into the development debate. Discussions of development policy are, as discussions on refugee protection seem to be, also in crisis, with many states not meeting their targets for development aid. If the argument on the reduction of solidarity to money and numbers is followed through, it is an approach which has to be covered by development budgets—and cannot be considered separately as an "extra." One proposal raised in the plenary session of the conference was the establishment of a solidarity fund—suggested as something that should not be linked to the return of refugees in any way.

Contributions to UNHCR and money spent on aid might also be seen as forms of solidarity. However, these financial determinations can be dangerous as well as useful: European states pay much more money for reception in the EU than on their contributions to the UNHCR budget. While their contributions to UNHCR could (and one might argue should) rise, the argument that money would be better spent on reception in the region than on reception in the EU brings the solidarity discussion back to one of "burden shifting." Another approach to this question would be to look at what makes reception practices in Europe so expensive (e.g., the building of reception centers and the issuance of vouchers in place of cash, as well as the prevention on asylum-seekers to enter the labor market). States in the west sometimes seem to be adopting increasingly expensive approaches—and perhaps reducing those costs should in fact be part of the search for a solution. Also, the burden to be shared has been exacerbated by measures designed to deny refugees the ability to be self-sustaining.

Many thinkers see a danger in putting the idea of solidarity into the form of an obligation between states. Such an obligation may, for example, harden the north-south divide, and create a sense of conditionality, making solidarity a prerequisite for protection, whereas there should be respect for the fact that protection of refugees is independent of burden-sharing concerns. The whole basis for legal protection would be severely undermined if its existing basis is questioned and challenged without new developments in terms of solidarity-conscious obligations.

Finally, the need to develop arguments in public debate for solidarity, and for accepting part of the responsibility in rich countries, was expressed. If solidarity has become a cutting-edge issue due in large part to its reduction to a discussion of money and numbers then it is surprising that there is, at present, no strong public pressure on this subject. Civil society clearly has not mobilized public opinion around the world to think beyond the parameters of prevention and deterrence that states are setting. More awareness of the impact of abstract discussions about burden sharing on the shifting of the burden and absence of responsibility recognition among states needs to be instilled. Global solidarity, from that perspective is not only about relations between states, or the obligations of state structures towards individuals, but also a matter of human solidarity: and expressions of support from those fortunate enough not to be refugees, to those forced to flee their homelands.

NOTES

Joanne van Selm has prepared this chapter on the basis of notes taken from the plenary session of the conference on this theme. The plenary speakers were Jens Vedsted-Henson (Aarhus University, Denmark); Peter van Wulfften Palthe (Dutch Ministry of Foreign Affairs), and Irene Khan, (then UNHCR). Conference rapporteur Ralph Wilde took the notes, and I am grateful to him for sharing them with me. Comments from the discussion are incorporated. While the contents of the chapter do not reflect the individual view of any single participant or of the author, the responsibility for the final presentation of the contents of the presentations and discussion in the chapter, including any errors, lie with the author.

1. Suhrke, Astri, "Burden Sharing during Refugee Emergencies: The Logic of Collective versus National Action," *Journal of Refugee Studies* 11, no. 4 (1998).

2. James C. Hathaway, ed., *Reconceiving International Refugee Law*, (Dordrecht: Martinus Nijhoff, 1999).

3. See Joanne van Selm, *Kosovo's Refugees in the European Union* (London: Pinter, 2000).

4

Regional Approaches to Forced Migration

George Okoth-Obbo, on Africa; Courtney Mireille O'Connor, on Latin America; Morten Kjaerum, on Europe; and Supang Chantavanich, on Asia

Over the five decades of the 1951 convention's impact on refugee protection, the universal convention has become the basis on which a number of regional initiatives have been built. Those initiatives have sometimes been meant to make application of the convention more meaningful in a regional context: it was, after all, originally drafted for the specific "problem" of Europe's refugees. In other regions, the subject of refugee protection has come onto the political agenda largely as a result of factors other than pure concerns about displacement. In this plenary session the organizers sought to address the regional developments in the world's major regions—or indeed to cast light on the absence of such developments. As such, the regions of Africa, Latin America, Europe, and Asia were selected for presentation. Each experiences refugee problems in different, and to an extent regionally specific, ways. Africa and Latin America have drafted regional supplements to the convention, each recognizing victims of war and conflict as refugees. These have their flaws in the current reality, but may also offer broader means for applying protection when it is recognized that there is a protection need that is not covered by the 1951 convention—both in those two regions and more widely. The EU is developing harmonized policies on refugee protection, in the context both of restrictions and of human rights agreements, and exporting these beyond its borders as other European states seek access to EU benefits beyond the migration discourse. In Asia, there has

31

been little attempt to regionalize refugee protection—many states have not even signed the convention or protocol.

AFRICA

If 1969 OAU convention is analyzed in relation to refugee protection both as a global problem and a regional phenomenon, it is seen to have its origins in globalizing motives.[1] The will existed to solidify the international refugee regime and apply the universal 1951 convention and 1967 protocol in the regional context. The OAU convention was not essentially the product, as is often claimed, of dissatisfaction among African states with the *legal inadequacy* of the 1951 convention and particularly its definition of a refugee. It was not elaborated to affect an African reform of, or rebellion against, the 1951 convention regime. In effect, it was the first effort to globalize the application of an instrument (the 1951 convention) that, although otherwise notionally "international," in reality was limited in application to Europe.

The OAU convention asserts the primacy of the international regime within Africa. It certainly does elaborate novel legal features geared to the specific needs and realities of the African continent. In this context, one of its most important overall values was to underpin asylum, refugee policy and practice in Africa in legal and humanitarian terms in the face of the destabilization and subversion already evident at that time in an exilic context. By creating a legally defined structure, coherence and predictability were brought to state actions and refugee behavior in the context of asylum and refugee protection.

However, even as it established Africa-specific catalogues, the 1969 OAU convention both affirmed and enhanced the international regime. Its "expanded definition" of a refugee is undoubtedly the OAU Convention's most celebrated feature. The provision was historically novel; has influenced developments in other regions (for instance the Cartagena declaration) and had persuasive force even in those regions where the convention otherwise does not apply. The convention's provisions on burden sharing and solidarity, the prohibition of *refoulement* and voluntary repatriation, were at the same time novel and representative of significant advances in both regional and global refugee law. Burden sharing, mentioned only briefly in the preamble to the 1951 convention is a central platform for the regime established by the OAU convention.

With regard to asylum, the obligations not to deny entry, to receive and to secure settlement of refugees are specifically mandated. These have since been reinforced by even more forthright provisions on the "right" to seek asylum spelled out in the African Charter on Human and Peoples' Rights. In contrast with the prohibition of *refoulement* in the 1951 convention, which contains exceptions, the OAU's equivalent provision contains an absolute prohibition. It also contains the first elaboration and codification in treaty terms of the principles and standards for the voluntary repatriation of refugees. Key among these is the voluntary decision of the refugee to return; safety, security, and full rights upon return; and the duty of the country of origin to cooperate in facilitating return.

For all these positive aspects, the convention has unfortunately also been relied upon to hinge other developments in international global jurisprudence and policy that are at least disputatious. Its expanded definition has been contrasted with the one in the 1951 convention to sustain the argument that the latter does not apply to groups or so-called civil war refugees. That convention's definition and its provisions on burden sharing and voluntary repatriation have also led some to see the OAU convention and Africa accordingly as the birthplace of the notion of temporary protection that flowered in western Europe in the 1990s (see below).

These views must be contended in light of both the legislative history of the OAU convention and its specific character as Africa's regulatory framework for refugees at the continental level. The OAU convention applied to Africa essentially the same fundamental notions that were the essence of the 1951 convention. It did not characterize or differentiate refugees based on numbers, nor are the protections it establishes attributed in a differential manner based on the cause of displacement. Nowhere does the convention periodize the duration of protection nor qualify the character, quantity, or quality of the protection to be provided. It was based on the same concept of extending protection for as long as the need endured. It also did not add qualifications to the idea that even during this protection phase, there would be the possibility for progressive movement towards solutions, such as integration or return. This approach to protection is well demonstrated in both legal and practical examples across the continent, although it is also true that, as elsewhere, things have been changing for some time, often to the detriment of genuine protection.

The OAU convention has served as an essential regulatory framework for refugees in Africa for thirty years. It has, above all, helped to bring coherence and predictability to asylum practice and refugee management in an environment where the refugee question often tends to become severely politicized. It has provided a reference point for dealing with refugees in an essentially humanitarian and friendly context, and mandated behavior on the part of both states and refugees themselves in favor of that construction.

All this having been said, historical and contemporary realities mean that the ampleness of the convention nevertheless must be looked at critically. The racist and postcolonial situations foreseen by the broad provisions in the definition of a refugee are all but finished. Now, the residual category of "events seriously disturbing public order" offers very limited capacity to deal with the broad range of refugee-producing situations in Africa today. The expanded definition has clearly reached the need for reform, particularly to more accurately reflect the contemporary causes of Africa's refugees and anchor the causal elements of flight more strongly in the need to protect life, liberty, and other human rights. In both cases, it stands in turn to learn from the approach of the Cartagena declaration on these issues.

There is a need for further development of the convention in other areas as well, including those in which deficits were apparent even already at its birth. The convention did not come equipped with provisions on refugee status management, a crucial shortcoming, particularly bearing in mind the cases of mass influxes and the mix among civilian refugees of exiles bent on extraconstitutional competition for power with the authorities in the country of origin. It was adopted without elaborate provisions on the safety of refugees nor on the management of refugee affairs in a predictable and coherent manner. It does not, in this connection, address the range of rights and accountability issues relevant to the personal legal relationship between the refugee and the state of asylum or with organizations such as UNHCR, or for that matter the OAU itself. Indeed, no operational role was foreseen for the OAU itself and even the supervisory one specifically mandated has proved impossible to realize meaningfully and effectively. Meanwhile, the convention also did not elaborate provisions on the refugees' quality of life, above all in regard to survival, social, and community rights. These, it is proposed, were not issues whose coverage should have been left to be computed only from the conjunctive formula of the convention.

In an era when it was far more critical to streamline the political imperatives underlying the refugee problem, these shortcomings may have been considered secondary. Today, the convention is in a position where it has to be legally ample. The challenge now will be to properly anchor a reform process along the axis of both region-specific priorities and those that must be drawn from the global sphere.

LATIN AMERICA

The Cartagena and OAU alternative definitions of refugee do not only facilitate prima facie recognition of large-scale influxes of asylum-seekers.[2] The "OAU/Cartagena standard" is an extremely useful evidentiary benchmark for the *individual* determination of refugee status under UNHCR's statute, the 1951 convention and their equivalents in national legislation. In certain jurisdictions both in and outside Africa and the Americas, proof of *elements* of the Cartagena and OAU definitions triggers rebuttable presumptions of well-founded fear and unavailability of national protection. One could argue, as the speaker here did, that it should do so in all. States consider refugees who meet the Cartagena or OAU alternative refugee definition—but outside the African and Latin American regions—to be of international concern. These refugees receive international protection and assistance on a mandatory basis from the international community through UNHCR, but on a discretionary basis from individual states. Over the past decade, this discretionary protection has tended to be made available in the form of "temporary protection" or "temporary protected status."

Many of these same states are forever seeking new ways to accelerate refugee status determination. Yet, in doing so, they have focused predominantly on ways to speed rejection, not recognition, of asylum claims. The OAU/Cartagena standard can and should be used to expedite individual refugee status recognition, in much the same way that other evidentiary benchmarks are used to "fast-track" asylum-seekers to rejection. The OAU/Cartagena standard's value lies not only in its ability to accelerate individual asylum proceedings in an objective, logical, and legally sound manner, however. It also offers states an opportunity to balance their expedited procedures in a humane way. Such a combination of objectivity and humanity can add to their apparent legitimacy in the eyes of both national constituencies and the international community.

The Cartagena declaration[3] resembles the OAU convention in that it reaffirms the fundamental relevance of the 1951 convention/1967 protocol definition, yet responds to the necessity, as demonstrated by the massive flows of refugees in and from Central America at the time of its adoption, to "enlarg[e] the concept of a refugee" to embrace the following:

> persons who have fled their country because their lives, safety or freedom have been threatened by generalized violence, foreign aggression, internal conflicts, massive violation of human rights or other circumstances which have seriously disturbed public order.[4]

Taken together, the broader set of criteria laid out in the OAU convention and the Cartagena declaration addresses the compulsion to leave one's homeland in search of refuge from threats to one's life, safety, or freedom due to foreign occupation, aggression, or domination; internal conflict; generalized violence; massive violation of human rights; or [other] serious disturbances of public order.

The Cartagena and OAU definitions reflect the interconnectedness of harm and fear in a country suffering serious disturbances of public order. They recognize the effect of the country situation on individual fear. The Cartagena declaration and OAU convention definitions also reflect the influence of individual suffering on the country situation. Of course, OAU/Cartagena criteria can be relied on alone outside the context of the 1951 convention/1967 protocol to grant refuge to persons in need of international protection. But, the country conditions to which they refer also provide a useful evidentiary benchmark in the assessment of well-founded fear and the availability of national protection within the context of the definitions contained in UNHCR's statute and the 1951 convention/1967 protocol.[5]

Prima facie recognition, usually applied in the circumstances of large-scale influx, relies entirely upon objective criteria. An understanding of this method of refugee status determination, therefore, allows one to make the intellectual leap from traditional, individual determination under the 1951 convention, on the one hand, to individual determination under the 1951 convention, reliant on the OAU/Cartagena standard with regard to well-founded fear and the availability of national protection, on the other. Prima facie recognition under the 1951 convention/1967 protocol relies on the legal presumptions—based on country information—that a harm constituting persecution is feared, that the applicant is the member of a targeted group, and that national protection is unavailable to her.[6] The OAU/Cartagena standard is also a useful tool for ensuring protection to persons falling *within* the terms of the 1951 convention/1967 protocol, but for whom time does not allow individual verification.

The refugee status determination authorities of some governments have tried to minimize recognition by arguing that persecution cannot exist in situations of armed conflict. Fortunately, such disingenuous legal contortionists are in the minority. Given the frequent interrelation between "serious disturbances of public order" and states of exception, the latter are often considered during examination of the two criteria where the OAU/Cartagena standard can trigger rebuttable presumptions: well-founded fear of persecution and the applicant's inability or unwillingness to avail himself of national protection.

In OAU/Cartagena situations, asylum-seekers may be more likely than in other situations to have been deprived during searches, detention, or military attack of their personal identity documentation, money, and other possessions requisite for lawful travel from one country to another. Such situations are yet another illustration of why illegal entry or irregular/nonexistent documentation should not be considered a controlling indicator of a claimant's credibility and, thereby, well-founded fear.

Identification of OAU/Cartagena conditions in a country is the converse of identifying a country as "safe." This does not mean that a well-founded fear cannot exist where OAU/Cartagena conditions do not obtain. It does mean, however, that the types of tumult enumerated in the broadened definitions of the OAU convention and the Cartagena declaration 1) are likely to contribute to the depth of fear experienced by the asylum-seeker, 2) may justify that fear, and 3) can limit his or her ability or willingness to avail themselves of the protection of that country.[7] Where OAU/Cartagena conditions prevail in the whole of the country, or in the place where the applicant might otherwise have found an "internal flight alternative," rebuttable presumptions of unavailability of national protection and well-founded fear should obtain.

Use of the OAU/Cartagena standard in favor of bona fide refugees should be part and parcel of the various acceleration and harmonization efforts in progress around the world. When applying it, governments need not fear the opening of the proverbial floodgates. Asylum-seekers will still need to prove that the harm they fear rises to the level of persecution and delineate the reason or reasons for persecution. As in all properly run refugee status determinations, just as applicants have the right to rebut presumptions and appeal rejection, so the relevant government agency will have the right to rebut presumptions and appeal rulings based on the OAU/Cartagena standard. Refugee status, regardless of its basis, will continue to be subject to cancellation. Finally, just as the objective OAU/Cartagena criteria enhance assessment of the well-founded nature of a fear and the availability of national protection, they can facilitate assessment of changes in—or cessation of—the circumstances that originally led to flight, and the related decision to repatriate.

EUROPE

Despite the increasing difficulties in getting access to EU countries to apply for asylum, in 1999 approximately 325,000[8] people applied for asylum in one of the member states.[9] In order to limit the number of people eventually obtaining refugee status, two features have been common throughout the last decade: i) the introduction of a more formalized safe third-country concept, and ii) more restrictive asylum practices. These developments have not only brought the international and regional human rights machinery closer to the issue of refugee protection, but have also highlighted the need for a more comprehensive refugee approach in Europe.

The safe third-country practices that emerged in the 1990s developed out of the 1970s concept of first country of asylum. In legal terms the concept was developed at the national level in the interface between the right to seek asylum but not to obtain asylum and the *non-refoulement* principle.[10] The first country of asylum issues, which had led to disputes between neighboring European states for decades, was eventually regulated in the Dublin Convention in 1990. However, no harmonized safe third-country procedures have developed in Europe.[11] Nonetheless, an elaborate system of readmission agreements has been put in place—an important precondition for any safe third-country policy to be effectuated. These agreements do not differentiate between groups of individuals being returned to the specific country, and thereby fail to oblige the receiving country to give the persons in question access to an asylum procedure. Consequently, the legal safeguards generally applying to the safe third-country concept do not offer the level of protection that is otherwise presupposed by the right to seek asylum and the *non-refoulement* principle, respectively.

Those who are not returned to a safe third country will have their asylum application treated in the asylum procedure. Throughout the years still more restrictive criteria have been applied at the national level. This has materialized in a fairly rigid assessment applied by immigration authorities when contradictions and inconsistencies occur in the story told by the asylum-seeker. Furthermore, states have interpreted the 1951 refugee convention in a still more restrictive manner. The restrictive application of the 1951 convention was one of the tools used for sending a signal to asylum-seekers that they should apply for asylum in other neighboring countries.

Parallel to the development of a more restrictive regime an increase in cases regarding refugees and asylum-seekers being brought to either the European Court on Human Rights or the UN treaty bodies has been witnessed. Apart from general growing human rights awareness in the post–Cold War period this evolution can be ascribed to the still more restrictive practices in Europe. Contrary to the refugee convention, the human rights conventions have courts or expert committees with jurisdiction to interpret the particular convention.[12] Asylum-seekers and refugees have used these options for petition when restrictive policies have led to violations of particular rights. When looking at the cases brought to the human rights bodies the issues raised generally concern the above-mentioned areas in relation to the right to seek asylum and discrimination.

In a number of cases the European Human Rights Commission and European Court on Human Rights have established a practice in relation to what could be called "inhuman return of an individual."[13] This practise derives from the prohibition against torture and inhuman treatment in article 3 of the European Human Rights Convention. The UN Committee against Torture (CAT) has established a practice that supplements the practice of the European Court on Human Rights.[14] The CAT has addressed the rigid assessment applied by immigration authorities when contradictions and inconsistencies occur in the story told by the asylum-seeker. This is in particular a problem when dealing with victims of torture. By using modern psychological knowledge CAT states that "complete accuracy is seldom to be expected by victims of torture and that such inconsistencies should not raise doubts about the veracity of the application for asylum."[15] This has led to several decisions where the committee would consider it a violation of article 3 to return the asylum-seeker. Furthermore, in relation to administrative procedures, the committee has stated that procedural regulations excluding the possibility to include political actions carried out by the applicant in the asylum country would not be compatible with article 3.[16] This way they uphold the old *refugee sur place* concept, which several European countries have tried to rule out in their practice.[17]

There are four conclusions to this brief introduction to some of the core problems in Europe that can be summarized as follows: (1) There is a need for a legal body that can interpret the 1951 refugee convention in an authoritative manner; (2) There is a legal lacuna in relation to those individuals who are not covered by the 1951 convention, but who can nonetheless not return to the country of origin; (3) There are no agreed mechanisms competent to decide safe third-country issues; and (4) There are no mechanisms in relation to mass influx situations.

Regionally, as well as internationally, there is a need for a refugee court or expert committee entrusted with the task to make authoritative interpretations of the 1951 convention.[18] As illustrated by European developments refugee law is today, to a large extent, developed by the human rights mechanism applying human rights law. The increased integration of refugee law into human rights law has offered a new dimension to refugee protection; however, it is unfortunate if the development of refugee law in its own right is neglected. Thus, an international or regional legal body should be established to make principal decisions on the 1951 refugee convention.

However, there may be individuals who are not covered by the 1951 convention, but who still cannot be returned because of the protection offered by article 3 of the European Human Rights Convention or article 3 of the CAT, or other humanitarian considerations. These persons are today protected by a variety of arrangements in the different countries: *Duldung,* toleration, de facto refugee status, etc. There has for many years been a need in Europe for a regional arrangement regarding subsidiary protection, like the one found in the OAU convention or in the Cartagena declaration. This issue is, however, closely linked to a legal body interpreting the 1951 convention since a formalized status in relation to subsidiary protection with the present restrictive tendencies may easily be a way for governments not to apply the 1951 convention. The one should not be established without the other.

In terms of procedural issues there is a need to establish criteria for safe third-country decisions and for how to ensure that the person is not in danger of *refoulement* in a chain reaction. Furthermore, there is still a need in Europe to clarify the situation in relation to mass influx situations and the application of temporary protection mechanisms. The EU Commission has taken an important first step in this regard by tabling a proposal for a council directive.[19] Contrary to previous attempts to make a joint action, the new proposal is in accordance with human rights standards as well as international refugee law.

While the wording of article 14 in the Universal Declaration on Human Rights—the right to seek asylum—has indeed become well-known, less attention is often paid to the fact that article 28 of the declaration stipulates that *"everyone is entitled to a social and international order in which the rights and freedoms set forth in this declaration can be fully realized."* Obviously, this places the international community under an obligation to establish mechanisms, structures, and policies that help secure the rights set forth in the declaration, including the right to seek asylum. And such mechanisms should therefore be established—not only in name or in form—but also in substance. As indicated these structures are not in place in Europe today. It is from the perspective of article 28 that the attempts to create an international refugee court or committee, a subsidiary protection standard and a scheme to regulate the safe third-country concept as well as temporary protection, should be viewed.

ASIA

Southeast Asia has witnessed continued flows of forced migration during the last three decades.[20] As the massive outflows of refugees from Laos, Cambodia, and Vietnam that started in 1975 terminated in the early 1990s, new waves of population displacements in Myanmar, Indonesia, and other countries in the region commenced or continued to take place at a significant rate. There are both old areas of origin like Cambodia and Myanmar and new ones like East Timor and Aceh in Indonesia. Country by country, the flows can be described as follows:

Cambodia

Population mobility continued massively after the repatriation of Cambodian returnees in 1993–1994. Approximately 300,000 persons were sent back to the areas of Battambong, Siem riep, and other major destinations with the assistance of UNHCR and UNBRO (United Nations Border Relief Operation). However, due to the lack of sustainable livelihood and land ownership in the areas where returnees were sent back, most returnees continued to move to other parts of the country, especially to Phnom Penh and other major urban and rural areas. A population census conducted in 1998 indicated that 26.8 percent of the total population had migrated from their birthplace with a higher proportion (56.6 percent) to urban areas than to rural areas (21.2 percent). Of the 31.5 percent of the population who lived outside their place of origin, 58.8 percent moved within the province, 35.5 percent moved to another province, and 5.9 percent moved outside Cambodia.

Most migrants in Cambodia are more or less permanently mobile. During 1979–1993, many of them were internally displaced because of the fighting between the Heng Samrin government on one side and the coalition of the Democratic Kampuchea (DK), the Royal Party (FUNCINPEC), and the pro-liberal faction on the other side. Once they were repatriated in 1993, they did not return to their places of origin but rather to the last place of residence before flight or to another preferred destination. Thus, most people are permanently on the move.

Myanmar

Myanmar is another country where both internal displacement and cross-border movements of people have taken place for decades. Political conflicts and the attempts of the ethnic minorities, especially the Mon, Karen, and Shan to secede since the end of World War II have rendered the country a place of fighting and violence. This was toppled by the pro-democracy uprise by university students and intellectuals in 1988 against the authoritative regime. Consequently, internal displacement continued to cross-border migration to Thailand and Bangladesh in the early 1990s. No studies give a comprehensive number of all migrants in and across Myanmar. But statistics of refugee population at the Thai-Myanmar seventeen border camps, amounting to approximately 120,000 persons, can roughly indicate a part of the total number of political refugees. The majority of this group comprised ethnic Karen, Karenni, and Mon. The Shan do not stay in refugee camps but blend with Thai people because of their cultural and language proximity. It is estimated that there are 3,000 Shan in Chiang Mai, a big city in the north of Thailand.

Indonesia

Political refugees in East Timor and Aceh (on Sumatra Island) are the two major groups of newly mobile people. In East Timor, 300,000 persons fled violence and massacre to stay in West Timor and other parts of East Timor, which are more peaceful. Thus, they are both internally displaced persons and refugees. The majority of the mobile groups are ethnic Timorese who are Christian and want to be independent from Indonesia. They were victimized by the militia East Timorese who are also Christian but do not want to separate from Indonesia.

As for Aceh, in 1989 in response to the Suharto's policy of settling thousands of transmigrants in this area, more than 6,000 troops have been sent to the province. Thousands of Achenese fled to neighboring Malaysia where many have languished in appalling conditions in detention camps for years. In addition, the number of internally displaced persons has increased continuously. The total number of refugees in twenty-eight locations in the districts of Pidie, North Aceh, and East Aceh had hit 130,000 in 1999.

Indonesia, as the biggest country in southeast Asia, has developed a population movement policy called "transmigration" since the 1970s. Due to the overpopulated settlements in Java island and under populated settlements

in Kalimantan (Borneo) and other islands, the government decided to relo-
cate its population from Java to those areas, resulting in a significant number of internally displaced persons due to the national relocation schemes.
This took place earlier to the recent forced migration in East Timor and
Aceh.

Other Countries

Laos and Vietnam are the last two countries in southeast Asia which also
adopted population relocation schemes. In Lao PDR, the hilltribal population in the highland areas, especially the Hmong, were brought to new resettlement areas in the lowland, partly due to the crop substitution policy,
which aims at eradicating opium growing among the highlanders and partly
due to the government's need to have a closer control of the Hmong among
whom some antigovernment movements have been formed with the support from overseas Hmong. In Vietnam, some relocation schemes were introduced but mainly not for political reasons, and the numbers are smaller
than in Laos.

New trends of involuntary population migration are emerging in the
southeast Asian region, comprising an increasing number of internal displacements; economic migration as a result of natural and man-made disasters; a continuation from IDP to cross-border asylum-seeker and refugee;
and development-induced displacement.

The Regional response to forced migration

During the 1990s when refugees from the Indo-Chinese states were persistent, a regional attempt to push forward the issue of forced migration and its
solutions was undertaken by the Association of Southeast Asian Nations
(ASEAN) through the Comprehensive Plan of Action (CPA), which introduced the two durable solutions of resettlement and repatriation of refugees.
The response was successful due to the tripartite cooperation among countries of destination, countries of origin, and UNHCR. In the new decade 2000,
the forced migration situation has become more complex and requires more
sophisticated responses from all parties concerned. Points that can be raised
from more efficient responses should cover the following:

- How can the 1951 Convention Relating to the Status of Refugee be used
  to cope with the increasing number of internally displaced persons in
  southeast Asia? As the convention only covers cross-border displaced
  persons, it is the International Committee of the Red Cross (ICRC) that
  has the mandate to assist IDPs in the region. But ICRC can only operate
  if it has the agreement and cooperation of the government of the coun-

try where the internal displacement is occurring. Therefore, in countries where there is no consent on ICRC operations, IDPs are left unassisted.

- How can humanitarian assistance properly be given to asylum-seekers in border area camps? UNHCR can help those people if the government of the country of first asylum allows it to do so. Nonetheless, those people do not have the full status of refugee. They are to be sent back when the situation improves. They are not entitled to other options of durable solutions (resettlement and local settlement). However, many have been staying in border camps for approximately fifteen years with such uncertain status and deprived of proper assistance. When the former high commissioner visited a Karen camp at the Thai-Myanmar border and made a remark that she was shocked by "the overcrowding and poor sanitation in the camp,"[21] she also mentioned that the Thai government did not do the best to aid those people. However, the Thai authorities argued that there were many Thai villagers nearby the camp who lived in poorer conditions than the Karen asylum-seekers. The country did not want them (the former) to have negative attitudes or show resistance to refugees.[22]

- How can a regional mechanism like ASEAN, or an international organization like IOM or UNHCR, cooperate with governments in southeast Asia to solve the problem of forced migration? With the principle of non interference with each nation-state, ASEAN will not be able to actively play a leading role in this regard. UNHCR and IOM cannot intervene in the nation's sovereignty. Consequently, the forced migration phenomenon, both internally and cross-border, will not be solved properly by existing regional and international mechanisms.

As forced migration in southeast Asia continues with new emerging characteristics such as the increasing number of IDP, life-threatening violence caused by economic hardship, the nature of temporary asylum, and the new form of development-induced displacement, the old mechanism of the international refugee regime seems to be unable to cope with the new realities. Indeed, it needs a better, sensitive regime that can address the root causes of forced migration as well as the protection of asylum-seekers deriving from various natures. The southeast Asian region still has a lot to do in order to develop such a new regime.

NOTES

This chapter has been compiled and edited by Joanne van Selm, who also wrote the introductory paragraph.

1. This is a summary of the presentation by George Okoth-Obbo entitled "The 1969 OAU Refugee Convention: A Collateralising Instrument." For a fuller treatment

of the thinking on which the paper is based, see, by the same author, "Thirty Years On: A Legal Review of the 1969 OAU Refugee Convention," *African Yearbook of International Law* 8, no. 3 (2000).

2. This is a summary of the presentation by Courtney Mireille O'Connor entitled "Legitimating Speed: Expediting Individual, 1951 Convention Refugee Status Determination Worldwide with Rebuttable Presumptions Triggered by the 'OAU/Cartagena Standard.'"

3. Although formulated in response to the Central American civil wars of the 1980s, the alternative definition contained in the Cartagena declaration—or a close equivalent—has been included in approved or draft legislation, or is implemented de facto, in at least nine countries throughout Latin America. Belize has adopted the refugee definition contained in the OAU convention. See, e.g., José H. de Andrade, "Regional Policy Approaches and Harmonization: A Latin American Perspective," *IJRL* 10, (1998): 389, 404 (Fischel de Andrade, *IJRL*).

4. Chap. 3 par. 3 (1984).

5. *Accord* I. Jackson, "The 1951 Convention Relating to the Status of Refugees: A Universal Basis for Recognition," *IJRL* 3, no. 3, (1991): 410–412.

> [T]he "good offices" procedure was based on the prima facie refugee character of the groups assisted, under the Statutory definition. In making this prima facie determination of refugee character, the High Commissioner used broad criteria based on the *objective* situation existing in the country of origin. The global result of the "good offices" procedure was explained by the High Commissioner as follows in 1965: "the refugees who benefit from 'good offices' are persons who are obliged by political events to leave their country and may reasonably fear for their security if they were forced to return there." This comes very close to a description of the type of situation covered by the so-called "broader refugee concept." It is significant, however, that this broader approach was not considered in any way incompatible with the 1950/1951 definitions. . . . *The "broader" concept should . . . be considered as an aspect of the Convention definition* and as an effective technical means of facilitating its broad humanitarian application in large-scale group operations. (Emphasis added)

Cf. G. Okoth-Obbo, *The OAU/UNHCR Symposium on Refugees and Forced Population Displacements in Africa—A Review Article, IJRL* Special Issue (Summer 1995): 98, where, in citing, inter alia, the Jackson article quoted above, he states as follows:

> [T]he historical and legal correctness of the argument that a large part of today's refugees, particularly the so-called civil war refugees, fall outside the material scope of the application of the 1951 Convention, remains open to at least reasonable difference of opinion. (Footnotes omitted)

See also Human Rights Watch/Helsinki, "Swedish Asylum Policy in Global Human Rights Perspective," 8, no. 14 (D)(September 1996): 4–5:

> Accelerated procedure for cases deemed "manifestly unfounded" should apply only to cases involving asylum seekers from countries where there is no more than an insignificant risk of persecution or other threat to life and freedom. These procedures *should not apply to applicants coming from countries afflicted by civil war or strife.* (Emphasis added)

6. See, e.g., 1994 *UNHCR* Note on International Protection, par. 27, which, in discussing the use of prima facie recognition under the 51CSR/67PCSR, states as follows:

> When circumstances in the country of origin are such that any reasonable person from a particular group would fear persecution, the "subjective element" of the refugee definition (i.e., "fear") can be presumed.

The court in *M.A. v. INS*, 899 F2d 304, 1990 (US) found that the standard of proof for a prima facie case of well-founded fear of persecution is a showing that "a reasonable person in his circumstances could have feared persecution if he were returned. . . ." (The standard of proof discussed in this case was that necessary to reopen an asylum decision—not to make a conclusive determination).

7. With regard to the effect of this tenet on manifestly unfounded claims, see, e.g., UNHCR exc. conceal. 30(d), which states that a claim that "relate[s] to . . . any . . . criteria justifying the grant of asylum [other than the Convention/1967 Protocol criteria]" cannot be considered manifestly unfounded or clearly abusive. Contra EC Ministers Resolution on Manifestly Unfounded Claims for Asylum (MUC Res.) (1992), sixth preambular par., par. 1(a) and 6(a).

8. Estimated from the Intergovernmental Consultations homepage www.igc.ch

9. This is a summary of the presentation by Morten Kjaerum entitled "Outline for a Regional Approach: Europe."

10. Kjaerum, M. "The Concept of Country of First Asylum," *IJRL* 4, no. 4 (1992): 514.

11. Lavenex, S. *Safe Third Countries*, (Budapest: Central European University Press, 1999), 76–78.

12. Clark, T. and Crépeau, F. "Mainstreaming Refugee Rights. The 1951 Refugee Convention and International Human Rights Law," *Netherlands Quarterly of Human Rights* 17, no. 4, (1999): 389–410.

13. Cf. Jens Vedsted-Hansen, Torturforbud som udsendelsesbegrænsning: Non-refoulement-virkningen af EMRK artikel 3 (The prohibition against torture setting limits to expulsion: The non-refoulement effect of article 3 of the European Convention on Human Rights), EU og Menneskeret, no. 2, May 1998, 49–57.

14. Kjaerum, M. "Flygtningeret—Menneskeret, Non-refoulement bestemmelsen i FNs Konvention mod Tortur" (The Non-Refoulements Prohibition in the UN Convention against Torture and Other Cruel, Inhuman or Degrading Treatment or Punishment), *EU-ret og Menneskeret, DJØF*, no. 2, May 1999, 8–17.

15. Communication 34/1995.

16. Communication 34/1995.

17. Cf. Terje Einarsen, Retten til vern som Flyktning, Bergen 2000, 606–611.

18. Terje Einarsen, 665ff.

19. COM(2000) final, Brussels 24.5.2000. (Editor's note—this directive has since been agreed upon).

20. This is a summary of the presentation by Supang Chantavanich on Asia.

21. *The Nation,* 18 October 2000 A1.

22. *Bangkok Post,* 20 October 2000: 6.

5

The Refugee Convention Applied: Moral, Medical, Ethical, and Judicial Questions and Limitations

Geoffrey Care, Edvard Hauff, Annemick Richters, and Loes van Willigen

The international developments in the last decade have seen an increasing number of people on the move. At the same time the striving for common defense of the economic and social interests within the EU has given European governments cause to take increasingly hard looks at measures to reinforce their borders against the "influx" of asylum-seekers. The emphasis in the European refugee debate and asylum policies nowadays lies on deterrence, restriction, and return, although recently attention has also been directed to immigration issues to fill needed job opportunities. This development makes the mental health problems of asylum-seekers even more complex than they already are at arrival in a host country.

The complexity of these considerations raises a number of moral, ethical, and judicial questions for professionals directly or indirectly involved in asylum procedures.

Requests for medical reports in connection with asylum applications have become quite common in European resettlement countries. Compliance with these requests can be quite time-consuming and frustrating. The experience of clinicians is that their reports often have little or no apparent impact on the decision by the immigration authorities. They themselves, and their staff, often become disheartened and this situation can easily trigger profound countertransference reactions[1] in the therapist and the whole treatment team.

The question is what the optimal role is, could be, or should be, for medical practitioners (psychiatrists, general practitioners, etc.) in such cases. What are their legal, medical, and ethical obligations?

Should the patients' therapist write the medical/psychiatric reports, or should specialized medical practitioners be employed for such tasks? To what extent should the decision makers in the asylum determination process consider such reports at all? Are medical practitioners (or other professionals) faced with particular ethical problems if they accept to act as experts for the immigration authorities?

All these and other questions will be discussed in this chapter, which is centered on a case history presented by a psychiatrist (EH). The case history is followed by a discussion about the moral dilemmas and ethical limitations in psychiatric care for asylum-seekers (AR).[2] After the relevant articles in international law, as well as the determination process, are discussed (GC). The chapter concludes with some observations, in which the results of the lengthy judicial procedure of the particular case are included.

A PSYCHIATRIC REPORT TO THE IMMIGRATION AUTHORITIES REGARDING NN/F, BORN 1965[3]

Mrs. NN, an asylum-seeker in Norway, had been in treatment at an urban community mental health center for a few months because of depression and symptoms of a post-traumatic stress disorder (PTSD).[4] When her application for political asylum in Norway was turned down, she requested, through her attorney, that the clinic send a medical report to the Ministry of Justice to be included in her appeal over the refusal. The report is based on information the patient herself had provided through her therapy, as well as on certain additional information from a patient's relative, XX.

Mrs. NN was born and grew up in a village in Iran. Her family experienced no special economic problems, and she went to school for seven years. As far as known, she suffered no mental illness in Iran. She was given away in marriage when she was fifteen years old. Her spouse was poor. He became a soldier and was a war prisoner in Iraq for eight years. At the time of applying for asylum she had two sons about six and seventeen years old.

Mrs. NN's problems started after one of her politically active brothers was arrested, imprisoned, and tortured severely. The patient put her house up for mortgage to raise bail for her brother to be given leave from prison. During leave, he managed to escape from Iran. The authorities then took her house and imprisoned her for a month. Her spouse, who had become a revolutionary guard, divorced the patient and took custody of their two children. He denied her contact with them. During her stay in prison, she felt completely at the mercy of the prison guards. She was hit several times and received little food. According to her own statements, she was interrogated several times during this month. During these interrogations she was tortured as the interrogator wanted information about her politically active brother. The torture consisted of dripping red-hot asphalt oil on her forearm. She was also given forty whip lashes as part of the torture. She denies having been submitted to sexual assault. However, she was pregnant during the imprisonment and had a miscarriage as a result of the abuse. In desperation from being denied visits by her children, she cut both her forearms with pieces of glass. After this, she was beaten by the guards and denied food for four days. She was on parole following the imprisonment.

After her traumatic experiences in her home country, Mrs. NN was in treatment with a psychiatrist in Iran for up to three months before going to Norway. She was treated with a number of different drugs. She was referred to the Norwegian psychiatrist (EH) about three months after arriving in Norway for assessment and treatment because of difficulties with sleep, worries, and possible visual hallucinations. She was found to be suffering from severe depression and post-traumatic symptoms. She was treated with antidepressants with good effect, as well as with supportive psychotherapy sessions. She was then referred back to her general practitioner.

Mrs. NN contacted the psychiatrist again after her request for political asylum in Norway had been turned down. She experienced a grave trauma reaction with severe sleep problems, anxiety, and depression. She lost 3–4 kilograms because she would throw up when trying to eat. She had an increase in nightmares about interrogation in her home country. Her thoughts of suicide were also reactivated. She was about to poison herself, but the thought of her parents stopped her. She was given antidepressants, and responded well to the medication again.

Then she started to deteriorate again and was troubled, anxious, and shaking. Her sleep problems were increasing; she had more nightmares and was very worried about the threat of being deported after her request for asylum was turned down. She was afraid of being sent back, and was not able to push away intrusive thoughts and memories from her time in prison. She had nightmares almost every night with dreams of prison and of being burnt. She tried to avoid talking about these experiences, and had increased symptoms when discussing them. She was afraid of losing control and going mad at not being able to push away the memories. She was irritable, but she usually managed to keep this to herself. She was also frightened by noise and loud sounds. Her ability to concentrate decreased, and she felt that she easily forgot things. Her thoughts of suicide then decreased again, but she stated it was possible that she would hurt herself should she be sent back. However, she did not really seem manipulative concerning the threats of suicide.

She feared being imprisoned again should she be returned to Iran, because of her breaking the parole, and because family members have been politically active in the opposition in Iran. She thinks that she will be imprisoned forever. She had received a letter from her eldest son in Iran saying that it will be dangerous for her to return to her home country.

End of the medical report:

Mrs. NN seems genuinely worried with regards to the threat of deportation. Her mood is fairly low. The patient is not oriented with regards to time. She cannot state correctly what year, month or day it is. She is able, however, to state the correct year according to the calendar in use in Iran. The patient has scars on both forearms. The scars are small and asymmetric, presumably caused by torture involving burning with hot oil. She also has several more symmetric scars along both forearms, 2 to 5 centimetres long, presumably caused from self-inflicted cuts with shards of glass while in prison.

Assessment and conclusion:

The patient is an asylum seeker from Iran, who is experiencing a crisis related to her request of asylum in Norway being turned down. Most of her family lives in Norway. She has a strong fear of being sent back to her home country, where she expects further imprisonment by the authorities. Her present psychological condition satisfies the criteria for a post-traumatic stress disorder. She also suffers from a depressive reaction partly in remission after treatment with antidepressants. There is no apparent basis for any psychotic or organic disorder, and it is plausible that the distortion in orientation is caused by the stressful situation she finds herself in, with a short stay in Norway and a regressive reaction psychologically. She is not acutely suicidal, but it cannot be ruled out that she might injure herself or commit suicide should she be deported and sent back to her home country.

A FOLLOW-UP REPORT SIX MONTHS LATER

After the patient's appeal to obtain permission to live in Norway was rejected, she experienced an acute worsening of her PTSD and depression. She went for emergency assessments at the community mental health center on several occasions. She had concrete plans to commit suicide and considered burning herself to death with fuel oil. She seemed to be under severe psychological stress and had lost a lot of weight. Her ability to understand the consequences of her actions was assessed as being limited. On the last emergency visit her condition had worsened, she seemed even more worn out and started to vomit and hyperventilate immediately as she entered the waiting area. She said she saw wolves running towards her, but it was not clear if this was a genuine visual hallucination or a pseudohallucination conditioned by a stress reaction. She was admitted the same day to the psychiatric emergency ward at the referral hospital for further observation.[5] She stayed there for six days. During her stay she set fire to herself without being severely hurt. She was then referred back to the Community Mental Health Center, and when she met for a new session there, she seemed helpless and her mood was markedly lowered. She sat prostrated and had problems concentrating. She told of nightmares while awake where she saw terrifying things when she was alone, dead people among them. She suffered severe sleeping problems and frequent bouts of vomiting. She received further follow-ups as an outpatient through the subsequent month. Then she was readmitted to the psychiatric emergency ward after a drug overdose. After discharge she continued to receive further follow-ups as an outpatient, but was admitted yet again following a new overdose. At the time of the writing of the follow-up report she had just been discharged again from the hospital.

End of the follow-up report for the Ministry of Justice:

Mrs. NN has been treated at the mental health centre intermittently for 1–2 years because of a depressive reaction and PTSD. At the time of the first intake, she appeared to be a level-headed woman with hope of a new life in Norway. It was fairly easy to establish contact with her and she collaborated well during treatment. Her response to antidepressants was good. During the time she has been in treatment, her psychological condition has deteriorated dramatically. She now appears desperate and chaotic, with repeated self-destructive actions. She is about to lose her social and emotional grip on life, and she functions on a near-psychotic level; periodically she is psychotic. [....] As a former prisoner with no familial or social support in her home country, she feels she has no future or possibilities for an acceptable life there.

On the basis of the development of the patient, my assessment is that there is a concrete danger for further self-inflicted harm which may result in the death of the patient should she be deported and sent back to Iran. The patient needs to be admitted for a long stay in a psychiatric hospital to avoid further decompensation and to treat her psychiatric disorders. An application for admission to the local psychiatric hospital for longer term in-patient treatment has been submitted, and while waiting she meets every second day at the community mental health centre, where she receives her medication for insomnia. Further medication is postponed until she is admitted to hospital. She also continues to have sessions with the psychiatrist as an outpatient while waiting.

After this report had been sent to her attorney Mrs. NN received her final rejection of her appeal for asylum permit in Norway from the Ministry of Justice. Her family, all of whom lived in Norway with refugee status, now were also quite desperate, and they borrowed money to be able to present the case to the court for a final appeal.

MORAL DILEMMAS AND ETHICAL LIMITATIONS
IN PSYCHIATRIC CARE FOR ASYLUM-SEEKERS

The case study of Mrs. NN presents various moral dilemmas for the care provider, which makes the case into a moral case. A case is a moral case when it is characterized by the presence of divergent and often irreconcilable rights, duties, interests, goals, and normative basic assumptions of the people or institutes involved.[6] A moral problem exists if there is uncertainty concerning the acceptability of a particular action. What is at issue is what a morally justifiable way of acting is.

The subject of psychiatry is mental disorders, commonly considered as manifestations of a behavioral, psychological, or biological dysfunction in the person. Many problems diagnosed by psychiatry as mental disorder, however, could often just as well, or perhaps even better, be described as normal reactions to abnormal social and cultural situations, such as in the case of refugees. Psychiatrists often realize that if the social and/or cultural situation of their patient does not change in those latter cases, they can do no more than palliative treatment, which ultimately can do more harm than good.

Common dilemmas in the psychiatric care for asylum-seekers, also present in the case of Mrs. NN, are manifold. What to do when the application of his or her patient for refugee status is expected to be rejected? Continue the therapy, which from a psychiatric perspective is necessary, or stop it and prepare the patient for a return to the country of origin? And what to do when continuing a treatment, which often is not necessary from a narrow psychiatric perspective, gives the asylum-seeker the right to stay in the country of asylum, while finishing the treatment means that he or she will have to leave to the country of origin where he or she, according to the psychiatrist, will have to fear for his or her life?

What to do when a female asylum-seeker does not want to talk about the sexual abuse experienced in detention because of culturally produced and constructed shame, and the psychiatrist's judgment is that at least in the current phase of treatment her wish should be respected, while her testimony of the abuse will contribute to be the evidence needed to be granted a residence permit?

The psychiatrist may be of the opinion, for the sake of policy and intervention programs, that the transformation of people traumatized by political violence into victims and patients with psychological and medical pathologies, like PTSD, is unwarranted because a social and political problem should not be made into a medical one that is subsequently "treated" at an individual level. But at the same time the psychiatrist knows that for the sake of justice to "the patient" it is necessary to medicalize the problem and present it is as PTSD to the authorities who have decisional power with regard to a refugee status. What to do?

Should the psychiatrist limit himself or herself to therapy or should he or she take social action by 1) mobilising people with the goal to get a residence permit for his or her patient; and/or 2) stimulate a debate within society about the moral problems the care for asylum-seekers raise (i.e., the public debates on euthanasia or abortion).

All these dilemmas in one way or another touch upon the question of what the scope and boundaries of professional psychiatric care are, or could and should be. Should care be limited to care according to a narrowly defined professional standard focused on an individual or does the psychiatrist also have a social or political responsibility. If so, what exactly does this responsibility entail? Should it be a responsibility of the psychiatrist as a professional or as a citizen?

BEYOND MODERNIST AND POSTMODERNIST ETHICS

The dilemmas presented cannot easily be solved by the application of the main medical ethical principles: beneficence or "doing good," nonmaleficence or doing no harm, respect for autonomy, and justice. In most cases, an attempt to do so will bring the moral dilemmas even more sharply to the fore. The most one can do is to try to determine—a difficult task—what is "the least harmful" and act upon that. The concept of autonomy is not so easily applied in many medical situations, the treatment of mentally disturbed patients being just one of them. Furthermore, autonomy is a contested concept from a cross-cultural point of view.[7] Doing justice seems the most difficult issue to tackle. A psychiatrist may want to make a contribution to this on an individual level (if only because without justice the therapy will never be effective), but it is generally agreed that the decision whether an asylum-seeker is granted a refugee status or not, should be a political decision and that justice should not only be done on an individual level but also at the level of the society in question. Other ethical approaches are needed to come to all-around moral deliberation about the cases in question.

The principle, modernist approach is the dominant one in medical ethics. Alternative postmodernist approaches (e.g., the phenomenological, the narrative, the hermeneutic, the discourse ethics, the care ethics, and the feminist approach) have taken issue with the presuppositions of the principle approach: individuality, rationality, and foundation in abstract principles.[8]

From a postmodernist perspective it has been argued that the modernist's search for codification, universality, and foundations in the area of ethics has been destructive of the moral impulse.[9] The postmodernist emphasizes the contextuality and relationality of human existence and furthermore that human and social life is full of problems, twisted trajectories, ambivalences, doubts, and moral agonies people have to learn to live with. "Postmodern ethics" is about facing the world without easy recourse to guiding codes or principles. It recognizes that the wholeness of a person as presupposed in modernist thinking is an illusion, and that people project multiple, inconsistent self-representations that are context-dependent and may shift rapidly. What is morally at stake in a particular case should be approached from a variety of perspectives. Every facet of a particular case has to be understood. Ethics is not a question of theoretical knowledge and of rational arguments but of practical insight, feelings, and emotions.

A key term in ethical discussion is "responsibility." In the modernism–postmodernism debate a "responsibility to act" in the world in ways that are justifiable is contrasted with a "responsibility to otherness." Responsibility in the modernist sense means inevitably closing off sources of possible insight and treating people as alike for the purpose of making consistent and defensible decisions about alternative courses of action. The modern cognitive machinery promises harmony, unity, and clarity and denies thereby the ineradicability of dissonance. The postmodernist vision accepts that ambivalence and disorder are aspects of life that we should embrace, not just temporary difficulties that need to be overcome by further analysis, or the application of even more structured ethical systems.[10]

If we go back to the case study of Mrs. NN we will most probably agree that the psychiatrist cannot keep the judicial system and its modernist reasoning and ethics out of his or her interaction with the patient. This inability easily leads to a juridification of the doctor-patient relationship. The psychiatrist who does not believe in the appropriateness of a modernist psychiatric approach towards his patient will recognize that there are no good solutions for the problems that he or she is confronted with. In discussions with colleagues and ethicists—using a "step-by-step approach"—the psychiatrist may find some norms and values for his actions. But each case will lead to a different weighting for those norms and values. Every "solution" leading to action will be a temporary one and will always leave the care provider with feelings of frustration because he or she has not been able to reach his or her professional or humanist goals.

THE PSYCHIATRIST AS DOUBLE AGENT

The moral dilemmas the psychiatrist is presented with in the care for asylum-seekers place him or her in the position of a double agent, which is a heavy burden to carry. Even though, like in the Netherlands, there is a special body to diagnose health problems of asylum-seekers for the Ministry of Justice—established in order not to damage the trust relationship between doctor and patient—the trust relationship is under strain all the time. This leaves the psychiatrist with feelings of betrayal towards the patient. At the same time the psychiatrist feels obligations towards his or her own state, which has to weigh its responsibility regarding its own citizens and the implementation of international human rights treaties. This in-between position inevitably causes feelings of frustration and not only betrayal towards the patient, but also towards human rights conventions and towards the state.

THE CONVENTIONS AND THEIR RELATION TO
THE HEALTH SITUATION OF AN ASYLUM-SEEKER

In the particular case of Mrs. NN, and asylum applications in general, the wording of the 1951 Convention Relating to the Status of Refugees and the 1967 protocol and other conventions which are today regularly encountered in making a decision, even though they may not give rise to any status under the 1951 convention, are:

- Article 1(2) (the refugee definition) and article 33(1) (the principle of *non-refoulement*): Refugee Convention 33(1), "No contracting state shall expel or return (*"refouler"*) a refugee in any manner whatsoever to the frontiers of territories where his life or freedom would be threatened on account of his race, religion, nationality, membership of a particular social group, or political opinion."
- Article 3 of the European Convention on Human Rights (ECHR): "No one shall be subjected to torture or to inhuman or degrading treatment."
- Article 5 of the ECHR, which deals with the right to liberty and security but is derogible, as is article 8(1), which reads: "Everyone has the right to respect for his private and family life, his home, and his correspondence."
- Article 3 of the Convention against Torture (CAT) (and similar, but differently worded article 7 of the International Convention for the Protection of Civil and Political Rights [ICPCPR], article 5 of the African Charter on Human Political Rights [ACHPR], and article 3 of the ECHR). Article 3(1) of the CAT read: "No state party shall expel, return (*refouler*), or extradite a person to another state where there are substantial grounds for believing that he would be in danger of being subjected to torture."

In the asylum determination process the medical situation of an asylum-seeker may be relevant in the following situations:[11]

1. The medical condition can give an answer to the question whether there is a need for protection, for example, if there is a fear for torture

or inhuman or degrading treatment in the country of origin (e.g., article 33(1) of the Refugee Convention, aricle 3(1) of the CAT).

2. The medical condition can be of such a nature that return to the country of origin leads to a possible inhuman and degrading treatment. For example, if there are insufficient possibilities for medical treatment (e.g., article 3 of the ECHR).

3. The medical condition can be a reason for inconsistencies in his asylum request. For example, in the case of post-traumatic stress reactions.[12]

THE REFUGEE DETERMINATION PROCESS

Part B of the *UNHCR Handbook on Procedures and Criteria for Determining Refugee Status* (the *Handbook*) offers guidance upon how a decision as to recognition of refugee status is to be reached. The prime obligation is upon the applicant to make out her claim for recognition, but it is, or should be, recognized that the duty to ascertain and evaluate the facts is shared between her and the decision maker. Sometimes the latter may have to produce the evidence.[13] This may be so with background material, and when the applicant is under a disability, an unaccompanied child, or a mentally challenged person.[14] The conclusions of the medical expert may dictate the decision-maker's approach to that evidence itself[15] apart from its influence upon the ability to return the applicant.

Severe persecution often leads to *"tainted"* evidence and thus adds difficulties toward reaching conclusions on the basic story. As with other evidence, and sometimes more so, it can influence a decision on whether what may happen upon return is likely to amount to persecution and inhumane treatment.[16] In the context of deportation, in the United Kingdom[17] there is a need to balance, on the one hand, the need to support a proper immigration policy, and on the other to give proper regard to the compassionate facts peculiar to the applicant. As recent cases under article 8 of the European Convention on Human Rights have emphasized there must be a *"proportional"* approach.

The applicant must tell the truth as best she can, and support her claim with whatever evidence she can obtain. The decision maker must evaluate the evidence, assess the reliability or credibility[18] of the applicant, and anyone she can find to support her story, and look at the overall plausibility of the story and, giving the benefit of any doubt remaining, reach a decision.[19] In telling her story an applicant is well-advised to get all the main facts the first time around. If not, she runs the risk of being disbelieved.

Dissecting the last paragraph, the system must enable her to tell her story: In some jurisdictions the legislation is either not readily available or it is not translated into a language that the applicant can understand. She is not obliged, at least in the United Kingdom or under the *Handbook* to produce corroboration,[20] nor is she obliged (paragraph 196 of the *Handbook,* notwithstanding) to give evidence herself or call a witness who could support her—but failure to do so must have some effect, and would readily find expression in a conclusion that there is something requiring explanation. Where there is none the tribunal may find the burden of proof is unsatisfied.

Telling the truth and being believed are of course two different things. For the decision maker hearing the story through an interpreter[21] and being unfamiliar with the culture or even the topography of a country can have a bearing on his or her conclusions. The importance of good representation can be crucial. Sometimes the background information is inherently conflicting, out of date, or incomplete. Countries do not, will not, or simply cannot share what they know, publicly at least.[22] More focused information may be necessary in order to allow the decision maker to come closer to a proper decision.

The Refugee Convention does not require particular procedures for refugee status determinations, though paragraphs 191 through 194 spell out the best practices in any determination. The EU is wedded to a Common Asylum Policy and all it entails.[23] Likewise, minimum standards have been adopted by the UNHCR. The International Association of Refugee Law Judges (IARLJ) includes among its aims both the fairness in the procedures and the application of the rule of law to all refugee determination procedures. This should be obvious, but is often obscured by governments who feel threatened. They sometimes enact a provision that places a time limit within which a claim must be made,[24] or within which to appeal or produce documents. Also presumptions are created or encouraged such as safe countries of origin or transit, relying on forged documents, or the route traveled, removing or limiting rights of appeal as a result thereof and linking nonadmissibility to the process.[25]

PRESUMPTIONS IN THE DETERMINATION PROCESS

There are many spoken presumptions, but regretfully there are also the unspoken ones. These vary from the racially prejudiced variety to the generalized categories of *"bogus," "spongers," "economic migrants,"* and to the *"if I decide this way I open the floodgates,"* or the more subtle *"well if he gets Exceptional Leave to Remain (ELR)[26] it achieves the main object."*

To the decision maker presumptions are a tool and used judicially a proper and inevitable one. Some are legal and some evidential. The common legal ones of "safe countries of origin" and "safe third- (first) country" are only as good as the information on which they are based. Rarely does one know this. They also suffer from the disadvantage that they are not amenable to swift adaptation to changing circumstances.

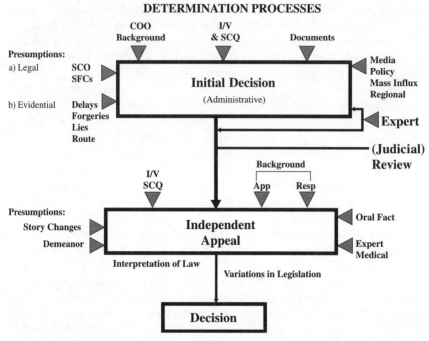

DETERMINATION PROCESSES

Figure 5.1.   The determination process and the aspects that might influence the outcome

Evidential presumptions, such as relying on forged documents, telling lies, failing to claim asylum in the first country arrived at or immediately on entering the host country, all have a place in this armory. The common difficulty is, once again, that they often depend upon the possession of detailed and reliable knowledge on the part of the decision maker. Without that they are no better than the decision makers' often fanciful view of life.[27] In this jurisdiction the sheer weight of numbers coupled with the power of the vote in some regions or the apprehensions related to security in others has to be recognized.

Generally, the standard that the applicant must be able to reach to be said to establish his claim may be a lighter one than would be found in the courts in civil cases—it may be *"a reasonable likelihood," "a real danger,"* or *"a real risk,"*[28] and the jurisdiction generally seems to permit a much more relaxed attitude to any rules of evidence that a country may have. Demeanor may be of little help though frequently lip service is paid to it.[29] The decision maker has a very difficult decision to make, however well he or she may be trained, however sympathetic or well-informed in most cases, at the end of the day the question *"is the story, as to those parts upon which his claim depends, essentially true?"* must be answered and in which direction will such a signpost point? Towards recognition or away from it? Experience in assessment of credibility is of very little use, since we never learn whether the assessment we made was right or wrong!

THE RELEVANT ASPECTS FOR THE DETERMINATION PROCESS IN THE CASE OF MRS. NN

The case of Mrs. NN raises most of the issues faced by applicants in presenting their case. In relation firstly to the medical evidence the most important aspects for the determination process are Mrs. NN's present state of health and mind and the prognosis. Also her present ability to tell the facts accurately and an assessment of the future (*"tainted evidence"*). Of further interest are the qualification and experience of the medical expert both in his field and of Iran. What formed the basis for the medical reports? How and where were the facts obtained by the medical expert?

The medical reports should show and be perceived as impartial. No conclusions and deductions should be expressed. Relevant are questions such as: at whose request were the medical reports made; and what is the etiology of PTSD? Given any reliable information on what facilities there are or may be available in Iran, how may this affect Mrs. NN if she remains at liberty, and if she does not? What are the effects of abbreviated time limits, and what are the effects of delay in the procedures?

To the decision maker the impartiality of the medical report of the psychiatrist is the guarantee of detachment that helps him to be better able to accept and rely on the report. The more "partisan" the psychiatrist seems, then the less likely it is that the decision maker will find the report useful.

Then the decision maker must take into account what training the decision maker has (if any!) What is the reliable *current* background information in Iran as far as it is material?[30]

Is there any other oral or documentary evidence? What are the possible definitions of persecution, a particular social group, or political opinion? Even of the agent of persecution or internal flight (protection)? Whether any other convention may apply (e.g., the CAT), and on what grounds? What may happen at port of entry if Mrs. NN would be returned?

While the decision maker—or appeal body—is not directly concerned with the welfare and living conditions of Mrs. NN, given her medical condition and the presence of members of her family in the host country, those factors could affect removal.[31]

BEST PRACTICES

There can be no single "correct" structure and none that can be said to be perfect. Professor Joe Carens' reflects[32] that any system should be able to tell, in an explicable manner, who may stay and who must go—and quickly. The EU's call for clear, simple, and common procedures, a level playing field reducing opportunities for the exploitation of differences from country to country, for harmonization, are indeed understandable and laudable, but from a courts' point of view not necessarily as effectual as governments expect them to be. The blame in this regard is frequently attributed (wrongly it is felt) to the courts themselves. The EU recognizes that to attain a single common structure may be an aim. The difficulty is that to reach this, first there is only agreement on minimum standards, and in the final stage there will only be a compromise. That compromise must be one which goes from the minimum, which the most conscientious and indeed rich countries will accept to the maximum, and which the poorest can afford.

One can only say for the time being that any structure must satisfy five criteria if it is to have a hope of reaching a defensible decision:

- it must be capable of being understood;
- it must be available;
- it must be capable of being independently reviewed both on fact and law;
- there must be adequate up-to-date background material; and finally
- the decision makers must be properly trained and resourced.[33]

Returning to the *Handbook*, the duty to ascertain and evaluate the relevant facts is a shared one. The applicant, whether she is fleeing persecution in a 1951 convention context or simply getting away from an intolerable situation that affords no access to protection (and may perhaps have been recognized under another refugee convention), is in a more vulnerable position than she would be in the host country itself. Nevertheless, she needs to be "sensitized" to her position and obligations in her host country.[34]

WHOSE JUSTICE, WHICH RATIONALITY?—
CONCLUDING REMARKS

The case study and the problems it raises for a psychiatrist are representative for what psychiatrists and other health care practitioners in Western countries are regularly confronted with in their care for asylum-seekers. They meet the consequences of all sorts of political-economic violence in the world in the form of the social suffering of individuals.

Rules, regulations, and protocols have been developed in order to help states decide about the asylum applications. In this development the state has to solve a moral double-bind: how to protect the interest of the state and its citizens while at the same time taking international human rights conventions seriously. Once the frameworks are ready for implementation they enforce a deterministic reasoning: In case of A then always B.

Psychiatrists, insofar as they are directly or indirectly involved in the decision-making procedures of the state, are asked to comply with this reasoning, while their profession asks, or at least due to its subject matter should ask, for a different kind of logic (e.g., moral engagement with the case instead of impartiality). They have to come to terms with the question of what is good, responsible, or ethical behavior in the dilemma presented. All the institutions the psychiatrist is confronted with (the psychiatric institution, the state and its judicial system, the United Nations) have their own perspectives of justice and rationality.

Some sort of "holistic ethics" might be of most interest to the patient, but the psychiatrist is often left with no more than situational ethics. In each different situation he or she has to decide, as rationally as possibly, what is good, responsible, and thus ethical behavior toward the patient in this particular context.

In the case of Mrs. NN, when facing a court hearing, the government finally decided to grant the applicant permission to stay in the country for humanitarian reasons.[35] The patient's condition became less critical, but as expected, she did not recover from her psychiatric condition after the decision was made. However, it was possible to establish a more secure and constructive treatment situation.

One could question if Mrs. NN should not have been given protection against inhuman and degrading treatment in an earlier stage. At face value one could conclude that based on the medical reports various articles of international and European conventions could have been applied.

Of course, the medical expert should not imply any usurpation of the decision-maker's duty to make a decision on the basis of what is heard and, on the basis of all the evidence, what is accepted. But, recognition should grow that the judicial determination process is (also) an intersubjective one, which can easily be influenced by (lack of) knowledge about backgrounds, presumptions, and hypes. In fact, although the position of a psychiatrist towards the patient is a different one than the position of a decision maker; in both relations with the asylum applicant countertransference reactions may occur.[36]

It was an achievement to get 139 countries to sign the 1951 convention. It will be a greater one to hold them to their obligations on a worldwide basis. The case history illustrates just how much work there is yet to be done, even in the countries recognized for their adherence to human rights and the rule of law. The judges can collectively harmonize the interpretation of the convention and explain where there are inevitable differences. They can ensure the presence of the rule of law and the best practices in all procedural matters. Some questions with regard to the role for medical practitioners in asylum procedures of their patients have stayed unanswered. Interdisciplinary discussions, as held around the case of Mrs. NN can contribute to finding the most appropriate answers.

NOTES

This chapter was first published as "When Ethics, Health Care, and Human Rights Conflict: Mental Health Care for Asylum," *Cambridge Quarterly of Healthcare Ethics* 11, no.3 (summer 2002). Reprinted by permission of the Cambridge University Press.

1. Which may vary from overprotection to denial and even "blaming the victim" reactions.

2. Parts of her contribution appeared in: Richters, A., "When Ethics, Health Care and Human Rights Conflict: Mental Health Care for Asylum Seekers. *Cambridge Quarterly of Health Care Ethics* 11, No. 3 (2002): 304–318.

3. The report has been adapted from the original ones, mainly to preserve the patient's confidentiality.

4. American Psychiatric Association. *Diagnostic and Statistical Manual of Mental Disorders*, DSM-IV. (Washington, D.C. 1994).

5. According to section 3 in the Norwegian Mental Health Act, which allows for up to three weeks of observation against the patient's will, if necessary.

6. Kleinlutenbelt, D., and Naaykens, A. "Morele dilemma's bij de psychiatrische hulpverlening aan asielzoekers," (Moral dilemmas in psychiatric assistance to asylum seekers), *Maandblad Geestelijke Volksgezondheid* 53 (1998): 623–638.

7. Richters, A. "Medical Ethics and Informed Consent: Cultural and Ideological Difference," in Willigen L. Van (ed.), *Medical Ethical Standards in Mental Health Care for Victims of Organized Violence, Refugees and Displaced Persons* (Amsterdam: Royal Tropical Institute, 1998): 71–79.

8. Widdershoven, G. *Ethiek in de kliniek: Hedendaagse benaderingen in de gezondheidsethiek.* (*Ethics in the clinic: Contemporary approaches in medical ethics*) (Amsterdam: Boom, 2000).

9. Bracken, P., Gillen, J.E., and Summerfield, D. "Ethical Issues in Mental Health Work with Refugees." in Willigen L. Van, (ed.), *Medical ethical standards in mental Health Care for Victims of Organized Violence, Refugees and Displaced Persons* (Amsterdam: Royal Tropical Institute, 1998).

10. Ibid.

11. Zwaan, K. "International Law, Medical Aspects and Asylum." Paper presented at the IARLJ European Chapter Conference, Dublin, May 16 & 17, 2002.

12. See *Kisoki v. Sweden.* CAT Communication no. 41/1996, 8 May 1996, 9.3.

13. See *Secretary for State for the Home Department (SSHD) v. Mohammed Bouheraoua.* QBD CO-878-98 25.5.00 per J. Dyson, par. 25.

14. See *R v. SSHD ex parte Kazim Kilic* CA(99-7005-4) esp. par. 39.

15. *Amrik Singh v. SSHD* (CA) [2000] Immigration Appeal Reports 340.

16. *D v. UK* 2.5.97 *Report* 37-III (available treatment for AIDS-quality of life) (1997).

17. Part 13, Statement of Changes on Immigration Rules.

18. Op. cit. 13.

19. See *Eleilmaran* (IAT UK) 00 THt/01369), 1.6.00.

20. Though in the United States absence of documentary support for an assertion seems to be expected at least.

21. See a United Kingdom IAT decision *Cavasoglu v. SSHD* (15357) for a robust defense of the right of the appellant to give evidence in whatever language he chooses.

22. Note the Centre for Information and Research on Exiles and Asylum-Seekers (CIREA) in the EU.

23. *Tampere 15–16* October 1999. Proposal for Council Directive Relating to Minimum Standards Concerning the Procedure for Granting and Withdrawing COM (2000) 578 final—2000/0238(CNS) Refugee Status in Member States, October 2000. See also *IJRL* 4, No. 11 (1999): 738 for a survey and some comment.

24. Decision of the Polish Supreme Administrative Court in 1999.

25. See *Dhesi* (UK IAT) (13879).

26. See a decision of the UK IAT (chaired by Mr. Rapinet).

27. See *Mendes 1996* (UK IAT).

28. But see *R. v. Karanakaran* (CA) [2000] ImmAR; 27 for a recent approach to fact-finding obligations in this jurisdiction; also see n. 14 above.

29. For an interesting and useful cautionary guidance on "credibility" findings see J. Webster in *R v. SSHD ex parte DGPatel* [1986] ImmAR 208: 212–214.

30. See *NZ* case of *RSAA 72427/99*.

31. The decision in Kilic above, n. 14 is useful also on all these issues.

32. In a paper presented to the Refugee Studies Program, Oxford, 1998.

33. Both these issues are being addressed by the IARLJ. It has developed a set of workshop materials and trained facilitators to run workshops. So far well over twenty-five judges have attended these courses. The question of background materials and access by judges to decisions in other countries is being addressed by Professor Hathaway and others, as well as the IARLJ. The EU makes attempts through CIREA and the OAU that has the machinery to assemble materials.

34. See the Conclusions of the Judicial Round Table (OAU/UNHCR) 17 November 2000, Addis Ababa.

35. This is the usual type of permission given to asylum-seekers in Norway. Only 1–3 percent of them get asylum.

36. Crépeau, F., Foxen, P., Houle, F., and Rousseau, C. *Multidisciplinary Analysis of the IRB Decision-Making Process. Summary Report.* (Montreal: University of Quebec, 2000).

6

Refugees: Whose Term Is It Anyway? *Emic* and *Etic* Constructions of "Refugees" in Modern Greek

Eftihia Voutira

The title of this chapter suggests an issue of appropriation of the term "refugee." The implicit subjects in this debate are the main actors in most forced migration situations: namely, the host society as a whole, the displaced, and the international organizations whose role is to protect refugee rights. I raise this question not rhetorically but anthropologically; my aim is to argue that the concept refugee not only has different connotations in different cultures but that the cultural meaning of the term refugee is an essential component of the way the legal definition is perceived and applied in an international context. For the sake of argument, I will assume that there is an *etic* view of refugees, which is normally identified with the "legal definition," enshrined in the 1951 convention and recognized on the official level by all states that are signatories to the convention. I call this view *etic* with special reference to the linguistic notion (e.g., phonetic/phonemic) as introduced by Kenneth Pike and elaborated upon by Marvin Harris, in order to denote the reference to the observer's attempt "to describe behavior from outside a particular system."[1] In contrast, there is an informal, and one might argue, more "muddled" use of the term in popular imagination. This use is largely predicated on an archetypal reference to flight or forced migration as an essential component of refugeeness independently of the other criteria that apply in determining refugee status.

As elaborated below, the term "refugee" has positive connotations in Greece and is used as a term of honor, unlike contemporary constructions of the term based on negative stereotypes casting refugees as a burden and state liability. This positive connotation is largely due to the collective perception of the "successful" integration and publicly acknowledged contribution of Asia Minor refugees to the twentieth-century Greek economic, social, and cultural development. Specifically, the meaning of the term refugee in modern Greek is informed and mediated by the collective memory of the Asia Minor refugees as a national asset (i.e., as integrated refugees), after their rehabilitation and effective adaptation into modern Greek society. This particular form of anachronism is an essential component of collective social memory construction and one that, as Paul Connerton has noted, depends on the regular repetition and reaffirmation of the past in the present through commemorative narrative enactments of significant events that mark the identity of a society.[2]

Whether the reception of the Asia Minor refugees was truly a "success" case depends not only on the time of assessment (long- versus short-term), but also on whose criteria are being applied and whether, to the extent that any received wisdom is sought to be reapplied elsewhere, the success is transferable to other cases of refugee settlement in other regions or in the same country at a later historical time.[3]

My main concern is not to make such an assessment, but rather to show the longer-term consequences of Greece's "refugee past" and to apply this to the case of Soviet Greek newcomers, the majority of whom are close relatives of those Asia Minor refugees that came from the Pontos during the 1918–1923 period. I will show that this issue has relevance in the way these recent arrivals, through their cultural associations, construe their refugee identity as an essential component of their financial expectations from the Greek state.

THE ETHNOGRAPHIC CONTEXT

Focusing on the post-1989 arrivals from the former Soviet Union (FSU), I give examples of the newcomers' preference for being called, and using as a term of self-ascription, "refugees" (*prosphyges*), rather than "repatriates" (*palinnostoundes*), or "returnees" (*epanapatrizomenoi*), as various Greek state actors have labeled them. As used in the context of modern Greek, the term repatriate (*palinnostoundes*) refers to the more recent Soviet Greek arrivals by distinguishing them from the political refugees of the Greek Civil War, who fled to communist countries and were granted the right to return to Greece (*epanapatrizomenoi*) after the end of the military junta (1976). As such, the term has particular social connotations and political implications; it refers to the east-west migration phenomenon that consists of a reshuffling of populations along ethnic lines across the old Cold War divide, allowing specific populations to return to their putative "historical homelands" (e.g., ethnic Germans, Greeks, Poles, Jews), a direct result of the liberalization policies of the late Soviet regime and eventual disintegration of the FSU. Thus, "Soviet Greeks," like the other ethnic minorities of the FSU that have a "place to go" in the west, have been granted "the right to return"—but still, many insist on being called refugees!

The ethnographic context drawn on is based on contemporary debates taking place in Greece as to whether the coethnic newcomers from the FSU are refugees or repatriates. This debate is paradigmatic of the problem that is addressed by the main hypothesis of my chapter—namely that the term refugee is not a rigid designator in the sense of denoting a "modality" that necessarily exists. Like other concepts and beliefs in any social context, the term refugee is a concept that correlates with other social institutions within society[4] and methodologically to understand its uses implies also understanding the wider workings of society.

In this particular cultural context refugee is a term adopted as a self-ascription by newcomer groups, asserting their membership in the Greek nation by using the concept, which by definition in its international legal sense excludes the co-ethnic component. (See condition 4 of article 1 of the Refugee Convention, which asserts that a refugee should be "outside his/her country of origin and be unable or unwilling to avail him or herself of the protection of that country"). Interestingly, the Soviet Greeks claim their refugeeness on the grounds of their Greekness only after arriving in their "historical homeland"—mainland Greece.

The situation seems odd and is used as an example in addressing the wider issue of the dialectic between the "local" meaning of refugee and the international convention usage. My aim is two-fold: a) to explore the limits of interdisciplinarity in forced migration studies by looking at how the concept refugee is used in the cultural context of modern Greek, and b) to suggest that what people *want* to be called has some relevance even if that meaning does not strictly correspond with the formal legal notion of refugee.[5] This approach also leads to a consideration of the researcher's stance in regard to his or her informants and to the official interpretation of the concept. My focus is on the *emic* construction of refugee in Greek—a term whose cultural connotations are based on the precedent of the mass forcible exchange of populations agreement between Greece and Turkey, under the Lausanne Treaty (1923). Accordingly, as I will argue, the positive meaning of the term refugee is embedded in the cultural knowledge that mainland Greek people share through their collective experience as socialized members of the nation.

THE CONCEPT REFUGEE IN GREEK

Conceptually, the notion refugee, like "diaspora," is a mass term that often overshadows the significant ethnological complexity involved in such identifications. Anthropologically, more than migration movement per se, refugees are seen as people in a state of liminality, betwixt and between, who, unless they are integrated into the state, remain, to use Mary Douglas' imagery of pollution, "matter out of place."[6] Typically, it is a term applied to the incoming groups, by the recipient groups (the host society), and in its twentieth-century context, a refugee is also a label that confers legal status on the bearers, who are entitled to financial assistance by the international humanitarian community and often compete with their hosts for available resources.[7]

In most languages the term 'refugee' has particular connotations relating to collective historical experiences. Seen as a decoding device, its usage is of particular interest in anthropological analysis since it discloses the values of the society that may acknowledge the presence of the phenomenon at its core.[8]

SOME HISTORY: DISCOURSES ON REFUGEES IN INTERWAR GREECE

The Romantic View

Under the principle of nation-state sovereignty, changes over a territory entail changes in the identity of the inhabitants of the regions that find themselves under this new authority. Border changes in this sense have a direct impact on questions of identity, membership, and belonging. Throughout the nineteenth and early twentieth centuries, the expanding territorial sovereignty of the Greek state to the north, the cultivation of the official state ideology of irredentism (the *Great Idea*), and the experiences of expulsions from different territories in the Balkans provided the context for a continuous debate on the uses of the term refugee and the corresponding obligation of the "homeland state" (Greece) to provide asylum: What did the term mean for a mainland Greek national? What did it mean for people who saw themselves as members of a larger Greek diaspora that extended beyond the boundaries of the Greek state? How should the term "*prosphygas*" (refugee) be used as a "label" for people fleeing conflict and disaster? These debates appear in the early twentieth century and as such they form part of an emerging discourse on refugees, by seeking to identify an appropriate response to what is perceived to be the refugee problem. In a document published in the Greek language newspaper *Melissa* in Odessa, itself a refugee journal whose editors fled from Bucharest in 1914, the writer presents a "romantic" view of the Greek exiles flooding the ports of Odessa, a major center of the Greek diaspora at the turn of the century.

> The term "refugee" (*prosphygas*) has acquired a new and unique meaning *(nean kai idiazousan semasian)* in the Greek language over recent years. It became a familiar term in the history of modern Greece, and fully identified with national struggles. . . . Refugees are not merely those in need of protection from others in order to survive and maintain their existence. Everyone who flees his homeland involuntarily (*akousios*) and tastes suffering (*xenitia*) and by necessity (*kat' anagen*) who is not able to return to his home is, and should be, considered a refugee.[9]

I call the view articulated in this passage "romantic" because of the explicit association the author makes of the Greek national struggles and the creation of refugees as the victims of "just wars" of liberation. The further criterion of coercion and persecution introduced as a determinant of refugee identity is seen here as a consequence rather than as a precondition of refugeeness.[10] The document suggests that refugees are valuable resources for their hosts. This optimistic account of the refugee experience and immediate adaptation into the host economy and society seems unrealistic, not only for us today, but also for Konstantinides' Greek-speaking audience of the time, confronted as they were by the continuous experiences of mass expulsions and forced migration of populations in Greece and other regions where the Greek diaspora lived. Thus, it can be usefully contrasted with the more "pragmatic" view that captures the other side of the debate, suggesting thus the spectrum of positions concerning Greek refugee discourse *before* the Lausanne Treaty, which set its own precedent concerning the usage of refugee in modern Greek.

Migrants and Refugees: The Pragmatist View

In his memorandum of 4 August 1921 to the Greek Ministry of Foreign Affairs, Archbishop Dimitrios Karapatakis, himself a survivor of post–World War I armed conflicts at the Anatolian/Caucasian border, offers an analysis of the changing situation in the Caucasus and redefines the relationship between migrant and refugee. The aim of the document is to address the question of a more effective intervention at the level of Greek national policy to the large influx of refugees. The latter are defined in terms of the "conditions of duress and uprooting, loss of property, and forced expulsions" by contrast to migrants who, "are people who deliberately decide to emigrate under conditions of peace and quietness."[11]

The description of the crisis and the call for intervention in Karapatakis' memorandum intimates the importance that the *scale* of an influx of newcomers can make in setting the requirements for state intervention. His basic argument is that current practices vis-à-vis refugees from the Caucasus should be stopped for two reasons: a) because there are no more substantive reasons for refugee flight from the Caucasus, and b) because the conditions in the camps jeopardizes the survival of the newcomers more seriously than if they stayed in their areas in the Black Sea. The underlying view is based on the interests of the refugees and in this sense it provides a compelling variant to other texts of the period, which tend to promote the interests of the receiving state. By identifying the main criterion of refugeeness to be flight from persecution, Karapatakis observes that the newcomers from the Caucasus are *no longer* refugees; they are immigrants because the causes for their original expatriation from the Caucasus have been eliminated (i.e., the advance of the Turkish Army, at the time of his writing, had stopped).

In order to deal with the plight of the more worthy, or "real" refugees, his recommendations include:

a) that asylum in Greece be given only to those who have been *uprooted two or three times*, migrants (i.e., "people who want to come for economic reasons to have a better life and to pursue commerce in Greece") should not be assisted.

b) that refugees be sent directly to their settlements, without having to go through the transit centers in order to minimize waste, suffering, and exploitation and be given the chance "to live like human beings and the opportunity to sow in the spring—something that would be profitable for themselves and the Greek state."[12]

Karapatakis' account captures, in summary form, the historical scene and the predicament of multiple forcible uprooting of masses of Greek Orthodox and largely Greek-speaking populations in the Balkans and eastern Anatolia at the end of World War I. His recommendations are also significant in that they anticipate the approach adopted by the Greek state in its assistance program that used the refugees as resources in national development.

REFUGEES AS IMMIGRANTS: THE INTERNATIONAL PERSPECTIVE

A third variant definition comes from one of the main protagonists of the post-Lausanne Treaty coordinating agency of assistance to the refugees, Refugee Resettlement Committee (RSC)—Charles Eddy. He introduces a novel criterion for the identity of the newcomers from Asia Minor to Greece that is predicated on their *ethnic membership* rather than their experience of persecution or political allegiance. "The refugees were immigrants it is true, but they were Greek immigrants coming to Greece, not aliens from a foreign shore."[13] Eddy's criterion reflects both the spirit and the letter of the Lausanne Treaty Exchange of

Populations Agreement between Greece and Turkey (Article 8), which labels the exchanged populations "immigrants" (*metanastai*) and sought the national homogenization of the populations in each country.[14]

Despite the official labeling of the newcomers as *immigrants*, the concept adopted on the societal level was that of the refugees. This practice intimates the resistance of popular imagination to adopt the meanings that appear to explain away the salient features of the "refugee experience" identified with the uprooting and loss of "home" and the denial of the newcomer's "Greekness" by the host population.

ELEMENTS OF "NATIONAL SUCCESS": GREEK COLLECTIVE MEMORY ABOUT THE "REFUGEE PAST"

Greece's "refugee past" has not until recently been part of standard "textbook knowledge" of Greek history.[15] There is, however, a remarkable consensus among scholars, politicians, and the refugees concerning the success of the 1923 settlement. In Greek academic writing, the case is often used as an example in disciplines such as international relations, history, and economics[16] and as such has contributed to the social construction of knowledge and the twentieth-century Greek collective memory regarding Greece's refugee past. The memory of the refugee past as a story with a happy ending is typically encapsulated in popular discourses by the often-repeated evocative phrase, "the Asia Minor refugees managed despite all odds to tame their fates and inject new blood into the old Greece."[17] Assuming a culturally homogenous state as a major political end, Kitromilides notes that "the whole effect of cultural evangelism of community construction worked out so well that Greece, after absorbing the Greek populations of Asia Minor and Thrace following the exchange of populations in 1923, emerged as one of the most ethnically homogeneous states in Europe."[18]

The term refugees has a positive connotation on the level of modern Greek collective representations. In one such affirmation, Leonidas Iasonides, a Pontic Greek refugee who repeatedly served as a member of the Greek Parliament with the *Komma Phileftheron* (Venizelos' Party) after the 1924 elections, stated:

> Many times, it has been said that we should finally stop being called 'refugees' since after 30 years we are all now natives, children of the same Greek homeland [*patrida*]. . . . The term 'refugee' is a term of 'honour' and we must insist on it, and not only we, the true refugees [*alethes prosphyges*], but the children of our children as well. [19]

As encapsulated in Iasonides' speech, the impact of the Asia Minor refugee experience on the meaning of the term refugee as a hereditary entitlement and term of honor has great relevance for understanding some of the contemporary expectations of newcomers and hosts in Greece. Such ideas have found resonance among the more recent Pontic Greek newcomers from the FSU, many of whom feel that they, also, are the descendants of what Iasonides refers to as, *alethes prosphyges,* "true refugees."

PERCEPTIONS AND DIFFERING EXPECTATIONS AMONG "OLD" AND "NEW" GREEK REFUGEES

The majority of the "Soviet Greeks," as I have called them for the sake of simplicity, arriving in Greece in the early 1990s do not speak modern Greek and, prior to leaving the FSU, had little understanding of their co-ethnics inside Greece. The older generations arriving from central Asia, Georgia, and southern Russia still speak the Pontic Greek dialect, which they refer to as *romeika.*[20] The rediscovery of an ethnic past inside the FSU coincided with liberalization policies introduced in the late *perestroika* years. Elements of such "ethnogenesis" were evident, for example, in the establishment of Greek festivals, including traditional dancing and singing throughout the regions they inhabited, which spread from the Ukraine to central Asia.

The people in Greece had somewhat unrealistic expectations of the newcomers, often mediated by collective perceptions about the country's "refugee past." The post-1989 formal encounter of the two groups began with a euphoric "rediscovering their long lost brothers." The media and politicians in Greece hailed the newcomers as members of the Greek nation, as "our own."

Those Soviet Greeks who had, in the early 1990s, faced the predicament of staying in the FSU or going to Greece had great expectations of their "historical homeland." Maintaining a distinct ethnic identity as Greeks under the old Soviet regime had often exacted high costs, the incentive, usually being ties to a "fatherland" abroad. The stronger the Soviet Greeks felt disillusionment with their Soviet past, and the greater their fear of economic and physical insecurity and the threat that minority rights would be undermined in the context of an emerging nationalist discourse in different regions of central Asia, Georgia, or southern Russia, the more they expected from Greece.[21]

The Soviet Greeks not only had higher expectations of their hosts than did their counterparts in the 1920s, they were also less suited to rural living and agriculture, in particular. Once inside Greece and dissatisfied with the treatment they encountered in their putative homeland, they were mobilized by Pontic Greek associations. The newcomers themselves began to use the language of the 1920 policies to further their cause and, aware of the positive connotations of refugees in the Greek context, seized upon the term as self-ascription in an attempt to achieve greater entitlements.

In an article entitled, "Who are we?" the president of the Thessaloniki Association of Pontic Greek Refugees from the FSU (*Syllogos Pontion Prosphygon apo tin teos Sovietike Enosi*), Y. Eleftheriadis, argued in favor of the refugee label as a term of self-ascription, by drawing on Greece's refugee past:

> Everyone knows about the exchange of properties as part of the Lausanne Treaty and the exchange of populations. Land property was distributed then to those refugees including those who arrived gradually from Russia until 1930.[22] (*Epistrophe*, October 1992:4)

The further elaboration of the Soviet Greek self-ascription as refugees is particularly telling.

> We, the Pontic Greeks from the FSU, are not merely 'repatriates' (*palinnostoundes*). We are refugees (*eimaste prosfyges*). [Because] if we, or our ancestors, had been able to catch the boats and come to Greece in 1920 then we would have had the right to the lottery for land distribution. In fact, however, by closing its borders, the S.U. deprived us of the right to resettle in Greece (*na metoikisoume stin Ellada*). Since Pontic Greeks were not able to leave the S.U., not of their own fault but because of coercion, they must now be considered by Greece as refugees from Turkey via the S.U. which had in the meantime closed its borders. If not, it follows that someone who was able to reach Greece from Turkey during the 1920–1930 period is a refugee, while another who fled from death and fell into the trap of the Stalinist regime—is not a refugee.[23]

In insisting on the use of the designation refugee as a term of self-ascription, other associations centered their criticism on the inefficient and ineffective manner in which assistance, mainly in the form of relief, was allocated to them by the state in a manner that marginalized and dehumanized the recipients.[24]

The Pontic Greeks' articulation of their demands encountered resistance at the level of state actors and the local population, who expected the newcomers to conform to the received wisdom concerning the 1923 refugees that the host population shared. Both policymakers and the locals tended to view the immigrating Soviet Greeks in a less favorable light than those who had been subject to a forced exchange of populations. Despite what has been described by some as "forced flight" and the nationalist and religious concerns facing the Soviet Greeks in the FSU, they were often perceived by their host Greeks to be "only" economic migrants. On the intragroup level, differentiations persisted; many of the Soviet Greeks who arrived in Greece in the early 1980s insist, "Those who come now are not real Greeks suffering under the Soviet regime; they are capitalists. They only come here to trade and make a better living."

Disillusionment with the newcomers was similarly voiced by a government official in Athens. In a personal communication of 6 May 1995, former Secretary of State V. Tsouderou found that instead of being appreciative of the material assistance and the training programs offered them, the Soviet Greeks were "*choosy* and ungrateful towards the Greek state."

Georgios Iakovou, a former Secretary of State of the Republic of Cyprus, who in 1994 was appointed as president of the Greek National Foundation on the grounds of his experience in managing the settlement of Cypriot refugees after the 1974 invasion, noted that:

> In Cyprus the refugees from the northern regions were "war refugees" and were received by the local people as the victims of that war . . . [while] in Greece the newcomers from Russia are not refugees—they come voluntarily to improve their lot. They are economic migrants, they don't speak the language, they have a different culture but they are officially ethnic Greeks so they share the same rights as other Greeks in terms of employment, protection and political rights. Yet what is still lacking is social solidarity with the native population.[25]

NEGOTIATING REFUGEENESS: TYPES OF REFUGEES IN GREECE

So far I have tried to show how the newcomers capitalize on the term refugee to express their dissent from the official labeling as originally used by the state. In this their activities have had some impact since much of the debate in the Greek Parliament today involves the recognition of the label *neoprosphyges* (new refugees) in contrast to the 1923 precedent.

The term also reflects another cultural assumption concerning the genuineness of the refugee label, which presumes that the only *true* refugees must be of Greek origin. This claim concerning those who are "ours" or "of us" is compatible with Hertzfeld's observation that the category on consanguinity is a dominant metaphor in the context of modern Greece in that it implies that "tolerance is self-evident towards one's consanguines and intolerant toward others."[26]

Greece's record on foreign asylum-seekers is limited. Their reception is biased because of these cultural assumptions, which imply that Sudanese, Palestinian, Ethiopian, Iraqi, or Afghani asylum-seekers are seen as "foreign refugees" and thus as essentially "others," whose treatment is to be guided exclusively by a rigid application of the 1951 Refugee Convention, which is not "common knowledge." Thus on the level of acceptance by the host society, the attitudes towards those who acquire "status" remain largely rigid and intolerant.

Seen from an *etic* perspective, Greece's institutional practice, since becoming a full member state of the EU in 1981, has been that of attempting but largely failing to follow a "Europeanized" and "harmonized" asylum policy and practice. Despite all its good intentions, the Hellenic Republic remains a "semiperipheral" European state, whose refugee protection standards and concomitant practice remain far behind those expected from an EU member state.

According to UNHCR statistics, in 1998 there was a decrease of asylum applications in Greece, contrary to the prevailing trend in Europe.[27] The relatively small refugee inflows in Greece is to be regarded as one of the main factors that have contributed so far to the inertia of the Greek state in the refugee protection domain. As usual, unprotected aliens such as refugees, especially when in small numbers, possess little political clout in a foreign host country, while the national electorates are at best indifferent towards them.

Given the substantial difference in numbers between refugees and "economic immigrants," and the fact that Greece is bound to effectively co operate in the prioritized area of common border (that is, immigration) control with the rest of the EU member states, Greece has shown a serious delay in initiating and developing a refugee protection regime.[28]

CONCLUDING REMARKS

In the preceding discussion I have distinguished between the cultural meaning of refugee in Greek and the current asylum practices of the Greek state. I have tried to make sense of the cultural specificity of the local conceptions of the term refugee by showing the sense in which the concept in modern Greek is a term of honor rather than shame and the way in which Soviet Greek newcomers capitalize on "Greece's long-term refugee past" in order to claim refugee compensation, which they perceive to be a more adequate sum than that of other repatriating labor migrants. In this they are mistaken since Greek asylum legislation is poorly defined and lagging behind in terms of protection, welfare, and refugee rights. In contrast, the repatriates receive privileged treatment and compensation in terms of membership (citizenship rights, subsidized housing for rural settlement, language training, and professional retraining). Yet this is not clearly understood by the newcomers from the FSU, who constitute the majority of the "new refugees" (*neoprosphyges*) as the Greek government has agreed to call them.[29] Their own perception is guided by the precedent of the 1923 "successful resettlement" which, as in the case of modern Greeks, is mediated by the long-term memory of Greece's refugee past. Given the acknowledgment that they are of the same "kin stock," these "new refugees" become a privileged class vis-à-vis other asylum-seekers or foreign refugees, whose rights and livelihoods remain under stress. This implies an interesting gap between the *emic* construction of refugees and the *etic* view of "asylum."

The above also suggests that there is a substantive methodological and ethical issue that is raised for the researcher who, like myself, has been studying the Soviet Greeks in the FSU and in Greece, using what Peter Loizos has called "the negotiated trust model."[30] According to this model, the researcher, rather than totally immersing herself into the community, enters the community "wearily and is greeted cautiously by the locals. The researcher seeks information while being painfully aware that the locals have secrets, which they may seek to keep."[31] Thus, trust and acceptance is something to be sought every step of the way rather than gained for good.

This leads me to ask the following: Can we follow a consistent and non-discriminatory use of refugee and "asylum" rights when our informants insist on a discriminatory approach? Do we have the right to disagree with our informants and to point out the inconsistencies and report matters differently than to what they would have us report? How much are we willing to trust such research from a disciplinary or an interdisciplinary perspective?

Another moral dilemma arises in attempting to interpret Greek state policy vis-à-vis the new refugees and other asylum-seekers: this policy remains inconsistent and discriminatory towards the foreign "others."[32] Even though Greece is bound as a signatory to the convention to protect the latter, it continues to privilege one category of coethnic newcomers. In this case, the concept refugee is a *label applied to a group,* not to an individual with acknowledged status, when the receiving state is willing to acknowledge the historical experience of their suffering. What remains problematic is the fact that while being willing to acknowledge suffering as constitutive of the refugee label, the policy remains preferential towards "our own" members of the nation and distrustful towards the suffering of "others." In the case of "foreign" refugees, their experiences have to be individuated and assessed on a case-by-case basis as recommended by the post–Cold War international humanitarian regime. According to this regime, the problem of asylum is not that of states fulfilling their international moral obligations by providing protection for refugees per se but that of controlling the "international migration crisis."[33]

The current vocabulary of forced migration as used and promoted by the humanitarian regime is meant to describe and accommodate, on an *etic* level, the varieties of situations refugees find themselves in. An acknowledged end of this regime is containment: a policy identified by Anthony Richmond and others as "global apartheid." The power of the metaphor relates to the underlying common mechanism of social control imposed by the use of an elaborate system of labels. From this standpoint, the fact that the modern Greek variant of asylum, which still lacks a coherent mechanism for distinguishing between varieties and categories of refugees, may be seen as a positive sign. Yet, it would be ironic to discover that once Greek asylum structures are up and running, they come to endorse inhumane approaches not only by not complying to international agreements but also by doing so.

NOTES

1. Pike, K. *Language in Relation to a Unified Theory of the Structure of Human Behaviour,* 2d ed., (The Hague: Mouton, 1967), 37. Within anthropology and in its relation to linguistics, the distinction between *etic* and *emic* has a long history and addresses the epistemological assumptions of the discipline itself. It refers largely to the capacity to infer the way "native people think" (*emic*), as opposed to offering an account of a culture in strictly observational terms (*etic*) (cf., Bloch, M. *How We Think They Think: Anthropological Approaches to Cognition, Memory and Literacy* (Boulder, Colorado: Westview Press, 1998). Here I am using the distinction to signpost the significance of looking at native constructions of refugee in modern Greek that are embedded within a set of cultural assumptions about Greece's refugee past. The specific use of this *emic/etic* distinction assumes that the concept refugee as defined by the convention, which plays the role of a binding document among states, would have different *emic* constructions when seen from the standpoint of the different cultures. See also Pike, K. *Talk, Thought and Thing: The Emic Road towards Conscious Knowledge* (Dallas, Texas: Summer Institute of Linguistics, 1993), chapter 5.

2. Connerton, P. *How Societies Remember* (Cambridge: Cambridge University Press, 1989), 12.

3. Voutira E. and Harrell-Bond, B. H. B. *"Successful" Refugee Settlement: Are Past Experiences Relevant?* in *Reconstructing Livelihoods,* Cernea, M. and McDowell, C., (eds.), (Washington, D.C.: World Bank, 2000), 58.

4. Gellner, E. *Concepts and Society,* in *Rationality,* Wilson, B. (ed.), (Oxford: Blackwell, 1974): 18.

5. In *Anatomy of Exile* (London: Harrap, 1972), 32, P. Tabori argues that most exiles resent outside classification, characterization, and generalization. This is true for a number of groups that have resisted the label, the most illustrious example being the White Russians, who preferred to use the term "exile," or *emigré* as a term of self-ascription, according to Chinyaeva, E. "Russian Emigrés: Czechoslovak Refugee Policy and the Development of the International Refugee Regime between the Two Wars," *Journal of Refugee Studies,* 8, No. 2 (1995): 144.

6. Douglas, M. *Purity and Danger: An Analysis of Concepts of Pollution and Taboo* (London: Penguin, 1970) and cf. Harrell-Bond, B. H. B. and Voutira, E. "Anthropology and the Study of Refugees," *Anthropology Today* 8, No. 4 (1992): 11.

7. Harrell-Bond, B. H. B. *Imposing Aid* (Oxford: Oxford University Press, 1986): 48–53.

8. Refugee research on Muslim cultures, for instance, has shown the degree to which the ideology of Islam, through its explicit reference to the flight of Mohamed from Mecca to Medina, prescribes the obligation to provide asylum to the *mohajer,* the person fleeing persecution (e.g., De Waal, A. "Refugees and the Creation of Famine: The Case of Dar Masalit, Sudan," *Journal of Refugee Studies* 1 no. 2 (1988): 127–140; Centlivres, P. and Centlivres-Demont, M. "The Afghan Refugees in Pakistan: An Ambiguous Identity," *Journal of Refugee Studies* 1, No. 2 (1988): 142–145. In the FSU, the term refugees (*biezanche*) was not used until recently, given that there was no place within the official ideology of the state to recognize the possibility of people fleeing from the system apart from the situation of defection construed as "treason." See Voutira, E. "Vestiges of Empire: Migrants, Refugees,

and Returnees in Post-Soviet Russia," *Oxford International Review* VII, No. 3 (Summer 1996): 52–59.

9. Konstantinides, N. "Oi Prosphyges," *Melissa* 14 no. 4, (1916): 50–51.

10. In this respect the view varies from the one enshrined in the UN 1951 Convention Relating to the Status of Refugees, which has become the main international legal instrument for the determination of refugee status in the post-World War II era. The UN Convention defines refugees as individuals—rather than groups—who have "the well-founded fear of persecution for reasons of race, religion, nationality, or membership of a particular social group or political opinion."

11. Karapatakis, G. "Memorandum on the Caucasian Migrants and Refugees from the Pontos (Ypomnima Peri ton Kaukasion Metanaston kai Prosfygon tou Pontou)," *Pontiaki Estia* 3 (May-June 1975): 28.

12. Ibid., 33.

13. Eddy, C. *Greece and Greek Refugees* (London: Allen and Unwin, 1931), 14.

14. For example, see Pentzopoulos, D. *The Balkan Exchange of Minorities and Its Impact upon Greece* (The Hague: Mouton, 1962), 32–33; and Psomiades, H. *The Eastern Question: The Last Phase: A Study in Greek-Turkish Diplomacy* (Thessaloniki: Institute of Balkan Studies, 1968), 12.

15. It is noteworthy that the revised national curriculum textbook of senior high-school readings includes a chapter on Greek refugees in general and an account of the cultural and economic contribution of the Asia Minor refugees to modern Greek society, see Andriotis, N. "To prosfygiko zitima stin Ellada, 1821–1930," (The Refugee Issue in Greece, 1821–1930), *Themata Neoellinikis Istorias* (Athens: Paidagogiko Institouto, Ypourgeio Ethnikis Paideias kai Thriskevmaton, 1999), 119–129, 165–171.

16. For example, see Psomiades, op. cit. 106; Tenekides, G. *Introduction, Exodus: Testimonies from the Western Asia Minor Regions* A (Athens: Centre for Asia Minor Studies, 1980) 15; Kostis, K. "The Ideology of Economic Development: The Refugees in the Inter-War Period," (I Ideologia tis Oikonomikis Anaptyxis: Oi Prosphyges sto Mesopolemo), *Deltio Kentrou Mikrasiatikon Spoudon* 9 (1992): 31–33; Mazower, M. *The Refugees, the Economic Crisis and the Collapse of Venizelist Hegemony, 1929–1932,* in Kitromilides, P., (ed.) "Mikrasiatiki Katastrophi kai Elliniki Koinonia," (The Asia Minor Catastrophe and Greek Society), *Deltio Kentrou Mikrasiatikon Spoudon* 9, Special Edition (1992): 119.

17. Yianakopoulos, G. (ed.), *Prosphygiki Ellada. Fotografies apo to Archeio tou Kentrou Mikrasiatikon Spoudon* (Refugee Greece. Photographs from the Centre of Asia Minor Studies), (Athens: Leventis Foundation and Centre for Asia Minor Studies, 1992), 23.

18. Kitromilides, P. *Imagined Communities and the Origins of the National Question in the Balkans,* in Blinkhorn, M. and Veremis, T. (eds.), *Modern Greece: Nationalism and Nationality,* (Athens: Sage, 1989), 50.

19. Iasonides, L. *Leonidas Iasonides: Collected Works* (Thessaloniki: Association Panagia Soumela, 1983), 84.

20. Mackridge, P. "The Pontic Dialect: A Corrupt Version of Ancient Greek?" *Journal of Refugee Studies* 4, No. 4 (1991): 335–340. All Soviet Greeks are not of Pontic Greek origin but they remain to date the most numerous and since the 1990s the most "visible" of the different categories of Greeks from the Soviet Union. In terms of their own self-identification, they call themselves *Romaioi* or use *Greki* as their formal Rus-

sian ethnonym. The adoption of the regional qualifier *Pontios* as a term of self-ascription only became possible after their arrival in and/or encounter with Pontic Greeks of mainland Greece. As one of my informants in the FSU put it, "We didn't know we were *Pontioi* before 1991. When Pontic Greeks from mainland Greece came here to the First Greek All-Union Congress in Yelendzik, we found out that we were not *Romaioi* but that we were *Pontioi*." Since then there have also been attempts to introduce the "regional category" Pontic Greek into Russian language publications by distinguishing between the general category of Soviet Greeks (*Sovetskikh Grekov*) and Pontic Greeks (*Pontiiskei Greki*) in Russian (e.g., Kuznechov, I. [ed.], *Pontiiskei Greki*, [Pontic Greeks], [Krasnodar: Studia Pontocaucasica, 1997]).

21. For a sociological study done in Greece that examines the issue of the expectations of the newcomers from the FSU *before* and *after* their arrival in Greece, concerning their reception and resettlement in the "homeland," with special reference to the groups that arrived in Greece between 1985–1989, see Kassimati, K. et al., *Pontioi metanastes apo tin Sovietiki Enosi: Koinoniki kai oikonomiki entaksi* (Pontian Immigrants From the Former USSR: Social and Economic Integration), (Athens: Ministry of Culture and Panteion University, 1992).

22. Eleftheriades, Y. "Poioi Eimaste?" (Who are we?), *Epistrophe* (October 1992): 4.

23. Ibid.

24. See Voutira, E. "When Greeks Meet other Greeks: Settlement Policy Issues in the Contemporary Greek Context," in *Crossing the Aegean: An Appraisal of the 1923 Compulsory Exchange of Populations Agreement between Greece and Turkey* (Oxford: Berghahn, 2002).

25. Iakovou, personal communication, 10 March 1995; cf., EIYAPOE, *Annual Reports*, (Athens: 1994, 1995, 1996).

26. Hertzfeld, M. *The Social Construction of Indifference* (Cambridge: Cambridge University Press, 1995), 28–30.

27. In 1998 there was a 40 percent increase from 1997 in the number of asylum-seekers in the rest of Europe. While in 1997 Greece received 4,400 asylum applications, in 1998 asylum applications numbered approximately 2,953. The acceptance rate (based on the number of definitive refugee status determinations) has also been one of the lowest among the EU states. The ratio between the number of asylum applicants lodged in Greece in 1998 and the total national population was also very low by EU standards: 4,020 inhabitants per asylum-seeker (UNHCR 1999).

28. Sitaropoulos, N. "Modern Greek Asylum Policy and Practice in the Context of the Relevant European Developments," *Journal of Refugee Studies* 13, No. 1 (2000): 105–117.

29. *Annals to the Greek Parliament* (22/1/1999), 3645–3668.

30. Loizos, P. "The Confessions of a Vampire Anthropologist," *Anthropological Journal on European Cultures* 3, No. 2 (1994): 35–38.

31. Ibid., 41.

32. Cf., Sitaropoulos, op. cit., 116.

33. Weiner, M. *The Global Migration Crisis: Challenge to States and to Human Rights* (New York: HarperCollins Publishers, 1995), 188–191.

7

Insisting on the *Jus Cogen* Nature of *Non-Refoulement*

Jean Allain

It has been said that "refugee law remains the unwanted child of states."[1] As such, states have, while giving lip service to the obligations enshrined in the 1951 convention, sought to limit the possibility of individuals to benefit from the rights to which they had agreed fifty years ago. The cornerstone of the 1951 convention remains intact after fifty years, but under attack. The provisions of article 33, which provides for the right of *non-refoulement*—precluding states from returning individuals to countries where they might face persecution—must act as the final bulwark of international protection. States may, individually or collectively, attempt to introduce policies that have the effect of violating the provisions of article 33, yet if it can be demonstrated that the notion of *non-refoulement* has attained the normative value of *jus cogens,* then states are precluded from transgressing this norm in anyway whatsoever. As such, much can be gained by insisting on the *jus cogens* nature of *non-refoulement.*

The 1951 convention sought to place beyond the pale of any state the possibility to *refoul* "a refugee in any manner whatsoever."[2] Yet, it would appear that of late, states have sought through collective efforts to do just that—to return refugees to "territories where [their] life or freedom would be threatened." This chapter considers the nature of the norm of *non-refoulement* to assess whether it is a norm of such importance to the international community that its derogation is prohibited. In other words, is the norm of *non-refoulement* a peremptory norm of international law—a norm of *jus cogens?* The relevance of this question is that if *refoulement* is beyond the reach of states, then the UN Security Council, through its resolutions may not seek to achieve collectively what states are prohibited from doing individually.

JUS COGENS

The notion of *jus cogens* is given voice in international law through articles 53 and 64 of the 1969 Vienna Convention on the Law of Treaties. These provisions provide that treaties may be invalidated upon their ratification or may later be terminated if their content "conflicts with a peremptory norm of general international law" when it is "accepted and recognized by the international community of states as a whole as a norm from which no derogation is permitted."[3] This is a manifestation of an international community that has determined that there are two types of laws that rule their behavior: *jus cogens* and *jus dispositivum. Jus dispositivum* are laws from which states may deviate, that is: there may be situations when states, although violating an international obligation, may claim circumstances that preclude their wrongfulness.[4] Norms of *jus cogens,* by contrast do not allow for such deviation—they are higher norms of which no violation is allowed. Under no circumstance may a state legally transgress the norms of *jus cogens,* as they are considered norms so essential to the international system that their breach places the very existence of that system in question.

The notion of *jus cogens* is, by international law standards, a relatively new concept. While embryonic forms were mentioned by both Grotius and Vattel, and found voice in separate and dissenting opinions of the Permanent Court of International Justice and the International Court of Justice,[5] it was not until the aftermath of World War II that the concept of *jus cogens* gained a foothold internationally. In 1953, Hersch Lauterpacht, in his role as Special Rapporteur of the International Law Commission, provided a draft convention on the law of treaties that included a provision whereby a treaty could be deemed void if it was inconsistent with "such overriding principles of international law, which may be regarded as constituting principles of international public policy (*ordre international public*)."[6] The incorporation of the notion of peremptory norms into the Vienna Convention acknowledged the fact that there were such principles that states could not simply legislate away. Those same principles were of such importance to the international community that it could not allow states to agree among themselves to abrogate them.

While the notion of *jus cogens* finds voice in the Vienna Convention, it should be made clear that peremptory norms may not be violated by states— full stop. It is not simply a matter of states finding their treaty obligations invalidated, as being in conflict with *jus cogens,* it is that any action that falls within the domain of *jus cogens,* be it a unilateral, bilateral, or multilateral act—customary or otherwise—is, by definition, prohibited as being illegal. Although erroneous, until recently the notion of peremptory norms was solely associated with the invalidation of treaties. While it is clear that *jus cogens* indeed exists as an international norm, the sole manifestation of its existence was inextricably linked to the Vienna convention. In other words, only if a peremptory norm conflicted with a treaty obligation was there a legitimate manifestation of the transgression of the concept of *jus cogens.* This, however, no longer holds.

Since the end of World War II and the establishment of the United Nations organization, the international community has slowly distanced itself from the conception of the "law of nations," replacing it with "international law," *stricto sensu.*[7] To make it plain, the community of states has moved towards the multilateral creation of law at the expense of the former system of bilateralism. In its wake, this movement has created an international system whereby there are interests not only owed to each other but to the community at large. The notions of obligations *"erga omnes"*[8] and "intransgressible principles"[9] come to mind as manifestations of this growing cosmopolitanism of international relations. Likewise, the conception of *jus cogens* is now finding voice beyond the Vienna convention, having been introduced by the special rapporteur dealing with state responsibility within the International Law Commission.

The regime of state responsibility[10] has moved under the guidance of the Special Rapporteur James Crawford, away from the notion of "international crimes"[11] towards differentiating between obligations owed to a single, wronged state and one due to the international community as a whole. First, in 1999, Crawford introduced the notion that compliance with a norm of *jus cogens* should constitute a circumstance that precludes the wrongfulness of an otherwise illegal act.[12] Second, the commission, in its deliberations during the summer of 2000, took Crawford's lead and adopted provisionally articles related to serious breaches of essential obligations to the international community, its consequences, and the ability to invoke responsibility over such breaches.[13] Crawford's justification for introducing *jus cogens* notions into the regime of state responsibility was due, in part, to give the concept its proper standing on the international plane. While the cases of invoking *jus cogens* as grounds for invalidating a treaty have been "very rare," the concept of peremptory norms has a wider breadth, which the commission has recognized. Crawford explains:[14]

> The problem stemmed partly from the way in which the system established by the Vienna Convention on the Law of Treaties operated in cases of *jus cogens.* The invocation of *jus cogens* invalidated the treaty as a whole. Such

cases were very rare. Usually, breaches of *jus cogens* occurred through the
continued performance of a perfectly normal treaty in the event of, for example, a proposed planned aggression or the supply of aid to a regime that
became genocidal. Such breaches were thus to be considered as "occasional"
or "incidental": they did not arise from the terms of the treaty as such but
from the circumstances which had arisen.

Thus, there is an acknowledgment that *jus cogens* norms exist beyond the parameters of simple treaty provisions; that state actions—whatever its basis—
could encompass violations of peremptory norms of international law.

What flows from this acknowledgment is that peremptory norms limit the
actions and interaction of states on the international plane. The question
then turns to the means of identifying such norms of *jus cogens,* which tran-
spire in international relations and whether the prohibition against *refoulement* meets those standards. If so, much can be achieved by insisting on the
jus cogens nature of the principle *non-refoulement,*[15] including holding the
UN Security Council and the EU accountable for actions that result in violations of the principle of *non-refoulement*, thus reducing the legitimacy of
their actions and providing the possibility of third states to challenge their
policies.

NON-REFOULEMENT AS A NORM OF *JUS COGENS*

To determine whether the norm prohibiting *refoulement*[16] has attained the
normative value of *jus cogens,* one must investigate the dual requirements of
its acceptance "by the international community of states as a whole" and "as
a norm from which no derogation is permitted." In other words, short of an
international convention stating that the norm of *refoulement* is *jus cogens;*
one must investigate its introduction into the *corpus juris gentium* via customary international law.[17] As such, state practice must be considered against
the backdrop of a double *opinio juris* whereby states must demonstrate that
they are undertaking their obligation not to *refoulement* on two grounds.[18]
The practice of states must not only be buttressed by an expression of *opinio
juris* that they are not forcibly repatriating because states believe themselves
bound by a legal obligation not to do so, but that states are also undertaking
this obligation because they believe it to be *jus cogens*.

At present, it is clear that the norm prohibition *refoulement* is part of customary international law, thus binding on all states whether or not they are
party to the 1951 convention.[19] Where the issue remains in flux is whether that
norm has achieved the status of *jus cogens*. The fact that *non-refoulement* is a
customary norm, means that state practice exists; but are states undertaking
not to *refoule* because they believe that the norm's status is *jus cogens?* The

most important *locale* for identifying the value attributed to the norm of *non-refoulement* is in the Executive Committee (EXCOM) conclusions of the UN-HCR. Such EXCOM conclusions are the consensus of states, acting in their advisory capacity, where issues of protection and hence *non-refoulement* are given voice internationally. Their pronouncements carry a disproportionate weight in the formation of custom, as they are the states most specifically affected by issues related to *non-refoulement*.[20]

The first tentative mention of the norm of *non-refoulement* being considered as *jus cogens* was broached by EXCOM in its conclusion no. 25 of 1982 where the fifty-seven states' members determined that the principle of *non-refoulement* "was progressively acquiring the character of a peremptory rule of international law."[21] By the late 1980s, EXCOM concluded that "all states" were bound to refrain from *refoulement* on the basis that such acts were "contrary to fundamental prohibitions against these practices."[22] Finally in 1996, the EXCOM members concluded that *non-refoulement* had acquired the level of a norm of *jus cogens* when it determined that the "principle of *non-refoulement* is not subject to derogation."[23] As such, the member states of EXCOM—those states whose interests are most specifically affected by the safeguarding of international protection and prohibiting *refoulement*—concluded by consensus that the norm of *non-refoulement* was in fact a norm of *jus cogens* from "which no derogation is permitted."

Further evidence of the *jus cogens* nature of *non-refoulement* is to be found in state practice, which has emerged in Latin America on the basis of the 1984 Cartagena Declaration on Refugees.[24] This declaration concludes, inter alia, that:[25]

> [. . .] the importance and meaning of the principle of *non-refoulement* (including the prohibition of rejection at the frontier) as a corner-stone of the international protection of refugees. This principle is imperative in regard to refugees and in the present state of international law should be acknowledged and observed as a rule of *jus cogens*.

As Joan Fitzpatrick has noted, the acceptance by Latin American states of the norm of *non-refoulement* as being *jus cogens* has been manifest in "intergovernmental bodies like the Inter-American Commission on Human Rights and the OAS General Assembly that have acknowledged the conclusions of the Cartagena colloquium with approval."[26] Finally, as a subsidiary means of determining the nature of *non-refoulement*, scholars have pointed to various elements of state practice and have determined that, in the words of Harold Koh, "[n]umerous international publicists now conclude that the principle of *non-refoulement* has achieved the status of *jus cogens*."[27]

Doubt that may linger, as to the *jus cogens* nature of *non-refoulement* due to the increased violations of the norm, should be set aside as being irrelevant to its legal standing. Although EXCOM has noted in its conclusion for the year 2000 that it is "deeply disturbed by violations of internationally recognized rights of refugees [including] *refoulement*,"[28] and in spite of the fact that UNHCR, itself, "*did* sign a *refoulement* agreement with Tanzania,"[29] this does not weaken the peremptory character of *non-refoulement*. As the International Court of Justice has noted in the *Nicaragua* case:[30]

> The Court does not consider that, for a rule to be established as customary, the corresponding practice must be in absolutely rigorous conformity with the rule. In order to deduce the existence of customary rules, the Court deems it sufficient that the conduct of States should, in general, be consistent with such rules, and that instances of State conduct inconsistent with a given rule should generally have been treated as breaches of that rule, not as indications of the recognition of a new rule.

Thus, although states may wish to backtrack from their obligations, having committed themselves to the *jus cogens* nature of *non-refoulement* they are estopped from acting as against the norm. As such, as long as there is an insistence on the nonderogable nature of *non-refoulement,* its status is secure.[31] In fact, by the twisted logic of the International Court of Justice, violations, if they are treated as such, strengthen the norm of *non-refoulement*. The court so explained in the *Nicaragua* case:[32]

> If a State acts in a way *prima facie* incompatible with a recognized rule, but defends its conduct by appealing to exceptions or justifications contained within the rule itself, then whether or not the state's conduct is in fact justifiable on that basis, the significance of that attitude is to confirm rather than to weaken the rule.

INSISTING ON THE *JUS COGENS* NATURE OF *NON-REFOULEMENT*

It is not a matter of simply insisting on the *jus cogens* nature of *non-refoulement* to ensure it maintains its status as a peremptory norm, but the demanding of its heighten status. The issue of insisting on the *jus cogens* nature of *non-refoulement* is that it is a norm that can—in no circumstance—be overridden.[33] Thus, beyond the states party to the 1951 convention, all states are bound to respect the obligation not to *refoule* individuals, either unilaterally or in cooperation with other states bilaterally or multilaterally. This leads to the conclusion that a collection of states forming an intergovernmental organization is not exempt from the peremptory nature of *non-refoulement* in its undertakings. That being the case, one must challenge the ability of entities such as the UN Security Council to violate such norms through its collective endeavors.[34]

The growth of internationalization qua globalization, which has manifest itself since the end of the Cold War, has meant that states have been willing to cooperate in new and expanding number of fields. This, in turn, has meant that increasingly states have moved to establish or reinvigorate intergovernmental institutions to undertake actions as collective. These institutions have, to some extent, escaped the scrutiny that ordinarily would be felt at the national level. With no true constituency to monitor their international activities and being one step farther removed from a general public to which they are accountable, states have sought, and many times achieved, collectively what they could not accomplish individually.[35] Thus, there is a need to hold intergovernmental institutions to their obligations and, in the case of *non-refoulement*, to ensure that states understand that they have agreed to its *jus cogens* nature and therefore must abide by such dictates.

The UN Security Council

The UN Security Council is endowed with the responsibility for the maintenance of international peace and security by the member states of the United Nations Organization. By virtue of chapter 7 of the UN Charter, the Security Council may take action when it perceives that there exists a threat or breach of the peace or an act of aggression.[36] Having so determined it may, by virtue of article 42, use force or may turn to the provisions of article 41 and take "measures not involving the use of armed force." In its role as the international organ vested with the "primary responsibility for the maintenance of international peace,"[37] the Security Council has near autonomy in its actions under chapter 7. Although its unfettered ability to act has been challenged through the *Lockerbie* case,[38] the member states have agreed "to accept and carry out the decisions"[39] of the Security Council. Further, by virtue of article 103, if there is a conflict between a state's UN obligations and its "obligations under any other international agreement, their obligations under the present charter shall prevail."

Following the dictates of article 103, if there was a conflict between an obligation towards a Security Council resolution on the one hand and an obligation under, say, the 1951 convention, then the obligation under the charter would prevail. Thus, prima facie, the Security Council could *refoule*, if it made a determination under chapter 7 that such an action was required as a means of restoring international peace and security. However, insisting on the *jus cogens* nature of *non-refoulement* places contemplation of such actions beyond the pale of Security Council actions. As Alain Pellet has noted, the Security Council "has an absolute obligation to respect *jus cogens*."[40] In mining the same vein, Bardo Fassbender has written that "obligations of states arising from decisions of the Security Council only lawfully arise 'under the present charter' (article 103) if those decisions are in accordance with the constitutional law of the international community, including the peremptory norms. . . ."[41]

Acting as ad hoc judge in the *Genocide* case, pitting Bosnia Herzegovina against Yugoslavia, Elihu Lauterpacht gave voice to the issue of *jus cogens* as it pertains to genocide and its relationship to article 103 of the charter:[42]

> The concept of *jus cogens* operates as a concept superior to both customary international law and treaty. The relief which Article 103 of the Charter may give the Security Council in case of a conflict between one of its decisions and an operative treaty obligation cannot—as a matter of simply hierarchy of norms—extend to a conflict between a Security Council resolution and *jus cogens*. Indeed, one only has to state the opposite proposition thus—that a Security Council resolution may even require participation in genocide—for its unacceptability to be apparent.

Returning to the notion of *non-refoulement*, by not insisting that it is *jus cogens* would give license to the Security Council—to draw the analogy used by Judge Lauterpacht—to set out resolutions which allowed for *refoulement*. The Security Council treaded quite close to such an exercise in 1991 when, with Security Council Resolution 688, it expressed its grave concern over Iraqi Kurds seeking safety in Turkey and Iran and considered that such "massive flow of refugees towards and across international frontiers . . . threaten international peace and security in the region."

While resolution 688 did not specifically call for the *refoulement* of Kurdish refugees, it had the effect of alleviating the pressure placed on Turkey "to provide aid and sanctuary for the 1 million starving and freezing refugees along its border."[43] By the willingness of the international community to acquiesce to Turkey's closed border policy and provide comfort to the Kurds by the establishment of a "safe haven," it "challenged the principle of nonrejection at the frontier"[44] as an element of the norm of *non-refoulement*. Guy Goodwin-Gill has noted that this resolution remains "ambiguous" and "controversial,"[45] in part, because while not saying so, it sanctioned Turkey's policy and sought to work around it.[46] In light of the action of the Security Council to accommodate Turkey one should consider the further insights provided by Judge Lauterpacht:[47]

> Now, it is not to be contemplated that the Security Council would ever deliberately adopt a resolution clearly and deliberately flouting a rule of *jus cogens* or requiring a violation of human rights. But the possibility that a Security Council resolution might inadvertently or in an unforeseen manner lead to such a situation cannot be excluded.

One need go no farther than examining the effects of the sanctions against Iraq to understand the nature of harm Security Council resolutions can cause.[48] Taken from this perspective, it is imperative to insist on the *jus cogens* nature of *non-refoulement* so as to ensure that the Security Council states understands that in its actions, either through the instituting of resolutions or through the effects of such resolution, that the norm of *non-refoulement* cannot be transgressed.

CONCLUSION

Having considered the norm of *non-refoulement* from the perspective of its *jus cogens* nature has demonstrated that states are estopped from violating its provisions either individually or collectively. Insisting on the *jus cogens* nature of *non-refoulement* goes beyond the policy considerations of inter-governmental entities such as the UN Security Council actions, which would violate an individual's right not to be returned to a state where he or she might face persecution. By playing this "trump" card, which places the individualized right of *non-refoulement* above all other considerations not meeting the threshold of *jus cogens* means that it can be utilized as a tool of the weak as against the strong. Thus, by insisting on the *jus cogens* nature of *non-refoulement*, not only can individuals challenge actions of states and their common manifestations, but can hold them accountable. A fundamental limitation of international law is the access granted to individuals to international adjudication.[49] Yet, the process of refugee determination inherent in the 1951 convention means that states must make decisions that are susceptible to review at the municipal level. Even if states are to act at the supranational or international levels, the decision to accept or reject refugee claims are carried out municipally. At this level, advocates can point to the *jus cogens* nature of *non-refoulement* and insist that, whatever the policy, wherever it may emanate from, it cannot, in practice, be applied in such a manner as to send a person back to a state to face possible persecution.

NOTES

This chapter was first published as "The Jus Cogens Nature of Non-Refoulement," *International Journal of Refugee Law* 13, no. 4 (2001): 533–558. Reprinted by permission of the Oxford University Press.

1. Byrne, R. and Shacknove, A. "The Safe Country Notion in European Asylum Law," *Harvard Human Rights Journal* 9, (1996): 187.

2. Article 33 (Prohibition of Expulsion or Return ["*Refoulement*"]) of the 1951 convention reads:

1. No Contracting State shall expel or return ("refouler") a refugee in any manner whatsoever to the frontiers of territories where his life or freedom would be threatened

on account of his race, religion, nationality, membership of a particular social group, or political opinion.

2. The benefit of the present provision may not, however, be claimed by a refugee whom there are reasonable grounds for regarding as a danger to the security of the country in which he is, or who, having been convicted by a final judgment of a particularly serious crime, constitutes a danger to the community of that country.

3. Article 53 (Treaties conflicting with a peremptory norm of general international law [*jus cogens*]) of the Vienna Convention on the Law of Treaties reads:

A treaty is void if, at the time of its conclusion, it conflicts with a peremptory norm of general international law. For the purposes of the present Convention, a peremptory norm of general international law is a norm accepted and recognized by the international community of States as a whole as a norm from which no derogation is permitted and which can be modified only by a subsequent norm of general international law having the same character.

While Article 64 (Emergence of a new peremptory norm of general international law [*jus cogens*] reads:

If a new peremptory norm of general international law emerges, any existing treaty which is in conflict with that norm becomes void and terminates.

4. Consider chapter 5 of the UN International Law Commission's 1996 draft articles on state responsibility detailing circumstances, which preclude wrongfulness including: consent of the other party; countermeasures; *force majeure*; distress; states of necessity; and self-defense. However, one should be aware of the recent inclusion of the following circumstance in the most recent draft by the commission, at: Article 21 (Compliance with peremptory norms), which reads: "The wrongfulness of an act of a state is precluded if the act is required in the circumstances by a peremptory norm of general international law." See generally, *International Law Commission Report*, A/54/10, 1999, 306–318.

5. See Micheal Byers, "Conceptualising the Relationship between *Jus Cogens* and *Erga Omnes* Rules," *Nordic Journal of International Law*, 66 (1997): 213–214.

6. Lauterpacht, H. *Report on the Law of Treaties*, UN Doc. A/CN.4/63 (1953), 155, as quoted in A. Mark Weisburd, "The Emptiness of the Concept of *Jus Cogens*, as Illustrated by the War in Bosnia-Herzegovina," *Michigan Journal of International Law* 17 (1995): 13.

7. See Nagendra Singh, "The UN and the Development of International Law," Adam Roberts and Benedict Kingsbury (eds.), *United Nations, Divided World* (1993): 388.

8. The lead pronouncement of the notion of obligations *erga omnes* was expressed by the International Court of Justice in the *Barcelona Traction* case (*ICJ Reports*, 1970) where, in a dictum, it determined:

33. . . . In particular, an essential distinction would be drawn between the obligations of a State towards the international community as a whole, and those arising vis-à-vis another State. . . . By their very nature the former are the concern of all States. In view of the importance of the rights involved, all States can be held to have a legal interest in their protection; they are obligations *erga omnes*.

34. Such obligations derive, for example, in contemporary international law, from the outlawing of acts of aggression, and of genocide, as also from the principle and rules concerning the basic rights of the human person, including the protection from slavery and racial discrimination.

For further consideration of obligations *erga omnes* see, André de Hoogh, *Obligations Erga Omnes and International Crimes: A Theoretical Inquiry into the Implementation and Enforcement of the International Responsibility of States* (1996).

9. The International Court of Justice spoke of such principles in its Advisory Opinion on the Legality of the Threat or Use of Nuclear Weapons (*ICJ Reports*, 1996), where it stated:

79. It is undoubtedly because a great many rules of humanitarian law applicable in armed conflict are so fundamental to the respect of the human person and "elementary considerations of humanity" as the Court put it in its Judgment of 9 April 1949 in the *Corfu Channel* case (I.C.J. Reports 1949, p. 22), that the Hague and Geneva Conventions have enjoyed a broad accession. Further these fundamental rules are to be observed by all States whether or not they have ratified the conventions that contain them, because they *constitute intransgressible principles of international customary law*. [Emphasis added.]

10. For items mentioned related to state responsibility see the "State Responsibility Project" of the Lauterpacht Research Centre for International Law, Oxford University, at www.law.cam.ac.uk/rcil.

11. Article 19(2) of the 1996 Draft Article on state responsibility reads:

An internationally wrongful act which results from the breach by a State of an international obligation so essential for the protection of fundamental interests of the international community that its breach is recognized as a crime by that community as a whole constitutes an international crime.

12. Op. cit., n. 3.

13. See International Law Commission, *State Responsibility—Draft Articles Provisionally Adopted by the Drafting Committee on Second Reading,* A/CN.4/L.600, 11 August 2000. The articles proposed are the following:

Article 41—Application of this Chapter
  1. This chapter applies to the international responsibility arising from an internationally wrongful act that constitutes a serious breach by a state of an obligation owed to the international community as a whole and essential for the protection of its fundamental interests.
  2. A breach of such an obligation is serious if it involves a gross or systematic failure by the responsible state to fulfill the obligation, risking substantial harm to the fundamental interests protected thereby.

Article 42—Consequences of serious breaches of obligations to the international community as a whole
  1. A serious breach within the meaning of Article 41 may involve, for the responsible state, damages reflecting the gravity of the breach.
  2. It entails, for all other states, the following obligations:
    (a) Not to recognize as lawful the situation created by the breach;

(b) Not to render aid or assistance to the responsible state in maintaining the situation so created;

(c) To cooperate as far as possible to bring the breach to an end.

3. This article is without prejudice to the consequences referred to in chapter II and to such further consequences that a breach to which this chapter applies may entail under international law. . . .

Article 49—Invocation of responsibility by states other than the injured state

1. Subject to paragraph 2, any state other than an injured state is entitled to invoke the responsibility of another state if:

(a) The obligation breached is owed to a group of states including that state, and is established for the protection of a collective interest;

(b) The obligation breached is owed to the international community as a whole.

2. A state entitled to invoke responsibility under paragraph 1 may seek from the responsible State:

(a) Cessation of the internationally wrongful act, and assurances and guarantees of non-repetition in accordance with Article 30;

(b) Compliance with the obligation of reparation under chapter II of Part 2, in the interest of the injured state or of the beneficiaries of the obligation breached.

3. The requirements for the invocation of responsibility by an injured state under Articles 44, 45, and 46 apply to an invocation of responsibility by a state entitled to do so under paragraph 1.

14. *International Law Commission Report*, A/54/10 1999, par. 306.

15. Here I challenge Guy Goodwin-Gill's assertion that "Although a sound case can be made for the customary international law status of the principle of *non-refoulement*, its claim to be part of *jus cogens* is far less certain, and little is likely to be achieved by insisting on its status as such." Guy Goodwin-Gill, *The Refugee in International Law* (1998), 168, n. 234.

16. The content of the norm of *non-refoulement* can be derived, in part, from the following EXCOM Conclusions:

General Conclusion On International Protection, EXCOM Conclusion No. 81, 1997

(i) . . . *non-refoulement*, which prohibits expulsion and return of refugees in any manner whatsoever to the frontiers of territories where their lives or freedom would be threatened on account of their race, religion, nationality, membership of a particular social group or political opinion, whether or not they have formally been granted refugee status, or of persons in respect of whom there are substantial grounds for believing that they would be in danger of being subjected to torture, as set forth in the 1984 Convention against Torture and Other Cruel, Inhuman or Degrading Treatment or Punishment;

and

Conclusion on International Protection, EXCOM Conclusion No. 85, 1998

(q) . . . *refoulement* in all its forms, including through summary removals, occasionally en masse, and reiterates in this regard the need to admit refugees to the territory of states, which includes no rejection at frontiers without access to fair and effective procedures for determining their status and protection needs.

17. Customary international law requires two elements: State practice sustained by the opinion of states, either overtly or through acquiescence, that they are undertak-

ing such practice because they are under a legal obligation to do so. See the *Nicaragua* case where the International Court of Justice speaks of settled practice and *opinio juris sive necessitatis. ICJ Reports*, 1986, par. 77.

18. See, for instance, the section entitled "Le double consentement," in A. Gómez Robledo, "Le *ius cogens* international," *Collected Courses of The Hague Academy of International Law* 172 (1981): 104–108; or Phillipe Cahier, "Cours général de droit international public," *Collected Courses of The Hague Academy of International Law* 195 (1985): 198.

19. Although questions remained as to the customary nature of the norm of *non-refoulement* during the Cold War era, it is clear that since the end of the Soviet era, the norm quickly attained a customary nature. Pre-1989, see Gunnel Stenberg, *Non-Expulsion and Non-Refoulement* (1989), 288; post-1989 consider the section entitled "The Principle of *Non-Refoulement* in General International Law," in Guy Goodwin-Gill, *The Refugee in International Law* (1998), 166–167.

20. This is so, because, as the International Court of Justice has noted, for a new rule of custom to evolve, practice "should have been both extensive and virtually uniform," but must also include the practice of states "whose interests were specifically affected." See the *North Sea Continental Shelf* cases, *ICJ Reports* 42, 1969, par. 73.

21. EXCOM Conclusion 25, *General Conclusion on International Protection*, 1982.

> b) Reaffirmed the importance of the basic principles of international protection and in particular the principle of *non-refoulement* which was progressively acquiring the character of a peremptory rule of international law.

22. EXCOM Conclusion 55, *General Conclusion on International Protection*, 1989.

> d) Expressed deep concern that refugee protection is seriously jeopardized in some States by expulsion and refoulement of refugees or by measures which do not recognize the special situation of refugees and called on all States to refrain from taking such measures and in particular from returning or expelling refugees contrary to fundamental prohibitions against these practices.

23. EXCOM Conclusion 79, *General Conclusion on International Protection*, 1996.

> i) Distressed at the widespread violations of the principle of *non-refoulement* and of the rights of refugees, in some cases resulting in loss of refugee lives, and seriously disturbed at reports indicating that large numbers of refugees and asylum-seekers have been *refouled* and expelled in highly dangerous situations; recalls that the principle of *non-refoulement* is not subject to derogation.

24. See Arthur Helton and Eliana Jacobs, "What is Forced Migration?" *Georgetown Immigration Law Journal* 13 (1999): 526.

25. See United Nations High Commissioner for Refugees, *Collection of International Instruments and Other Legal Texts Concerning Refugees and Displaced Persons: Regional Instruments* (1995), 206, par. 5.

26. Fitzpatrick, J. "Temporary Protection of Refugees: Elements of a Formalized Regime," *American Journal International Law* 94 (2000): 284.

27. H. H. Koh, "The Haitian Centers Council Case: Reflections on Refoulement and Haitian Centers Council," *Harvard International Law Journal* 35 (1994): 30.

28. EXCOM Conclusion 89, *Conclusion on International Protection*, 2000.

29. Goodwin-Gill, G. "Refugees: Challenges to Protection," Conference Paper: Commemorating UNHCR at 50: Past, Present, and Future, 16–18 May, 2000, New York, 4. (Emphasis in the original).

30. Case concerning *Military and Paramilitary Activities in and Against Nicaragua, ICJ Reports*, 1986, 98.

31. Secure unless there emerges a new norm of *jus cogens* in line with Article 64 of the Vienna Convention, op. cit., n. 3.

32. Ibid.

33. Lauri Hannkainen has argued that because article 33(2) of the 1951 convention provides the possibility of an exception, then the norm of *non-refoulement* can never attain the status of *jus cogens* because there is, built into the provision, the possibility of derogation. However, as Paul Weis noted, in his commentary on the *travaux perpartoire* of the 1951 convention, the "notion of proportionality has to be observed" between the "danger entailed to the refugee by expulsion or return" and "the menace to public security." Further, as has been noted more recently by Dugard and Van den Wyngaert, since the norm of *non-refoulement* has been recognized as *jus cogens* by states it must "trump" even extradition treaties where issues of human rights violations are concerned. Lauri Hannkainen, *Peremptory Norms (Jus Cogens) in International Law: Historical Development, Criteria, Present Status* (1988), 261–263; Paul Weis, *The Refugee Convention, 1951: The Travaux Preparatoires Analyzed with Commentary* (1995), 342; and John Dugard and Christine Van den Wyngaert, "Reconciling Extradition with Human Rights," *American Journal International Law* 92, (1998): 194–195.

34. As has been noted by a Trial Chamber of the International Criminal Tribunal for the former Yugoslavia (ICTY) in a case related to SFOR (UN Stabilization Force) and its cooperation with the tribunal: "On its terms, Article 29 [related to state cooperation] applies to all states, whether acting individually or collectively. In principle, there is no reason why Article 29 should not apply to collective enterprises undertaken by states, in the framework of international organizations and, in particular, their competent organs such as SFOR in the present case." *Prosecutor v. Simic et al.* case, *Decision on Motion for Judicial Assistance to be Provided by SFOR and Others*, Trial Chamber III, 18 October 2000, par. 64.

35. Consider, for instance, the example of the role of the European Court of Justice and the fact that it "pushed for economic integration where states themselves could not." Jean Allain, "The European Court of Justice is an International Court," *Nordic Journal of International Law* 68, (1999): 272–273.

36. See Article 39 of the UN Charter.

37. Article 24(1) of the UN Charter.

38. Consider for example, Vera Gowlland-Debbas, "The Relationship between the International Court of Justice and the Security Council in Light of the *Lockerbie* Case," *American Journal of International Law* 88 (1994): 643–677; or more generally, Mohammed Bedjaoui, *The New World Order and the Security Council—Testing the Legality of its Acts* (1994).

39. Article 25 of the UN Charter.

40. "Là, je pense, s'arrête le balancier: Le Counseil de sécurité a l'obligation absolue de respecter le *jus cogens* et la Charte des Nations Unies. Ce sont les limites, et les

seules limites, à son action." Alain Pellet, "Société Française pour le droit international," *Le Chapitre VII de la Charte des nations unies*, Colloque de Rennes (1995), 237.

41. Bardo Fassbender, *UN Security Council Reform and the Right of Veto: A Constitutional Perspective* (1998), 126.

42. Separate Opinion of Judge Lauterpacht, Further Request for the Indication of Provisional Measures, *Application of the Convention on the Prevention and Punishment of the Crime of Genocide* (Bosnia and Herzegovina v. Yugoslavia), Order, 13 September 1993, 440.

43. Teson, F. R. "Collective Humanitarian Intervention," *Michigan Journal of International Law* 17, (1997): 344.

44. Goodwin-Gill, op. cit., n. 15, 289. Earlier in his text Goodwin-Gill notes: "Turkey's decision to close its border to Kurdish refugees, and the support or non-objection of a substantial number of members of the international community, if it did not breach *non-refoulement* (understood as a general principle of international law that includes the dimension of nonrejection at the frontier), certainly consolidates the exception." Id., 141.

45. Id. p. 286.

46. As has been noted "UN Resolution 688 is important both for what it does and does not say." Bill Frelick, "Refugee Rights: The New Frontier of Human Rights Protection," *Buffalo Human Rights Law Review* 4, (1998): 265.

47. Op. cit., n. 42, 440–441.

48. Consider the following excerpt from Andrew K. Fishman, "Between Iraq and a Hard Place: The Use of Economic Sanctions and Threats to International Peace and Security," *Emory International Law Review* 13 (1999): 687 (footnotes in the original omitted):

> In Iraq, two million men, women, and children have died over the span of nine years. This is the legacy of the United Nations sanctions regime imposed on Iraq. Critics of the sanctions consider the system a modern holocaust and a heinous crime against humanity. Yet the passage of time and the death toll exacted from the Iraqi people has caused neither the UN nor the primary advocates of the sanctions regime, the United States and Great Britain, to reexamine the policy or acknowledge the profound moral dilemma it raises. In an interview broadcast on the CBS television program "60 Minutes," interviewer Leslie Stahl asked then United States UN Ambassador Madeleine Albright the following question: "Half a million Iraqi children have died—more children than died in Hiroshima. Is the price worth it?" Albright responded: "yes, we think the price is worth it."

49. See Jean Allain, *A Century of International Adjudication: The Rule of Law and its Limits*, 2000.

8

Turkey, UNHCR, and the 1951 Convention Relating to the Status of Refugees: Problems and Prospects of Cooperation

Kemal Kirişçi

Turkey was a drafter of the 1951 Convention Relating to the Status of Refugees. The convention was ratified and became part of national law in 1961.[1] Asylum-seekers from the Soviet Union and eastern Europe were granted asylum and many subsequently resettled. Mass influxes in 1988, 1989, and 1991 involving in total approximately 900,000 refugees, and an ever increasing number of asylum-seekers arriving from countries east and south of Turkey, however, led to changes in this liberal attitude. Asylum-seekers began to be viewed increasingly as a national security concern leading to the application of the "'geographical limitation." Turkish officials began to argue that Turkey's obligations under the convention do not extend to asylum-seekers and refugees originating from non-European countries. UNHCR tried to fill the gap and succeeded in developing a temporary arrangement with Turkish authorities that provided for some degree of protection and status determination for such asylum-seekers. However, this arrangement did not always protect asylum-seekers and refugees from *refoulement* by Turkish authorities. The situation was also aggravated when the Turkish government in 1994 adopted its own legislation on asylum and status determination.[2] Over just a couple of years the situation evolved from bad to worse as Turkey's violations of the rights of asylum-seekers and refugees attracted serious and concerted criticism from western governments as well as major international human rights advocacy groups.[3]

Yet, it is possible to claim that starting from roughly 1997 the Turkish government has become more cooperative and a certain degree of improvement in its implementation of the 1951 convention has occurred. There has been a significant drop in the number of deportations, acknowledged by some western government reports. Closer cooperation between UNHCR and the Turkish government to improve the training of Turkish officials dealing with asylum-seekers and refugees developed.[4] Furthermore, there have been a number of court cases against the government that have resulted in rulings supporting claims made by asylum-seekers and refugees. As a result the government in 1999 revised the 1994 Asylum Regulation and introduced some amendments to address the source of some of the complaints.[5] Most significantly, there are signs that Turkish officials are increasingly open to discussing the possibility of lifting the "geographical limitation."[6] Until recently this would have been considered a taboo. What is happening in Turkey? How can these changes be explained? Are they of a permanent nature? What are the prospects of Turkey actually lifting the "geographical limitation"? Will Turkey consider integration as a permanent solution next to its preferred policy of resettlement and repatriation?

This chapter addresses these questions and argues that many of the improvements that have occurred can be attributed to a successful strategy employed by UNHCR in winning the trust and goodwill of Turkish officials. This included the development of training and education programs on refugee law and practice, encouraging the use of administrative courts to appeal decisions of the Turkish Ministry of Interior (MOI) and assisting civil society groups involved in the promotion and protection of the rights of asylum-seekers and refugees. Undoubtedly, Turkey's aspiration to become a member of the EU is another important factor.

The chapter is divided into two sections. The first examines the development of the Turkish practice towards asylum and refuge and the nature of the problems associated with this practice. The second section evaluates the role and challenges confronting UNHCR and the international community in their bid to contributing to the improvement in Turkey's implementation of the convention.

TURKISH GOVERNMENT PRACTICE AND POLICY

There are three major legal sources of Turkish refugee policy. The first is the Law on Settlement adopted in 1934 (Law 2510).[7] According to this law only individuals who are of "Turkish descent and culture" can migrate to and settle in Turkey or acquire refugee status. Article 3 defines a refugee as someone who has arrived in Turkey, not with the intention of settling, but has sought asylum as a result of compulsion and has the intention to stay in Turkey temporarily.

The article goes on to clarify that only those refugees who are of "Turkish descent and culture" can choose to stay on and integrate. Who falls within this definition has been left to the Council of Ministers but in practice it has included Turks from the Balkans, as well as Albanians, Bosnians, Circassians, Pomaks (Bulgarian-speaking Slav Muslims), and Tatars. A small proportion of immigrants and refugees were also admitted from countries to the east of Turkey such as Kazaks, Kyrgyz, Turkmens, Uzbeks, and Uyghurs.

The second major legal source is the 1951 convention. Turkey was among a group of countries that pushed for the introduction of a geographical and a time limitation to the convention as expressed in article 1.B(1)(a). Accordingly, Turkey accepted to be bound by the terms of the convention for refugees fleeing persecution in Europe as a result of events prior to 1951. In 1967 when signing the 1967 Protocol Relating to the Status of Refugees, Turkey accepted to lift the time but chose to continue to maintain the geographical limitation. Since the Maltese decision to lift the geographical limitation in Europe, Turkey remains the sole "persistent objector" together with Monaco. As the archives of Turkish Foreign Ministry are closed to the public it is difficult to find the exact reasons for supporting the limitation.

Lastly, there is the regulation on asylum, introduced in November 1994, which aimed to take over refugee status determination from UNHCR as previous practice had entailed. The regulation created two categories of asylum-seekers. The first, mainly those who came from Europe, could benefit from the protection of the convention. The second involved asylum-seekers coming from outside Europe who sought from Turkey the right to demand asylum in a third country. It was the official determination to implement this ill-designed regulation that led to a major crisis between Turkey and the international community over the right of asylum-seekers and refugees.

The favorable treatment accorded to asylum-seekers from eastern Europe can basically be attributed to two political reasons. Extending status and assistance to *eastern bloc* refugees was regarded as the natural extension of anticommunist policy. The second reason is that these asylum-seekers were in manageable numbers and readily accepted for resettlement in western countries. Consequently, there never were any of the economic, political, and social problems often associated with integrating refugees. Furthermore, the costs of shelter and resettlement were borne by international agencies, such as the International Catholic Migration Commission and UNHCR.

The flow of asylum-seekers from eastern Europe came to a virtual halt with the collapse of Communism. However, the eruption of violence and ethnic strife in the former Soviet Union territories and the Balkans has led to displacement of Muslim and Turkic groups and their flight to Turkey. Although these countries appear to be considered part of Europe and therefore the 1951 convention applies, Turkish authorities have refrained from granting refugee status for fear of serving as a "pull factor" in addition to offending the governments in the respective countries of origin, in particular Azerbaijan, Russia, and Uzbekistan.

Instead, a compromise approach has been adopted. Applicants are either allowed to stay in the country on an unofficial basis or permitted to benefit from the law that allow persons considered to be of Turkish descent to settle, work, and eventually obtain Turkish citizenship. The pull factor might have been the consideration when a large group of Chechen refugees turned up at the Turkish border in Georgia in February 2000.[8] In spite of considerable public opinion in support of their admission into Turkey the government insisted that these refugees were safe in Georgia and that Turkey was providing humanitarian assistance.[9] There is also the case of Meshketian Turks (also known as Ahiska Turks). These are people who have tried to return to their ancestral homes in Georgia where Stalin had displaced them to Central Asia. Some have been trying to seek asylum in Turkey claiming mistreatment and persecution especially in the Krasnador region of Russia.[10] In their case, too, Turkey has been reluctant to grant them asylum. Instead, an estimated 15,000 Ahiska Turks have settled with their relatives in various parts of Turkey.[11]

Pragmatism has also been the approach in dealing with the estimated 20,000 Bosnian Muslims from former Yugoslavia who sought asylum in Turkey after 1992 and Albanian refugees who were brought to Turkey from Macedonia under the Humanitarian Evacuation Program during spring 1999, as well as the roughly 18,000 Kosovars who entered Turkey for protection.

Prior to the introduction of the 1994 Asylum Regulation, Turkish national law had no provisions governing the status of asylum-seekers and refugees coming from outside Europe. Instead, Turkish refugee policy was based on the general provisions of the Law on Settlement (No. 2510), the Citizenship Law (No. 5682), the Passport Law (No. 5683), and the Law on Sojourn and Movement of Aliens (No. 5687). However, a policy based on pragmatism and flexibility was permitted to evolve during the 1980s as a growing number of Iranians fleeing Ayatollah Khomeini's regime began to arrive. The absence of visa requirements for Iranian nationals made their entry into the country relatively easy. There are no accurate statistics on their numbers, although a member of the Turkish Parliament put the total of Iranians that came through Turkey between 1980 and 1991 at 1.5 million. Generally, these people found their way to third countries by their own means while only a small proportion approached UNHCR. Turkish officials granted those Iranians whose cases were being examined by UNHCR, or those who were waiting to be resettled, residence permits.

From the late 1980s onwards, asylum-seekers from countries other than Iran also began to benefit from this arrangement, including many Iraqis, but also nationals of Afghanistan, Somalia, Sri Lanka, Sudan, and Tunisia, as well as Palestinians. The Iraqis can be viewed in two groups. The first consisted of those who came during the mass exoduses of 1988 and 1991 but did not wish to be repatriated. Most of these refugees have been resettled in third countries while a few continue to receive residence permits from Turkish authorities.[12] The second group is composed of those from northern Iraq who sought refuge in Turkey after 1991. Turkish authorities refused them the right to seek asylum arguing that northern Iraq was safe from persecution. Turkish authorities reserve the right to deport such persons. However, some of them did nevertheless approach UNHCR in Ankara and had their refugee status recognized. On many occasions, Turkish officials refused to allow them to leave the country when they did not have passports with valid entry stamps into Turkey.

These developments also coincided with a period when Turkey faced increasing criticism over deportations of persons that the international community considered to be genuine asylum-seekers or refugees. This was accompanied by growing pressure from western governments and refugee advocate organizations on Turkish officials to respect the principle of *non-refoulement* for "nonconvention" refugees. They argued that the forced return of asylum-seekers and refugees constitutes a breach of Turkey's international legal obligations. *Non-refoulement* is considered not only a pillar of the 1951 convention but is also fast acquiring the status of customary rule of law, making it binding even on countries not party to the convention.[13] There were also increasing arguments that Turkey as a party to the European Human Rights Convention had additional obligations.

These pressures partly explain why it became necessary for Turkey to legislate the Asylum Regulation in November 1994. This Regulation was an attempt to bring status determination under the control of the MOI without actually lifting the geographical limitation. In accordance with Turkey's commitments under the 1951 convention, the Regulation limited the right to refuge to asylum-seekers coming from Europe. On the other hand, individuals coming from outside Europe would first have to convince Turkish authorities that they had a plausible case for asylum. Only those who succeed in doing that would then be given the possibility of approaching UNHCR for resettlement out of Turkey if recognized as a refugee by UNHCR.[14]

Until the mid-1980s Turkish authorities had to cope with a manageable flow of convention refugees who were often promptly resettled in the West. There were few incidents of overstay or violations of Turkish laws. However, the situation began to change when growing numbers of Iranians and other non-Europeans began to seek asylum. The situation was aggravated by the mass influxes of Iraqi Kurds in 1988 and 1991, Bulgarian Turks in 1989, and Bosnian Muslims in 1992–1993. In five years close to 900,000 people sought asylum in Turkey. These movements taxed Turkey economically, and in the case of Kurds, Turkish officials felt Turkey's national security was endangered. Against the background of international criticism there was also a frustration that Turkey was not getting any recognition for the economic and other sacrifices entailed by the assistance and protection it was actually extending to refugees from northern Iraq.

These criticisms were particularly potent as they came at a time when there was growing concern that Iran was assisting Islamic terrorist groups in Turkey as well as the Workers' Party of Kurdistan (PKK), a radical Marxist-Leninist group advocating the establishment of a separate Kurdish state by armed struggle. Officials feared that Islamic fundamentalist and PKK activists were mingling among those entering the country that might otherwise have a valid claim for asylum.

Another motive for the adoption of the Asylum Regulation was the need to prevent or control illegal migration. Economic difficulties in former communist countries and a liberal visa regime increased the number of illegal migrants in Turkey. A growing number of illegal foreign workers came mostly from neighboring Black Sea countries but also from Iraq, Iran, and African countries. Turkey also became a transit country for a growing number of illegal immigrants from Middle Eastern, Asian, and African countries trying to reach western Europe.

The new status determination procedure was accompanied by a very strict five-day time limit for filing an asylum application with the Turkish police. The regulation called for the outright deportation of those who did not meet this deadline. The regulation granted the right to receive a residence permit for those asylum-seekers and refugees whose files were being processed for resettlement by UNHCR while calling for the expulsion of those who either failed to be resettled within a reasonable period of time, left undefined, or failed to receive refugee status from UNHCR. The regulation called for close cooperation with international organizations and UNHCR while also acknowledging the principle of *non-refoulement* and providing for the possibility to seek an administrative review of a negative decision.

The regulation, at face value, seemed an improvement. Firstly, it appeared that Turkey would be taking over the task of status determination. This even led to some expectations that Turkey might be planning to lift the geographical limitation. Secondly, a relatively clearer set of procedures gave the impression that the asylum process would acquire greater transparency and predictability. Third, the reference in article 29 to "a refugee or an asylum-seeker who is residing in Turkey legally can only be deported by the Ministry of the Interior within the framework of 1951 Geneva Convention . . . or for reasons of national security and public order" seemed an unequivocal recognition of the principle of *non-refoulement,* clearly a major step forward. Previously, *non-refoulement* for non-Europeans was not clearly recognized and was often a source of conflict. Lastly, a liberal reading of the Asylum Regulation also seemed to suggest the prospect for greater cooperation with international organizations including UNHCR.

However, the practice that evolved in the first few years was disappointing. It provoked massive international criticism and condemnation. Amnesty International, United States Committee for Refugees, and many other refugee advocacy groups issued reports critical of the Turkish government.[15] Problems included the fact that the Turkish authorities were clearly unprepared to assume the task of actual status determination, having neither the knowledge, nor the requisite skills to undertake the process.

The most serious problem concerned deportations. The regulation calls for the deportation of those persons whose case has been rejected or was not filed within a five-day time limit. Furthermore, the regulation required that those who had illegally entered the country file their applications in the (remote) provinces where they entered. Refugee advocates argued that deportations on narrow technical grounds are violations of the *non-refoulement* principle. They argued that the turning back or sending back of recognized refugees or asylum-seekers who may have a genuine case constitutes a violation of this principle even if they may have entered the country illegally or not met the deadline. There was the impression that the time limit had more to do with deterring prospective asylum-seekers and discouraging people from seeking asylum in Turkey than a particular administrative function.

Another particularly difficult problem was the status of refugees who had been in the country illegally but had their asylum applications processed and accepted by UNHCR prior to the Asylum Regulation coming into force. Often, these were refugees whose resettlement was arranged but who were unable to leave the country as they risked being deported. Those who did attempt to leave the country were considered by Turkish authorities to be in violation of the Asylum Regulation and prevented from leaving the country for their respective resettlement destinations. Technically, they would have to be deported. They remained trapped in Turkey as a crisis developed between UNHCR and the international community on the one hand and Turkish authorities on the other. By 1996, more than 3,300 such people were caught in this stalemate.[16]

The regulation provides for the appeal against decisions relating to status determination. However, the major weakness with this procedure was that the "appeal" is an administrative review and not a judicial one.

In March 1997 alone, the MOI ordered the deportation of close to 600 persons deemed to be in the country "illegally." This number included many refugees who had been processed and recognized by UNHCR but were illegally present in Turkey. By August 1997, what was called a "one-time-solution" was reached. This arrangement allowed refugees to exit Turkey to their respective countries and gave UNHCR until February 1998 to finalize pending status determination cases. Subsequently, recognized refugees would be allowed to leave for their respective resettlement countries while rejected cases were expected to return to their country of origin.

This arrangement turned out to be the product of a new, more flexible, and cooperative frame of mind on the Turkish side.

In 1997, another positive development in relations between the Turkish government and UNHCR occurred when the MOI instructed its officials in border towns to direct asylum-seekers to UNHCR field officers. By 1998, a series of seminars and conferences for Turkish officials organized by UNHCR with funding from western governments were initiated. More importantly, coordination between UNHCR in Ankara and the MOI had improved to such an extent that for all intents and purposes UNHCR regained its role of status determination. Starting from 1997, a number of deportation cases were appealed before local administrative courts and favorable rulings were obtained. In 1999, the Turkish government increased the five-day time limit to ten days. A significant reduction in deportations was also achieved by 1999, and UNHCR officials in the border towns were allowed access to illegal immigrants with a view to reaching potential asylum-seekers.

THE ROLE AND CHALLENGES CONFRONTING UNHCR AND THE INTERNATIONAL COMMUNITY

The early 1990s was a period when Turkish officials suspected the international community and, in particular, the West was supporting the PKK and the cause of Turkish Kurdish nationalists. Furthermore, this was a period in which Turkey came under sustained criticism from the international community, and particularly nongovernmental organizations, for human rights violations against Kurds. Many officials believed that these criticisms had malicious intent and were used as an excuse to lend support to the cause of the PKK. Hence, the general mood was one that left little room for cooperation with the external world.

The key task for UNHCR seemed to be to rebuild the old goodwill and confidence on which cooperation between Turkey and UNHCR had previously been based. UNHCR began by offering itself as a partner for the implementation of the 1994 Asylum Regulation.

One of the first breakthroughs came when UNHCR succeeded in persuading the Turkish authorities to launch a publicity campaign. At first Turkish officials seemed rather apprehensive, as there was the concern that such publicity might actually attract asylum-seekers to Turkey. However, there was also recognition that this could mean a possibility of reducing the number of asylum-seekers illegally present in the country. This would mean greater control over the movement of people. In return UNHCR committed itself to encouraging asylum-seekers who approached them to register with Turkish authorities too. The results were mixed. There was increased awareness among asylum-seekers of the regulation and the number of registrations with Turkish authorities especially in border towns did modestly increase. However, the five-day time limit for filing applications continued to constitute a major problem as did *refoulement*. At the same time this project helped to create a climate for further cooperation between UNHCR and Turkey.

Subsequently, UNHCR was able to convince Turkish authorities to organize training conferences and seminars on refugee law and status determination for Turkish officials. Participants not only left better informed, there was evidence of significant changes towards asylum-seekers and refugees.[17] These training seminars and close cooperation between Turkish officials and UNHCR have created a team of officials who are well-informed and cooperative. One drawback is, however, that these officials are frequently redeployed from one service or department to another, meaning the opportunity to build institutional memory and a body of expertise is wasted.

The training programs were gradually expanded to include a wider range of actors such as judges, prosecutors, and gendarmes. The seminars became critical exercises in confidence-building, cooperation, and informal forums for negotiations and the resolving of outstanding problems, such as the five-day time limit and the question of whether Turkey is bound by the principle of *non-refoulement* given its geographical limitation to the 1951 convention.

There was a general acknowledgment that a violation of a time limit for handing in applications should not constitute a basis for deportation. Not surprisingly, in January 1999 the Turkish government introduced an amendment to the regulation increasing the time limit from five to ten days. One other area where UNHCR played an initially discrete but critical role in improving Turkish refugee policy is in the use of courts to protect and advance the rights of asylum-seekers and refugees. A military judge has argued that article 125 of the Turkish Constitution makes it possible for administrative decision to receive judicial appeal.[18] Actually, writing back in 1980, a Turkish scholar had argued that it was possible for a foreign national to challenge in court an administrative decision preventing the entry or calling for the expulsion of a foreigner.[19]

In 1978, the Council of State (Danıştay) had ruled against the state for expelling a Swedish TV crew without providing clear evidence of a violation of the law requiring such an expulsion.[20] In spite of this precedent and a general legal opinion that asylum-seekers and refugees could appeal against an order of deportation by the state, this had never occurred. A lack of confidence in the Turkish police and appeal system coupled with a fear that challenging authorities in court might adversely affect their case had deterred asylum-seekers or refugees from choosing to go to court to challenge the authorities.

The opportunity to break this timidity occurred in July and October 1997 when two administrative courts ruled in favor of two Iranian refugees against the MOI decisions calling for their deportations for violating the time limit clause of the 1994 Asylum Regulation. In both cases the Iranian asylum-seekers had been recognized as refugees by UNHCR in Ankara and their re-settlement to third countries had been arranged. The problem had arisen when UNHCR sought the cooperation of the Turkish government to assist the Iranians to leave the country.[21]

In both cases the courts ruled that the interpretation of the regulation by the MOI was at fault and that what was critical was the actual substance of the cases and not the time limit. The courts argued that duly ratified interna-tional legal instruments such as the 1951 convention constituted part and parcel of enforceable Turkish laws and hence had to be respected. The courts argued that the MOI had failed to cite any evidence to show that these persons were not actually refugees and hence annulled the deportation or-ders. The MOI appealed but the Council of State upheld the decision of the lower court.[22]

Another critical judicial ruling challenging Turkish practice came from the European Court of Human Rights (ECHR). Turkey is a party to the European Human Rights Convention and since 1987 has recognized the right of indi-viduals to petition the European court. The case involving the expulsion of an Iranian woman duly recognized as a refugee by UNHCR is an important case taken to the European level. The Turkish authorities called for her ex-pulsion on the grounds of entering Turkey illegally in violation of the regu-lation. The appeal made to an administrative court calling for a stay of exe-cution was rejected. Subsequently, the case was taken to the ECHR that not only found the case admissible but also ruled that there was "a real risk of the applicant being subjected to treatment contrary to article 3 if she is re-turned to Iran." More importantly, in terms of Turkish refugee policy the Court held that:[23]

> The Court is not persuaded that the authorities of the respondent State con-ducted any meaningful assessment of the applicant's claim, including its argua-bility. It would appear that her failure to comply with the five-day registration requirement under the Asylum Regulation 1994 denied her any scrutiny of the factual basis of her fears about being removed to Iran. In the Court's opinion, the automatic and mechanical application of such a short time-limit for submit-ting an asylum application must be considered at variance with the protection of the fundamental value embodied in Article 3 of the Convention.

There can be no doubt that these judicial rulings have influenced the prac-tice of the MOI and are likely to contribute positively to a better protection of the rights of asylum-seekers and refugees in Turkey in future.

It would be unrealistic to attribute all the improvements in Turkish refugee policy to UNHCR. A number of western governments played a key role and particularly, those governments with a long track record of accepting refugees for resettlement. Among these are the United States, Canada, Australia, and the Netherlands. Canada and the Netherlands supported training programs while the United States has agitated for better respect for the human rights of asylum-seekers through diplomatic channels, and together with Australia has facilitated resettlement of refugees, especially those with politically complicated backgrounds. More recently, the EU too has become a critical player. It has provided modest support for some Turkish nongovernmental organizations with programs for asylum-seekers. Furthermore, since the Helsinki Summit of December 1999, when Turkey was included among the candidate countries for membership, the EU has more actively campaigned for improvements in Turkey's refugee policy. In both the Accession Partnership Document adopted in December 2000 and the Progress Report on Turkey under the section on justice and home affairs the EU has called for a series of policy changes. Most importantly, the EU has called on Turkey to harmonize its asylum legislation with the EU *acquis*. In this respect it has called on Turkey to lift its geographical limitation, improve border control, open reception facilities for asylum-seekers and refugees, put in place administrative structures to perform status determination, sign readmission treaties with EU member states, and adjust its visa regimes to conform with EU standards.

CONCLUSION

In spite of the significant improvements in Turkish asylum and refugee policy major problems persist. Turkey continues to maintain its geographical limitation. In effect this means that for asylum-seekers coming to Turkey as a result of events outside Europe the only permanent solution is resettlement or repatriation. As table 8.1 indicates the numbers involved actually are not that significant. Since the adoption of the 1994 regulation 20,085 persons have filed asylum applications with the Turkish authorities. Of these, 7,343 have been recognized as refugees. Most of these refugees have subsequently been resettled. Except for Iranian cases the recognition cases are not particularly high. It should also be noted that there is high number of pending cases awaiting a final decision. Asylum-seekers who have had their cases rejected are informed that they need to leave the country within two weeks. However, this decision is rarely actively pursued. The Turkish authorities simply do not have the resources to actually deport such individuals.

Turkey's current asylum and refugee processing capabilities are severely limited. This in many ways explains why, contrary to the letter of the Regulation, status determination continues to be done by UNHCR. Turkey is far from having the infrastructure and the resources to meet the standards for the social and economic rights of refugees laid down in the

1951 convention, which is why, during the Cold War and since, Turkey encouraged resettlement of refugees rather than assisting their integration in
Turkey. Furthermore, the existing laws of Turkey, in particular the Law on
Settlement, in their current form technically do not allow for the integration of refugees who are not of "Turkish descent or culture." Yet, it should
be noted that even those refugees who technically could fall within this
definition have not been encouraged to seek such a status.

A further problem is that persons who are technically illegally present in
the country and even if duly recognized by UNHCR, are at risk of being *refouled.* The magnitude of the problem is best illustrated by the discrepancy
between statistics of protected persons maintained by government and UN-
HCR, respectively (as illustrated by tables 8.1 and 8.2).

One other problem that asylum-seekers in Turkey face has to do with
every individual's right to seek an independent and transparent appeal
against administrative decision affecting their basic human rights. Since 1996
Turkish courts have actually been used to appeal against decisions of the
MOI. On a number of occasions the courts have overturned the decisions
against asylum-seekers and suspended orders of deportation. In the case of
at least one asylum-seeker the ECHR received an appeal against a decision
of the MOI as well as a Turkish local court ruling that the Court subsequently
ruled against.

Against this background it is somewhat surprising to note that UNHCR decisions are not open to appeal by courts or independent bodies.[24] UNHCR
practice only allows for a possibility for an asylum-seeker to seek an internal
review of a rejected case. This clearly falls shorts of international legal stan-

**Table 8.1.   Statistics Concerning Applications Under the 1994 Asylum Regulation as
of 1 November 2000**

Country	Applications	Accepted Cases	Rejected Cases	Pending Cases	Cases Not Assessed
Iraq	8,961	2,335	2,809	3,296	114
Iran	10,713	4,946	750	4,469	172
Afghanistan	184	27	16	126	15
Russia	32	16	13	—	—
Uzbekistan	40	1	15	—	18
Azerbaijan	25	3	20	—	2
Other European*	30	6	18	—	1
Other**	100	8	63	22	1
Total***	20,085	7,343	3,705	7,913	356

*Includes: Albania, Bosnia, Bulgaria, Macedonia, Ukrainia, and Yugoslavia.
** Includes: Algeria, Bangladesh, China, Congo, Egypt, Eritrea, Ethopia, Jordan, Lebanon, Libya, Kuwait, Kyr-
gyzistan, Pakistan, Palestine, Ruanda, Sierra Leone, Somalia, Sudan, Syria, Tunisia, and Zaire.
*** Not appearing in the table but included in the total for applications are 768 applications that were sub-
sequently withdrawn.
Source: Data obtained from the Foreigners Department of MOI.

Table 8.2.   Aggregate UNHCR Statistics for Asylum-Seekers and Refugees in Turkey as of 30 November 2000

Year	Applications	Accepted	Rejected
1998	6,838	2,230	3,013
1999	6,605	1,903	4,266
2000	5,285	2,106	4,012
Total	18,728	6,239	11,291

Source: Statistics obtained from the Ankara Branch Office of UNHCR. The discrepancy in aggregate of accepted and rejected cases and the actual total results from cases that get carried to the following year.

dards as expressed in article 14 of the International Covenant on Civil and Political Rights of 1966 and article 6 of the European Convention on Human Rights that call for the right of appeal against administrative decisions in a fair and public hearing held by an independent and impartial tribunal. The diplomatic immunity from jurisdiction that UNHCR enjoys closes the possibility of its decisions being reviewed in Turkish courts. A solution could be to allow contested cases to be reviewed by an ad hoc body of internationally recognized refugee law experts such as a European Legal Network on Asylum supported by the European Council on Refugees and Exiles.

For a long time Turkey resisted restrictions on its sovereign authority to control immigration. In a way, Turkey has been tamed and has come to accept that international law does bring restrictions to state freedom. This is most visible in the case of a growing respect for *non-refoulement*. All that still remains of traditional Turkish policy is that it is a "persistent objector" to lifting the geographical limitation to the 1951 convention. The credit for this change goes to a wide range of actors, but no doubt UNHCR has been a central player in nudging Turkey towards a better implementation of the 1951 convention.

Yet at the same time Turkey is still far from being an ideal implementer of the convention. It continues to resist the lifting of the geographical limitation and shies from developing the facilities for doing its own status determination. Resettlement or repatriation remains its preferred solution and it offers very little room for local integration for refugees who are not of Turkish descent or culture. However, since it became a candidate for membership to the EU, Turkey is under growing pressure to align itself with EU *acquis* on asylum.

The cumulative effect of these efforts would most likely lead to a Turkey that increasingly tightens its border and develops policies to deter asylum-seekers and illegal immigrants. A Turkey that tightens up control may actually end up aggravating illegal immigration and making a larger group vulnerable to human rights abuses. Hence, ironically, this may create a situation whereby the pre-1994 asylum and refugee policies would appear in comparison to be more liberal and permissive.

NOTES

1. *Official Gazette (Resmi Gazete)*, 5 September 1961, No. 10898. Ratification of the 1967 Protocol Relating to the Legal Status of Refugees in July 1968 published in *Official Gazette*, 14 October 1968, No. 13026.

2. *Official Gazette*, 30 November 1994, No. 22217. "The Regulation on the Procedures and the Principles Related to Mass Influx and Foreigners Arriving in Turkey Either as Individuals or in Groups Wishing to Seek Asylum from a Third Country." Hereafter referred to as "the regulation" or "Asylum Regulation."

3. See, for example, the following reports: *U.S. Department of State: Turkey Country Report on Human Rights for 1996* (Released on January 1997 obtained from www.state.gov.), B. Frelick, *Barriers to Protection: Turkey's Asylum Regulations* (Report issued by the U.S. Committee for Refugees, July 1996, Washington, D.C.), and *Turkey: Refoulement of Non-European Refugees—A Protection Crisis* (Amnesty International Secreteriat, London, Document EUR 44/031/1997).

4. Both developments are raised in *1999 U.S. Department of State on Human Rights Practices: Turkey* (Released in February 2000 obtained from www.state.gov.), and *2000 Regular Report From the Commission on Turkey's Progress Towards Accession* (November 2000, European Commission, Brussels), 64.

5. *Official Gazette*, 13 January 1999, No. 23582.

6. Interviews with Ministry of Foreign Affairs and Ministry of Interior officials, 12 and 14 December 2000.

7. *Official Gazette*, 14 June 1934, No. 2733. This Law has since been heavily amended but the basic articles that define who can be an immigrant and refugee remain unchanged.

8. *Milliyet*, 22 February 2000 reported that there was a group of 104 Chechen refugees at the border at minus 30° C.

9. *Radikal*, 25 February 2000.

10. Ossipov, A. "Constructing Conflict in the Former Soviet Societies: The Case of Meskhetian (Ahiska) Turks," paper presented at the *Workshop on Ahiska (Meshketian) Turks: Identity, Migration and Integration*, 14–15 December 2000.

11. Opening speech given by Abdulhaluk Cay, State Minister responsible for immigrants and refugees at the *Workshop on Ahiska (Meshketian) Turks: Identity, Migration and Integration*, 14–15 December 2000.

12. According to statistics from the Aliens Department there were as of 1 November 2000 still 120 Iraqis from the 1991 mass influx of refugees with residence permits in Turkey.

13. Goodwin-Gill, G. *The Refugee in International Law* (London: Clarendon, 2d ed., 1996), 167.

14. For an official translation of the text of the Regulation and an early evaluation of it see K. Kirişçi, "Is Turkey Lifting the 'geographical limitation'?: The November 1994 Regulation on Asylum in Turkey," *International Journal of Refugee Law* 8, No. 3 (1996). For a more critical analysis of the Regulation see B. Frelick, "Barriers to Protection: Turkey's Asylum Regulations" *International Journal of Refugee Law* 9, No. 1 (1997).

15. See note 4.

16. *Chronological History of 'One Time Solution,'* UNHCR, Ankara, 7 December 1998.

17. *İltica ve Mülteci Konusunda Seminer* (Seminar on Asylum and Refuge) held at Neva Palas Oteliö Ankaraö, 28 Eylül, 02 October 1998.

18. Odman, T. *Mülteci Hukuku* (AÜ. SBF. İnsan Hakları Merkezi Yayınları, No. 15, Ankara, 1995), p. 187.

19. Duran, L. "Yabancıların Türkiye'den Sınırdışı Edilmesi," *İnsan Hakları Yıllığı*, Yıl 2, 1980.

20. For the ruling see *Danıştay Dergisi*, Yıl 8, Sayı 30–31, 1978, 50.

21. For a detailed legal analysis of the role of courts in asylum cases see T. Tahranlı, "Sığınmacı, Mülteci ve Göç Konularına İlişkin Türkiye'deki Yargı Kararları Konusunda Hukuki bir Değerlendirme," in *Sığınmacı, Mülteci ve Göç Konularına İlişkin Türkiye'deki Yargı Kararları* (2001, UNHCR, Ankara).

22. It should be interesting to note that very shortly before the Council of State issued this ruling UNHCR had actually organized together with the Council of State and the Turkish Bar Association a *Panel on the Role of the Judiciary and International Refugee Law in the Turkish Context*, 9 December 1998, Ankara. The Head of the Council of State was the host and gave the opening speech to the Panel.

23. European Human Rights Court (Fourth Section) *Case of Jabari v. Turkey* (Application No. 40035/98), Judgment, Strasbourg, 11 July 2000, 7–8.

24. See M. Alexander, "Refugee Status Determination Conducted by the UNHCR," *International Journal of Refugee Law* 11, No. 2. This article's analysis also includes the practices of the UNHCR Branch Office in Ankara. Questions with specific reference to the practices of UNHCR in Ankara was also raised by N. Yuca, "Türkiye'deki Sığınma Prosedürü ve Problemleri" (Turkish Asylum Procedures and its Problems), paper presented at the conference on *Turkey and EU Enlargement* by the Centre for Research and Policy on the European Community, Ankara University, 5 December 2000.

9

Whither the Accountability Theory: Second-Class Status for Third-Party Refugees as a Threat to International Refugee Protection

Jennifer Moore

The international refugee definition does not discriminate between victims based upon the persecutor's affiliation or nonaffiliation with the state. While the majority of asylum states recognize this principle of equal access under the "protection theory,"[1] a minority of states including France and Germany currently subscribe to a much more restrictive concept of agency. Under the "accountability theory," asylum is limited to individuals who fear persecution at the hands of entities for whose abusive acts the state is deemed responsible. In accountability jurisdictions, so-called "third-party refugees"[2]—those who fear persecution by nonstate agents—are denied protection.

This chapter cautions that the accountability theory strikes at the very heart of international protection, by threatening the international consensus underlying the provision of asylum to refugees. Part II presents a conceptual analysis of the accountability theory and its fundamental inconsistency with the principle of refugee protection. This philosophical approach is followed in Part III by a pragmatic examination of the impact of the accountability theory in the context of a regional burden-sharing regime that allows a European state, under certain circumstances, to return an asylum-seeker to the country of first asylum. Part III concentrates on two asylum cases from the United Kingdom: *ex parte Adan and Aitseguer*,[3] decided by the United Kingdom House of Lords, and *T.I. v. United Kingdom*,[4] a case ultimately brought before the European Court of Human Rights.

In *ex parte Adan and Aitseguer,* the House of Lords blocked the return of a Somali woman and an Algerian man to Germany and France, respectively, where they had previously sojourned. The Law Lords reasoned that both countries would likely return the asylum-seekers to their countries of origin because they feared persecution by nonstate agents.

Contrastingly, in *T.I. v. United Kingdom*, the European Court of Human Rights refused to block England's return of a Sri Lankan "third-party refugee" to Germany, despite his previous denial of asylum by administrative bodies in that country for lack of state complicity in his feared persecution. Notwithstanding, its endorsement of the protection theory, the Court permitted T.I.'s return to Germany based on its speculation that he might be eligible for an alternative temporary form of protection under the German Aliens Act.

Taken together, *ex parte Adan and Aitseguer* and *T.I. v. United Kingdom* clarify that when an asylum-seeker arrives in an accountability theory jurisdiction first, and moves on to a protection jurisdiction second, it matters little that a majority of states subscribe to the broader protection principle, if in fact she risks removal to a country that may return her to persecution by nonstate agents. In a European legal climate which places severe limits on "forum-shopping" by refugees, the protection theory cannot afford to be embraced by a mere majority of states. Rather, protection for victims of both state and nonstate persecution should be the consensus of all members of the international community. Moreover, protection theory adherents must refuse to return asylum-seekers to accountability jurisdictions until such time that the protection theory has universal application.

THE PROTECTION THEORY AND
ACCOUNTABILITY THEORY: THESIS AND ANTITHESIS

The definition of a refugee set forth in article 1 of the 1951 Convention Relating to the Status of Refugees does not define the character of the actor whose persecution is feared by the asylum-seeker. A refugee is someone outside her country of origin with "a well-founded fear of being persecuted for reasons of race, religion, nationality, membership of a particular social group or political opinion" who is either *"unable or unwilling* to avail [her]self of the protection of that country."[5] UNHCR, the agency responsible for providing protection and assistance to refugees worldwide, instructs that the silence of the Refugee Convention regarding the agency of persecution must be read expansively, such that "offensive acts . . . committed by the local populace . . . can be considered as persecution . . . if the authorities *refuse, or prove unable*, to offer effective protection."[6]

As clarified by Guy Goodwin-Gill in his treatise on international refugee law, "the issue of state responsibility for persecution . . . is not part of the refugee definition."[7] Further, Goodwin-Gill explains, "there is no basis in the 1951 Convention . . . for requiring the existence of effective operating institutions of government as a precondition to a successful claim to refugee status."[8] Thus, according to both conventional international law and scholarly interpretation, the state is *not* the necessary agent of persecution, *nor* is a functional state backdrop to persecution a prerequisite to the provision of surrogate international protection to refugees.[9]

Despite international legal dictates regarding the agency of persecution, state practice differs considerably regarding the recognition of the equal claim to international protection on the part of refugees fearing nonstate agents of persecution. A majority of western asylum states, including Australia, Belgium, Canada, the United Kingdom, and the United States, subscribe to the so-called "protection theory," which encompasses victims of unofficial and official persecution alike.[10] However, a minority of European states, including Germany and France, have crafted the more restrictive "accountability theory," which bars protection to refugees fleeing persecution by certain nonstate actors.

The accountability theory as a basis for the denial of refugee status has a more limited application to the specific context of a so-called "failed state," as demonstrated by Germany's denial of asylum to refugees from Somalia and Afghanistan in recent years. However, it has also been applied more generally by France and some of its neighbors to refugees from any state, embattled yet functional, which is unable to provide protection in a given circumstance, often due to internal armed conflict.

In the case of the broadest application of the accountability theory, refugee protection will only be granted in two situations: either the state must be the persecutor, or the state must be *unwilling but able* protect against persecution by nonstate agents.[11] Where the state lacks the capacity to prevent or punish persecution by other entities, whether insurgents, clans, subclans, or criminals, the victims of such persecution are legalistically placed outside of the refugee definition. The technical significance of the accountability theory is that it replaces the more embracive *"unable or unwilling* to protect" standard in paragraph 65 of the UNHCR *Handbook* with a more demanding *"unwilling but able* to protect" requirement. The human result is that refugees fleeing varying degrees of state dysfunction are left out in the cold.

While a denial of status to those refugees fleeing nonstate persecution is a clear violation of the spirit of the 1951 Refugee Convention and a significant dilution of the availability of international protection in those states that subscribe to the accountability theory, unfortunately the problem is not so contained or containable. The tear in the fabric of international protection caused by the accountability theory becomes an unraveling hole in the context of a regional burden-sharing regime in which a EU member may return an asylum-seeker to the first Union member through whose territory she transited.[12] It is the combination of the accountability theory and the application of the first asylum country concept that is most threatening to both abstract principles of refugee protection and the very practical plight of individual refugees. The threat is particularly evident at present to those asylum-seekers in Europe who happen to pass through Germany or France before seeking asylum in a country such as the United Kingdom.

RECENT ASYLUM JURISPRUDENCE IN THE UNITED KINGDOM UNDER THE DUBLIN CONVENTION AND THE 1996 ASYLUM AND IMMIGRATION APPEALS ACT: *EX PARTE ADAN ET AL.*

Two recent asylum cases in the United Kingdom deal with one or more individuals fearing nonstate-sponsored persecution, and both involve the possible removal of one or more asylum-seekers to Germany or France as provided under United Kingdom law. In the first case, the United Kingdom House of Lords, affirming the Court of Appeals, protected the asylum-seekers concerned from returning to Germany and France, respectively.[13] In the second, the European Court of Human Rights allowed the United Kingdom to return an asylum-seeker to Germany.[14] In both cases, the United Kingdom recognized that the accountability theory was in violation of the spirit of the 1951 convention, and yet this finding did not consistently prevent return to a country found to perpetrate such a violation. The differential outcome of the two asylum cases argues powerfully that the availability of refugee protection to victims of state and nonstate persecution alike is a core value of the 1951 convention that must be recognized by all members of the international community.

The asylum-seekers in *ex parte Adan* were Lul Adan, Sittampalan Subaskaran, and Hamid Aitseguer. Adan, a Somali woman, alleged past persecution and the fear of future persecution by a rival clan in a situation of total governmental collapse in her native country. The German authorities had denied her asylum claim before she reached the United Kingdom. Subaskaran, a Sri Lankan man, claimed past and future persecution by the insurgent guerrilla force known as the LTTE or Tamil Tigers. His application had also been denied previously in Germany. Finally, Aitseguer, an Algerian man, had experienced and feared persecution by Islamic fundamentalists; he passed through France on his way to applying for asylum in the United Kingdom.

In each case, the United Kingdom Secretary of State had summarily dismissed their claims, having certified that each applicant was returnable to either Germany or France as a safe country of first asylum under the Dublin Convention and the 1996 Asylum and Immigration Appeals Act (hereinafter calles the 1996 act).[15] Appeals of the Secretary's decisions by Adan, Subaskaran, and Aitseguer were consolidated and decided by the United Kingdom Court of Appeals in July of 1999, in a judgment that affirmed the protection principle as the correct interpretation of the international refugee definition. The House of Lords then granted leave to appeal in the cases of Adan and Aitseguer, and decided their cases in December of 2000, affirming the judgment of the Court of Appeals.

Ex Parte Adan, Subaskaran, and Aitseguer in the Court of Appeals

The heart of the Court of Appeal's decision lay in its principled assessment of the protection and accountability theories.

In finding both the German and French variants of the accountability theory to be in violation of the Refugee Convention, the United Kingdom Court of Appeals declared the protection theory to be required by the Refugee Convention. In so concluding, the court provided a very clear articulation of the protection theory itself:

> the issue we must decide is whether or not, as a matter of law, the scope of Art. 1A(2) extends to persons who fear persecution by non-State agents in circumstances where the State is not complicit in the persecution, . . . whether because it is *unwilling or unable* . . . to provide protection. We entertain no doubt that such persons . . . are entitled to the Convention's protections.[16]

In what might be characterized as an academic discussion offered to assist future adjudicators in determining the application of the 1996 act's safe country provisions, the Court of Appeals cited one of its own earlier decisions regarding third-country transfers, declaring that "[w]hat is required is that there should be no real risk that the asylum-seeker would be sent to another country otherwise than in accordance with the convention."[17] The court then proceeded to find that the accountability theory is "as a matter of law at variance with the convention's true interpretation."[18] However, the court chose to culminate its decision, not with this broad-based invalidation of the accountability theory, but with the more qualified statement that "the Secretary of State, in administering Section 2(2)(c) of the Act of 1996, is only concerned with the question whether there exists a *real risk* that the third country will *refoule* the refugee in breach of the convention."[19]

The legal representative for the Secretary of State had argued in *ex parte Adan et al.* that Germany and France had alternative legal forms of relief from *refoulement* that would ensure that the convention was not violated in practice, despite any denial of formal refugee status under the accountability theory. Fortunately, from the perspective of the applicants, counsel was not able to provide meaningful evidence of "the efficacy of the[se] other forms of protection."[20] For this reason, the court was not required to resolve affirmatively whether the availability of temporary or lesser forms of protection in lieu of asylum in third countries would satisfy the United Kingdom's obligations under the convention or the 1996 act. Rather, the Court of Appeals was able to conclude that the Secretary must entertain the merits of the asylum applications of Adan, Subaskaran, and Aitseguer, and could not return them to Germany and France.

Ex parte Adan and Aitseguer in the House of Lords

Failed States, Embattled States, and the Accountability Theory

After the Court of Appeals ruled in favor of Adan, Subaskaran, and Aitseguer, the secretary of state sought leave to appeal the cases of Adan and Aitseguer in the House of Lords. Leave was not sought by the Secretary as a means of effecting the removal of Adan and Aitseguer to Somalia and Algeria, respectively, but rather in order to secure guidance from the House as to future cases involving alternative applications of the accountability theory. As Lord Steyn specified,

> the House gave leave to appeal in the cases of Adan and Aitseguer . . . . [to] consider *whether there is a material difference between a state where governmental authority has collapsed* (as is the case in Somalia) *and a state where governmental authority exists but is too weak to provide effective protection against persecution by non state actors* (as is the case in Algeria).[21]

The two applications of the accountability theory considered by the House of Lords in *ex parte Adan and Aitseguer* might be termed the "failed state" and "embattled state" alternatives. Under the failed state variant, Germany denies asylum to applicants such as Adan from a handful of dysfunctional and ungoverned countries like Somalia.[22] Contrastingly, the broader embattled state alternative is the basis for the denial of asylum in France and other accountability jurisdictions to applicants such as Aitseguer from states like Algeria that, while functional, are unable to provide individuals with effective protection from persecution by nonstate agents. Of the two accountability alternatives, Germany's failed state approach has a more limited application, and would serve to deny asylum to refugees only when they feared persecution by nonstate agents in countries in which state authority was not only ineffective but also nonexistent.

Having posed the question, the House held that the two variants of the accountability theory are equally incorrect interpretations of the international refugee definition. As Lord Steyn concluded:

> The relevant autonomous meaning of article 1(A)(2) of the Refugee Convention is therefore as explained in *Adan [I]*. Like the Court of Appeals I would hold that

there is no material distinction between a country where there is no government (like Somalia) and a country [where] the government is unable to afford the necessary protection to citizens (such as Algeria). Both are covered by article 1(A)(2).[23]

Therefore, with regard to the primary issue framed by Lord Steyn, the House quite succinctly dismissed the accountability principle by directly citing its own 1999 precedent in *Adan (I)* and squarely affirming the Court of Appeals in *ex parte Adan, Subaskaran, and Aitseguer.*

Third-Country Transfers under the Refugee Convention

In light of the relative ease with which the House of Lords framed and resolved the main issue on appeal in *ex parte Adan and Aitseguer* as described above, it is noteworthy that the Law Lords also grappled extensively with what at first blush was a more abstract and peripheral issue. Throughout all four of the separate opinions, the Lords probed the protection and accountability principles in light of the so-called "proper interpretation" of the Refugee Convention.[24]

As a threshold matter, the Lords clarified their duty to interpret the Refugee Convention and to instruct the secretary of state as to their determination. On this basis, the Law Lords repeatedly stressed that the conventional refugee definition has "one true meaning,"[25] a "true construction,"[26] "one autonomous interpretation,"[27] "an authoritative interpretation,"[28] and an "international meaning."[29] The House of Lords then affirmed the "proper interpretation" of the convention "[t]hat persecution may be by bodies other than the state" as "accepted in *Adan (I).*"[30]

Through a close reading it becomes clear that the essential ruling in *ex parte Adan and Aitseguer* was not simply that the House of Lords would continue to reject the accountability principle and would recognize third-party refugees from both failed and embattled states under the *Adan (I)* protection principle. Rather, the House also felt compelled to address a deeper question: was the United Kingdom prohibited from sending third-party refugees to accountability jurisdictions on the strength of that same protection principle? With regard to the cases of Adan and Aitseguer, the Law Lords responded with a resounding "yes."

The Secretary of State had argued before the House that there was "a permissible range of interpretations" of the Refugee Convention,[31] notwithstanding, his agreement that *Adan (I)* was the proper rule in Great Britain. Given this margin of appreciation, he maintained that he was permitted to return Adan and Aitseguer to Germany and France as safe countries of first asylum under section 2(2)(c) of the 1996 Asylum and Immigration Act, despite the likelihood that their claims would be denied on accountability grounds. The Lords rejected the secretary's reasoning, most pointedly in the opinion of Lord Steyn:

> The Secretary of State wrongly proceeded on the twin assumption that there is a band of permissible meaning of article 1A(2) and that the practice hitherto adopted in Germany and France falls within the permissible range. The Secretary of State materially misdirected himself. His decisions must be quashed.[32]

By addressing the practical exigencies of prospective third-country transfers under domestic law, the House of Lords applied the *Adan (I)* protection principle in a new context. In so doing, the House confronted the prospect of "chain-reaction *refoulements,*" finding such indirect forced returns in violation of article 33 of the Refugee Convention.[33] In the words of Lord Steyn:

> it is a long standing principle of English law that if it would be unlawful to return the asylum seeker directly to his country of origin where he is subject to persecution . . ., it would be equally unlawful to return him to a third country which it is known will return him to his country of origin.[34]

Lord Hutton went even further in proclaiming the *non-refoulement* principle as "an important human right . . . notwithstanding that the state . . . is not complicit in [the feared] persecution."[35] He then concluded that section 2 of the 1996 act could not serve "to take away that right from Ms. Adan and Mr. Aitseguer," and therefore that the secretary of state was prohibited from returning them to either Germany or France.[36]

While unanimously affirming the lower court's decision regarding Adan and Aitseguer, it is significant that the House of Lords did not reiterate the Court of Appeal's reasoning in all respects. Specifically, the House of Lords did not rely upon the "real risk" test cited by the lower court. Rather, the Law Lords unambiguously rejected the accountability principle and overturned the secretary of state's decisions to return Adan and Aitseguer to Germany and France. In so doing, the House clarified that the protection theory is the correct interpretation of the convention, and protects third-party refugees from nonstate persecution in both failed and embattled states. Moreover, *ex parte Adan and Aitseguer* discourages "chain reaction refoulements" of refugees to likely persecution by nonstate agents by prohibiting indirect returns through accountability jurisdictions.

Nevertheless, the "real risk" test cited by the Court of Appeals is largely untouched by the House of Lords in *ex parte Adan and Aitseguer.* Therefore, despite the success of Adan et al. in fighting their returns to Germany and France, and the notable validation and extension of the protection theory by the House of Lords, there may be a small but important piece of unfinished business in the aftermath of *ex parte Adan and Aitseguer.*

The "real risk" test rearticulated by the Court of Appeals in *ex parte Adan, et al.* remains a possible factor in cases involving the possible transfer of asylum-seekers to third countries, particularly those that may have specific measures for temporary protection that fall short of the durable status of asylum. The real risk test would appear to contemplate a case-based investigation of a state's interpretation and application of the Refugee Convention that may in practice tolerate returns to accountability theory jurisdictions. Because the House of Lords felt it was in no position to evaluate the claimed alternative forms of protection in Germany, arguably the real risk analysis became moot in Adan and Aitseguer's case. However, it was the very claim of meaningful alternatives to asylum in Germany that led to a different outcome when another third-party refugee petitioned the British Secretary of State, and ultimately the European Court of Human Rights. The case of *T.I. v. United Kingdom* will be examined next.

T.I. v. UNITED KINGDOM

T.I. v. United Kingdom was the case of a Sri Lankan who alleged past persecution by both the LTTE insurgents and the Sri Lankan government, as well as a fear of future persecution by both state and nonstate agents were he to be returned to Sri Lanka.[37] According to T.I.'s testimony, he was first captured, interrogated, and forced into servitude by the Tamil Tigers over a two-year period. In 1995, after escaping from an LTTE settlement, he was arrested by Sri Lankan soldiers on two different occasions, both leading to his interrogation regarding suspected LTTE affiliation and numerous instances of torture, including severe beatings, whippings, and burnings. A doctor involved in the treatment of torture victims issued a report on T.I.'s behalf concluding that his extensive scars, as well as his psychological attributes, were characteristic of survivors of torture, and moreover that his testimony regarding the detention centers in which allegedly he had been incarcerated in Sri Lanka were consistent with descriptions given by other Sri Lankan asylum-seekers.

T.I. alleged a prospective fear of persecution upon return to Sri Lanka, based upon probable ongoing suspicions that government officials would have as to his LTTE association. In this context, his testimony highlighted the potentially graphic impact of his extensive scars as immutable evidence of past torture and hence past suspicion of involvement in insurgent activities, which might in turn provoke further suspicion and inhuman treatment in the future.

T.I. claimed asylum in Germany in 1996 and his application was denied, first by the state refugee status determination authority in 1996, and then by an administrative court in Bavaria in 1997. The first decision was grounded in the finding that T.I.'s alleged torture, if it occurred, was due to "excesses of isolated organs [that] . . . cannot be imputed to the Sri Lankan state."[38] The Administrative Court's denial was based contrastingly on an unwillingness to attribute persecutory acts by the Tamil Tigers to the Sri Lankan state, as well as an adverse finding regarding T.I.'s credibility.

With reference to the United Kingdom Court of Appeal's decision in *ex parte Adan*, it is noteworthy that where Sittampalan Subaskaran claimed a fear of nonstate persecution, T.I. alleged both state and nonstate persecution, which might be thought to strengthen his prospects in an accountability jurisdiction. However, the German authorities not only refused T.I. protection due to the nonstate character of the Tamil Tiger's abuse, as in *Adan*, but also out of an apparent refusal to attribute acts by state officials to the state.

After the second adverse decision in his case, T.I. left Germany for Italy and then the United Kingdom, where he claimed asylum in September 1997. Analogous to the early stages of the asylum case of Subaskaran, T.I.'s asylum claim was denied in 1998 by the secretary of state without consideration on the merits, based on a finding under section 2 of the 1996 Asylum and Immigration Act that he was returnable to Germany as a safe country of first asylum.

Unlike Mr. Subaskaran, however, when T.I. appealed to the Court of Appeals later in 1998, the court upheld the secretary's determination, finding that the secretary "was entitled to conclude that the German authorities do not adopt an approach . . . outside the range of responses of a Contracting State acting in good faith to implement its obligations under the [Refugee] Convention."[39] When T.I. was denied leave to appeal to the House of Lords, he sought "leave to remain . . . on compassionate grounds," further judicial review on medical grounds, and a request for reconsideration of his case based on the Court of Appeals decision in *ex parte Adan et al.*, all unsuccessfully.[40]

After being denied asylum by the secretary of state and losing in the Court of Appeals, T.I. petitioned the European Commission of Human Rights on September 28, 1998. He claimed that the United Kingdom, in finding him removable to Germany, had violated a number of provisions of the European Convention on Human Rights, including article 3 regarding prohibition against torture and inhuman treatment.[41] The Commission transferred competence to examine T.I.'s application to the European Court of Human Rights, and the court's decision was rendered on March 7, 2000.

As layered as the factual and procedural tapestry of T.I.'s case is the thicket of legal claims and analysis set forth by the applicant, opposing counsel and the various adjudicatory bodies. An added dimension not present in *ex parte Adan* is the involvement of the European Court of Human Rights.

Although asylum is not a subject of the European convention, article 3 has been interpreted by the court to bar a country from returning an individual to torture and inhuman treatment analogous to the Refugee Convention's prohibition against *refoulement* to likely persecution. In fact, in *Ahmed v.*

Austria, the European court in 1996 blocked the return of a Somali national to his country of origin, where he feared persecution by a paramilitary faction led by the warlord General Aideed.

Ahmed is an important decision for the European court given that no less than three vital legal principles emanate from this case. The court concluded in *Ahmed* that: (1) article 3 regarding prohibition against inhuman treatment serves as protection against certain forms of persecution; (2) in addition to prohibiting affirmative inhuman acts by a signatory, article 3 also bars a signatory from returning an individual to a jurisdiction in which such inhuman treatment may occur; and (3) article 3 protects against inhuman treatment by nonstate agents, as well as state officials.[42] The third *Ahmed* ruling is particularly significant in that it borrows the protection principle from international refugee law and applies it in the context of human rights law and the European convention.

Affirming its willingness to apply the second *Ahmed* principle to T.I.'s threatened return to Germany, the court held in *T.I. v. United Kingdom*, "that the indirect removal in this case to an intermediary country, which is also a contracting State, does not affect the responsibility of the United Kingdom to ensure that the applicant is not, as a result of its decision to expel, exposed to treatment contrary to Article 3 of the convention."[43] Moreover, the court recognized the inconsistency between its own jurisprudence regarding protection from nonstate human rights abuses (i.e., *Ahmed* principle 3) and the accountability theory as utilized by Germany to deny refugee protection where the state is not complicit in the alleged persecution.

Despite its apparent favorable application of *Ahmed*, as well as its implicit condemnation of the German accountability theory, the European court refused to block the United Kingdom's removal of T.I. to Germany. The reason for the court's decision was ostensibly its finding that T.I. would not *necessarily* be returned by Germany to Sri Lanka, despite his denial of asylum. The court examined several provisions of the German Aliens Act, and concluded that T.I. might be eligible for one or more alternative forms of protection that are not limited to victims of state-sponsored persecution.

In particular, the court examined section 53(6) of the German Aliens Act, "which grants a discretion to the [German] authorities to suspend deportation in case of a substantial danger for life, personal integrity, or liberty of an alien. This applies to concrete individual *danger resulting from either state or private action*."[44] The European court found that T.I. would be eligible to seek section 53(6) protection, and that "the apparent gap in protection resulting from the German approach to non-state agent risk is met, at least to some extent, by the application by the German authorities of Section 53(6)."[45]

In order to reconcile the court's willingness to apply article 3 of the convention to block deportations that may *result* in inhuman treatment in another country, with its unwillingness to block T.I.'s return to Germany, it may be useful to examine the Court's qualification of its earlier statement of *Ahmed* principle 2. Like the United Kingdom Court of Appeals in *ex parte Adan et al.*, the European court does not state that the mere possibility of treaty violations is sufficient to find that individuals may never be returned to a particular jurisdiction. Rather, the court states that article 3 "imposes an obligation on the contracting states not to expel a person to a country where substantial grounds have been shown for believing that he would face a real risk of being subjected to treatment contrary to Article 3."[46]

Just as it articulates the *Ahmed* principle in the form of a "real risk" test, the Court phrases its final determination that T.I. may be returned to Germany in terms of a negative assessment of his likelihood of return by Germany to Sri Lanka: ". . . the Court finds that it is not established that there is a real risk that Germany would expel the applicant to Sri Lanka in breach of Article 3 of the convention."[47]

The good news in *T.I. v. United Kingdom* is that article 3 of the European convention is still held to prohibit return to persecution by nonstate agents (*Ahmed* principle 3), and that the Court requires a signatory state like Germany to provide alternatives to asylum in the case of victims of nonstate agents of persecution. The more sobering news is that the court was willing to deny protection to T.I. on the basis of a purely discretionary form of relief from deportation, despite the fact that the German government had "not provided any example of Section 53(6) being applied to a failed asylum-seeker in a second asylum procedure."[48] Moreover, the court does not address the very real disadvantage that even if section 53(6) protection were provided to T.I., it amounts to a temporary suspension of deportation, rather than a conference of durable legal status on a par with asylum.

CONCLUSION

T.I. v. United Kingdom—together with the domestic proceedings in the United Kingdom that preceded it—illustrates the vulnerability of a refugee protection regime that lacks consensus regarding the status of victims of nonstate agents of persecution. The abstract right of all refugees to protection may be proclaimed, and the withholding of asylum to victims of nonstate agents may be officially condemned, while de facto returns to persecution are tolerated. So long as the accountability theory is applied, even in a limited number of jurisdictions, the rights of third-party refugees may be honored in the breach.

The "real risk" in allowing returns to accountability jurisdictions lies not only in the very real possibility of chain reaction returns to persecution in the case of individual asylum-seekers, but also in the propagation and perpetuation of a double standard that will negatively impact far greater numbers of refugees. The principle of nondiscrimination, enshrined in the Refugee Convention and international human rights law more generally,[49] does not tolerate an interpretation of the refugee definition that forces victims of non-state persecution to rely on the discretionary kindness of temporary relief from forced return rather than the durable protection of asylum. Thus the strongest principled and practical statement that protection adherents can make in the face of accountability doctrine is in refusing to return asylum-seekers to accountability jurisdictions, as demonstrated by the British House of Lords in *ex parte Adan and Aitseguer*.[50]

NOTES

A version of the paper was published in volume 13 of the International Journal of Refugee Law, *IJRL* 13, No. 32 (2001). This chapter is an excerpted and revised version of that article, from which many of the footnotes have been omitted. Thanks to UNM law graduate Melissa Ewer for her valuable research assistance, and to Aninia Nadig for her thoughtful editorial assistance.

1. The protection theory also may be referred to as the "persecution theory." The protection/persecution theory focuses on the *fact* of persecution and the *lack* of protection. In contrast, it is the *character* of the persecutor that is the overriding concern of the accountability theory.

2. See *Adan v. Secretary of State for the Home Department* [1999] 1 A.C. 293 [*Adan I*] 306A–B. Lloyd Berwick held that "for those who are sometimes called 'third-party refugees' . . . if the state is unable to provide protection . . . the qualifications for refugee status are complete." See below, n. 72.

3. *R. v. Secretary of State for the Home Department, ex parte Adan and Aitseguer* (U.K. House of Lords, 19 December 2000) [hereinafter *ex parte Adan and Aitseguer*], affirming *R. v. Secretary of State for the Home Department ex parte Adan, Subaskaran, and Aitseguer* (U.K. Court of Appeals, 23 July 1999) [hereinafter *ex parte Adan et al.*].

4. *T.I. v. United Kingdom* (European Court of Human Rights, 7 March 2000); *IJRL* 12, No. 244 (2000).

5. Convention Relating to the Status of Refugees [hereinafter Refugee Convention], 28, July 1951, 189 UNTS 150, art. 1(A)(2); emphasis added.

6. U.N. Office of the High Commissioner for Refugees, *Handbook on Procedures and Criteria for Determining Refugee Status under the 1951 Convention and the 1967 Protocol relating to the Status of Refugees* (1979) [hereinafter the UNHCR *Handbook*], par. 65; emphasis added.

7. Goodwin-Gill, G. S. *The Refugee in International Law,* 2d Ed. (Oxford: Oxford University Press, 1996), 73.

8. Ibid., 73–74.

9. See also, Atle Grahl-Madsen, *The Status of Refugees in International Law* (A. W. Sijthoff-Leyden, 1966), 191, 192, and James Hathaway, *The Law of Refugee Status* (Toronto: Butterworths Canada Ltd., 1991), 124. See generally, Jennifer Moore, "From Nation State to Failed State: International Protection for Human Rights Abuses by Non-State Agents," *Columbia Human Rights Law Review* 31, No. 82 (Fall, 1999).

10. *Ex parte Adan and Aitseguer*, opinion of Lord Slynn of Hadley, par. 3 and opinion of Lord Steyn, par. 6. See also, J. Moore, *op. cit.*, 108, n. 70.

11. This restrictive definition of agents of persecution was set forth in 1996 in a nonbinding resolution of the EU. See Joint Position 96/196/JHA Defined by the Council on the Basis of Article K.3 of the Treaty of the European Union on the Harmonized Application of the Definition of the Term "Refugee" in article 1 of the Geneva Convention of 28 July 1951 relating to the Status of Refugees, 1996 O.J. (L63/2), par. 5.2 [suggesting that persecution requires human rights abuses perpetrated, "encouraged or permitted" by the state]. It is also reflected in the so-called "Sri Lankan Tamil Case" decided by the German Federal Constitutional Court [FCC] in 1989. See BVefGE 80, 315, decision of July 10, 1989, 2 BvR 502/86, 1000/86, 961/86 [German FCC suggesting that political persecution requires persecution by the state].

12. See Convention Determining the State Responsible for Examining Applications for Asylum Lodged in One of the Member States of the [European] Community [Dublin Convention], 16 June 1990, Article 7(1) ["The responsibility for examining an application for asylum shall be incumbent upon the member state responsible for controlling the entry of the alien into the territory of the member states . . ."]

13. *Ex parte Adan and Aitseguer*, Lord Steyn's opinion, par. 24 and 23, affirming *ex parte Adan et al.*, in the Court of Appeals, 9; above, n. 3.

14. *T.I. v. United Kingdom* 19; above, n. 4.

15. *Ex parte Adan et al.*, Court of Appeals, 6–7, citing Section 2(2)(c) of the 1996 Act.

16. Ibid., 16; emphasis added.

17. Ibid., 14, citing *ex parte Canbolat* (Court of Appeals) [1997] 1WLR 1569, 1579 A–C; emphasis added.

18. *Ex parte Adan et al.*, Court of Appeals, 15.

19. Ibid., 19; emphasis added.

20. Ibid.

21. *Ex parte Adan and Aitseguer*, Lord Steyn's opinion, par. 11; emphasis added.

22. Such dysfunctional countries will likely lack international recognition as states. See also *ex parte Adan and Aitseguer*, Lord Slynn's opinion, par. 2 and 6.

23. *Ex parte Adan and Aitseguer*, Lord Steyn's opinion, par. 23, referencing the House of Lord's earlier decision in *Adan v. Secretary of State for the Home Department* [1999] 1 A.C. 293 [hereinafter "*Adan I*"].

24. *Ex parte Adan and Aitseguer*, Lord Slynn's opinion, par. 14.

25. Ibid., Lord Steyn's opinion, par. 17.

26. Ibid., Lord Steyn's opinion, par. 21.

27. Ibid., Lord Steyn's opinion, par. 22.

28. Ibid., Lord Hutton's opinion, par. 7.

29. Ibid., Lord Hobhouse's opinion, par. 11.

30. Ibid., Lord Slynn's opinion, par. 14 and 12.

31. Ibid., Lord Steyn's opinion, par. 1.

32. Ibid., Lord Steyn's opinion, par. 24. Also worthy of note is the House's response to the Secretary's reliance on the 1996 Joint Position of the European Union on the harmonized application of the definition of term refugee. The 1996 EU Joint Position takes a proaccountability approach, requiring "persecution by third parties" to be "encouraged or permitted by the authorities" if it is to "fall within the scope of

the Geneva Convention . . ." Par. 5.2. Lord Steyn economically responded that "[c]ounsel [for the Secretary] put too much weight on this document." *ex parte Adan and Aitseguer*, Lord Steyn's opinion, par. 18. See also above, n. 15.

Lord Steyn's view is supported by the position of the European Council on Refugees and Exiles [ECRE] in its analysis of "Non-State Agents of Persecution and the Inability of the State to Protect—the German Interpretation" (London, September 2000) [ECRE NSA Report] ["Apart from its nonbinding nature, the joint position can hardly be adduced as showing a consistent common state practice that favors the strict application of the accountability theory"]. See ECRE NSA Report, nn. 60–62 and related text.

Moreover, with regard to the potential negative impact of the House's decision on the EU harmonization process, or as "an implicit criticism of the judicial departments of Germany and France," Lord Steyn responded that "[t]he sky will not fall in." "National courts can only do their best to minimize the disagreements. But ultimately they have no choice . . . . The House is bound to take into account the obligations of the United Kingdom government. . . ." Lord Steyn's opinion, par. 18.

33. Refugee Convention, 189 UNTS 150, Article 33: "No contracting state shall expel or return ("*refouler*") a refugee . . . to the frontiers of territories where his life or freedom would be threatened . . ."

34. *Ex parte Adan and Aitseguer*, Lord Steyn's opinion, par. 14.

35. Ibid., Lord Hutton's opinion, par. 11.

36. Ibid., Lord Hutton's opinion, par. 11 and 12.

37. *T.I. v. United Kingdom*, above, n. 4, 3–4.

38. Ibid., 4.

39. Ibid., 5.

40. Ibid., 5–6.

41. Ibid., 1; [European] Convention for the Protection of Human Rights and Fundamental Freedoms [hereinafter European Convention], 4 November, 1950, Article 3, 213 UNTS 222, Europ. T.S. No. 5.

42. See, generally, *Ahmed v. Austria*, 24 Eur. H.R. Rep. 278 (1996), par. 10, 21, 35, and 41–47. See also *T.I. v. United Kingdom*, 15, citing *Ahmed*. See also *Soering v. United Kingdom*, 161 Eur. Ct. H.R. (Ser. A)(1989), par. 82 [clarifying that a party to the European Convention is obligated "not to put a person in a position where he will or may suffer [inhuman] treatment or punishment . . ."]

43. *Ex parte Adan and Aitseguer*, 16.

44. *T.I. v. United Kingdom*, 10; emphasis added. The court goes on to specify that in early 1999, twenty-four Sri Lankans benefited from Section 53(6) protection, all of whom alleged nonstate sources of danger. Unlike T.I., however none of these individuals had sought temporary protection after being denied asylum in the first instance. Ibid., 18.

45. Ibid., 17, 18. It should be noted that the European Council on Refugees and Exiles [ECRE] does not share the confidence of the European court regarding the efficacy of section 53(6) of the German Aliens Act. In its recent study of German policy regarding third-party refugees, ECRE noted that "[i]n 1999, of the applicants for political asylum in Germany . . . [o]nly 1.55 percent were granted the temporary suspension of deportation pursuant to Section 53 of the Aliens Act." 2000 ECRE NSA Report, n. 6 and related text. See also above, n. 32.

46. *T.I. v. United Kingdom*, 15, citing *Ahmed* at par. 39–40; emphasis added. Compare *ex parte Adan et al.*, 14.

47. Ibid., 19; emphasis added.

48. Ibid., 18.

49. Refugee Convention, art. 3. See also International Covenant on Civil and Political Rights, 19 December 1966, art. 2, 999 UNTS 171 and European Convention, art. 14.

50. See *ex parte Adan and Aitseguer*, Lord Steyn's opinion, par. 24.

10

The Geneva Convention and the European Union: A Fraught Relationship

Carl Levy

For a brief moment in the spring of 1999, the acceptance of Kosovar refugees by member states of the EU seemed to signal the emergence of a new policy that did not necessarily treat refugees in an increasingly restrictive manner. Since the early 1990s, refugees and asylum-seekers had been squeezed into the margins of all European receiving states. Suddenly and perhaps for only a brief moment they were treated with great humanity.[1] It looked as if the much weakened Geneva Convention was getting its second wind. In earlier interventions I examined the development of refugee policy in the context of EU policymaking and the relationship between third-country nationals, refugees, asylumseekers, and the policies that have unfolded since the signing of the Treaty of Amsterdam.[2] The roles of the Geneva Convention and the amending instruments have been a ghost at this banquet.[3] They were always present in the political and policy discussions. They were cited in grave and respectful tones as soft and hard law was passed that effectively undermined their intent.[4] Here I would like to carry out a synoptic overview of "the state of health" of the refugee convention in the EU fifty years later.

HISTORICAL OVERVIEW

Legal scholars note that asylum law is protected by the binding universality of international law; the immigration policy of a sovereign state is guided by the flexible particularities of its national immigration policy.[5] However, for a historian or social scientist, the fiction that the Geneva Convention was outside the grimy world of political economy and politics has always been difficult to swallow. Joly's classification of the 1960s and 1970s as a period of uncoordinated liberalism when refugees and asylum-seekers in western Europe were easily accommodated in the general flow of labor migrants or welcomed as victims of the Cold War tells another story.[6] Similarly her classification of the 1980s and 1990s as an era of harmonized restrictionism carried out through intergovernmental agreements rather than community law implies that the Geneva Convention will only thrive under certain benign conditions. But the economic boom of the late 1990s led to tighter labor markets in Europe so that the restrictionist juggernaut might be slowed down. By 2000 there were certain straws in the wind in Europe (but perhaps not the eponymous British home secretary). Various European and UN-connected research bodies were claiming that the EU needed more immigration to protect future shortfalls in pension systems.[7] Many governments in the EU opened their labor markets to skilled information technology workers from the developing world.

The Geneva Convention and its supplements have always been at the mercy of economic and political cycles. At first it was a guilty reaction to the extermination of the Jews (some of the diplomats in Geneva may had remembered a meeting at Evian in 1938). It was conceived in a period that stretches from the Nuremberg war crimes tribunal, the discovery of human rather than civil rights, and the naming of genocide. Thus, its definition of the persecuted refugee hounded by ideologically and/or racially driven state machines had the era of Hitler and Stalin very much in mind. (Indeed, the recent controversies about "nonstate agents" and mass displacement that cannot be easily placed in this older time-bound definition has become one of the great sources of debate between UNHCR and the member states of the EU). The Geneva Convention was born during the Korean War and lived its youth and adolescence under the polarities of the Cold War and it only entered its troubled middle age when the Cold War started to fade in the 1980s.[8] The massive flows of forced migrants from the former Yugoslavia and the developing world in the last fifteen years of the twentieth century may have effectively killed it. And in the developed world it was western Europe, which adopted the UNHCR recommendations as the template for refugee and asylum policy. The United States kept the UNHCR at arm's length during most of the Cold War. The United States openly employed its asylum and refugee policy as a tool in its struggle against the eastern bloc. Allies and clients from Indochina or Cuba were welcomed but asylum-seekers from El Salvador or Chile were not. Even after 1980 when the United States changed its laws and the UNHCR opened an office in Washington, D.C., Reagan's policy that supported "warrior refugees" in camps on the border with Afghanistan, Angola, Cambodia, or Nicaragua meant tensions persisted.[9] Thus, the undermining of the UNHCR's mission to set the standards of protection for individual asylum-seekers became evident in the middle 1980s when the governments of western Europe turned away from the model set by the UNHCR earlier. Indeed in the 1990s the vast majority of the refugees and asylum-seekers in Europe were not recognized under the Geneva Convention. If they had been "convention" refugees they would have had equal access to the welfare state and the labor markets of their host nations as any other citizen or long-term resident. Due to political and economic reasons mainstream politicians no longer endorsed this policy.[10] Therefore, by the middle 1990s over 90 percent of the asylum-seekers and refugees in Europe were either awaiting determination of their status or were given de facto statuses that gave the varied access to welfare entitlements and the labor market. The trend throughout Europe was to substitute cash benefits for payments in kind for both those persons awaiting determination of their claims or for even the more legally secure de facto refugees. There was also a trend to isolate them from the general public or disperse them throughout the territory of a host nation.[11] But they were not immediately deported and a large percentage of asylum-seekers and the temporarily protected managed to stay on in Europe. This was because if, as I have just argued, the granting of convention status became increasingly rare, the European states could still not abandon the bedrock concept of *non-refoulement*. The only country in the industrialized world that seems to have maintained an increasingly successful policy of deportation was Australia.[12] But the recent diversion of boatloads of asylum-seekers on the high seas by the Australians is not unique in the developed world.[13] The Americans practiced this on a much wider scale towards Haitians in the 1980s and 1990s.[14]

The Geneva Convention, as we understand it, is probably on its deathbed. Indeed the first session of the conference in South Africa to which this volume is dedicated, dealt with the contentious issue of a variety of types of temporary protection that have effectively replaced convention status.[15] In any case it might be hypocritical to harp on the fading of convention status in western Europe. Most of the world's refugees have always lived in the developing world, where very poor countries have had to shoulder a disproportionate amount of the effort. As is well-known, the UNHCR budget that helps nations such as Pakistan or Iran is far outstripped by the home office budgets in Europe and devoted to preventing refugees ever reaching the EU.[16] In any case, the regional amendments to Geneva in the 1960s recognized that the Eurocentric nature of the 1951 treaty had to be amended. However, even in Europe the Geneva Convention has only been geographically relatively widespread since the end of the Cold War. While it is true that the aspirant candidates for the EU had to show their good faith by serving as the EU's buffer zone in the 1990s. In order to become a buffer zone that qualified as a series of "safe third countries" they had to incorporate the Geneva

Convention into their law.[17] Turkey has still not expanded geographical coverage beyond Europe but is trying to reform its laws.[18] But even Italy only expanded the coverage of the Geneva Convention beyond Europe at about the same time it became a country of immigration rather than emigration.[19] Thus, perhaps one could argue that the dying Geneva patient had one more rally as the twentieth century ended.

EUROPEAN HARMONIZATION AND BURDEN SHARING

In the rest of this chapter, I will examine the tensions between the EU and UNHCR in terms of the issues arising from the wars of the Yugoslav succession in the 1990s and the attempts by the EU to harmonize asylum and immigration policy during the same decade. I will cover the issues arising from Yugoslavia first because out of these tragic events the UNHCR proposed the concept of temporary protection, which in its own way has come to threaten the existence of the Geneva Convention itself. This will be followed by a discussion of harmonization. But it is best to issue a health warning immediately.

Even in 2002 real harmonization of EU asylum and immigration policy is still very much a future aspiration. Much of the effective legislation (the Dublin Convention and the Schengen Implementing Convention) is intergovernmental. The European laws, even those new installments passed after the Treaty of Amsterdam became operational in 1999, are either still proposals or soft and squishy.[20] And even the projected hard laws that are supposed to be passed within five years of the treaty coming into effect will be couched in terms of minimum guarantees. Thus, in a certain sense this will allow different member states to pursue their own distinctive forms of refugee and asylum-seeker policies even if the trend will be towards some sort of harmonization. Hailbronner's comprehensive and sober account of European refugee and asylum law comes to the conclusion that policy developments since the Treaty of Amsterdam form the *possible* framework for a European asylum and refugee law area.[21]

This leads us to my second health warning. Since the early 1990s much of the rhetoric about harmonization has really been about "balance of effort" or perhaps more realistically expressing the feelings of the participants involved, "burden sharing."[22] While the internal logic of the Single European Market, "Schengenland," the Treaty of Amsterdam and its aftermath may mean that supranational harmonization is inevitable, nevertheless the real driving forces in the 1990s were strategic battles between nation-states over the control of the inflow of third-country nationals over their borders. And this led to a barely hidden confrontation between Germany and her partners. The Germans were particularly keen on a common policy to ensure that in future Yugoslav-type crises they would not receive a disproportionate number of refugees. This meant "burden sharing." Their major partners were prepared to discuss sharing the burden of military and civilian intervention in Bosnia or Croatia, or the disastrous policy of Orwellian newspeak "safe havens."[23] But they left the room or pretended not to hear when the subject of receiving refugees under temporary protection came up. However, as the Kosovo crisis of the spring of 1999 demonstrated, temporary protection cannot work without burden sharing. Tony Blair and Gerhard Schröder remained on civil terms during the crisis in the spring of 1999 even if other German *Land* politicians were more candid.[24] But the combined effects of public clamor and diplomatic pressure forced the United Kingdom government to agree to accept potentially thousands of refugees, although in the end this amounted to little because NATO's "humanitarian" war succeeded in reversing the flow of Kosovar Albanians.

In the longer term the Germans have been rather successful in forcing other member states to take in asylum-seekers and refugees. In 1999, 366,000 individuals applied for asylum in the EU 15.[25] Although Germany still took in the largest percentage of asylum-seekers annually, that had been reduced from over 60 percent in 1992 to 20.8 percent in 1999. The British took in 20 percent of the total in 1999, an increase of 53 percent from 1998, and the figures in 2000 made Britain the largest recipient of claims in Europe, although Germany may have outstripped Britain in 2001. The next largest nation in 1999 was Switzerland with 12 percent and then the Netherlands with 9 percent. The buffer zone policy, the looming necessity for the CEEC candidates for the EU to ingest the Schengen *acquis*, and the Kosovo crisis witnessed dramatic increases from low totals, if not of the total European percentage, of the intake of asylum-seekers and refugees, in that part of Europe. Bulgaria's intake increased by 62 percent, the Czech Republic's intake increased by 77 percent, Slovenia by 74 percent and the Slovak Republic by 157 percent. Transit countries have become receiving countries. Hungary received more applications than Denmark and Finland combined.[26] Non-EU 15 nations of Europe (including Norway and Switzerland) received a further 90,975 refugees on top of the already mentioned total for the EU 15. But admittedly, this was also due to the fact, as mentioned earlier, that the CEECs have become fully paid-up members of the Geneva Convention, so just as the Mediterranean member states had created asylum policies in the early and middle 1990s, the CEECs followed suit a few years later.

Perhaps more significant is the per capita number of refugees each nation of Europe received in 1999. Thus is the average number of asylum applications per 1,000 inhabitants for the EU 15 for 1999 was 0.98, Luxembourg received 6.78, Belgium 3.5, the Netherlands 2.49, Austria 2.49, and Ireland 2.09. Among the "big five" in the EU, the United Kingdom received 1.55, Germany received 1.16, France received 0.52, Italy received 0.21, and Spain received 0.21.[27]

These data raise some very interesting questions about burden sharing but they certainly do show that by the year 2000 the Germans had statistically resolved this issue, at least between major refugee-inducing crises. And this was done outside the self-denying ordinances of supranational regulation.

There has been much speculation about the effects of supranational regulation in the EU on the future of the Geneva Convention. It had been argued that the intervention of the European Court of Justice and other instruments in future policy might protect the legacy of the Geneva Convention.[28] This is hard to predict, but we do know that instruments like the UN Convention on Torture and the European Convention on Human Rights have been used by member states to allow unsuccessful applicants for convention status in their countries to stay under a variety of humanitarian de facto statuses.[29] However, this as I have argued, has reduced the Geneva Convention to its core: the sanctity of *non-refoulement*. Thus if we want to assess the real impact of harmonization on the Geneva Convention in Europe in the 1990s we have to examine the intergovernmental attempts at coordination and the reactions by the UNHCR to them.

UNHCR, it must be stressed, has not always been the most consistent defender of *non-refoulement*. As Loescher demonstrates in his history of the Office, UNHCR reinvented itself as the world's greatest humanitarian agency in the post–Cold War 1990s.[30] Thus the emphasis shifted from the protection of refugees on the umbrella of the convention to relief of distress for refugees in border camps in the developing world and Europe or for Internally Displaced Persons (IDPs) in both. This led to compromises at times with the refugee generating ethnic cleansers and on the Bangladesh/Burma border and in the African Great Lakes region to the movement of refugees to areas of extreme danger and indirectly to the deaths of thousands of civilians. Similar dubious policies also occurred in Europe. The actions of UNHCR in Bosnia, Croatia, and Kosovo over the past decade have been subject to much comment.[31] Thus the UNHCR has been accused of colluding with ethnic cleansers by accepting the presence of so-called safe areas in Bosnia. Or it has been accused of being a tool of NATO in Kosovo since the official "war aim" of the intervention was to reverse the ethnic cleansing of Kosovo, which these critics argue did not begin in earnest until NATO, without UN sanction, started to bomb Serbian positions. It is further argued that when the exodus of Kosovar Albanians entered Macedonia the UNHCR was overwhelmed and in fact was only rescued by the logistical support of NATO. More generally, some commentators argue that the presence of UNHCR aid helped sustain the war in Bosnia through the siphoning off of its aid into the illicit markets used by combatants and criminals.[32]

In defense of UNHCR, it must be said that its policymakers and brave workers were the pawns of big power politics. From 1992 until early 1995 the United States, the EU, the Russian Federation, and other interested parties could not agree on a joint position towards Bosnia. Significant military intervention was ruled out, thus the unprecedented massive program by UN-HCR became a substitute for policy, indeed a fig leaf to hide the confusion and shame of many of the great powers. This led to the fall of Srebrenica and the ensuing massacre that hearkened back to the initial events that had created the Geneva Convention in the first place in 1951. But the "safe areas" were always dependent on a credible deterrent, as Kofi Annan has ruefully acknowledged.[33] The war ended with the reverse ethnic cleansing of the ethnic group that had been the original beneficiary of ethnic cleansing. But due to the bitter suspicions of the Serbs, UNHCR has had a far smaller impact on the hundreds of thousands of refugees in Serbia in the late 1990s.

The activities of UNHCR in the European context had a new and complex dimension because of its role in tending to the needs of internally displaced persons. But the reason why its mandate could be expanded in this direction was due to the fact that European nations would only accept some of the displaced under temporary protection if a good deal of the refugees were kept in the region.[34] Whether one believes that more massive placements of refugees would have aided ethnic cleansing and therefore was immoral, the fact remains that this implicit contract underpinning the regime of temporary protection undermined the credibility of the definition of the refugee as understood from the Geneva Convention. In this respect UNHCR could not argue with great confidence against the EU when it tried to regionalize the movement of several thousand Kurds fleeing Turkey in 1997, if in effect it had accepted a far greater regionalization in Bosnia several years earlier. Of course this issue came up in a much bigger way during the Kosovo crisis of 1999 when the connections between temporary protection, burden sharing, and the treatment of IDPs was made more transparent.[35] The Macedonian government demanded that refugees be airlifted out of their country for fear that the unbalancing of the ethnic make-up of the country would lead to civil war and NATO needed Macedonia to mount its intervention into Kosovo. Thus the EU accepted burden sharing and UNHCR worked closely with NATO, even if it did complain that certain family groups had been split up in the rush to evacuate refugees to Turkey. In both Bosnia and Kosovo UNHCR worked closely with military forces. This met with criticisms from certain quarters. It may also be true that UNHCR's initial organization in Kosovo was not up to par, nevertheless one cannot but agree with the assessment made by UNHCR during its jubilee:[36]

> All too often during the 1990s, humanitarian organizations such as UNHCR were left to deal with problems which were essentially political in nature. In each case, the limits of humanitarian action were clearly demonstrated. As High Commissioner Ogata emphasized with growing insistence throughout the decade, emergency relief operations should not be treated as a substitute for timely and firm political action to address the root causes of conflict.

In the aftermath of the Dayton Peace Agreements, UNHCR became intimately involved in addressing the root causes of conflict, and this has continued in Kosovo. Here too the creation of the temporary protection regime has placed the guardian of the Geneva Convention in a delicate position. Temporary protection seems to mean that certain groups affected by war or natural disaster are granted refuge so long as these conditions pertain. When they are removed, it has been argued, they should be brought back home. This position is fraught with many difficulties.[37] UNHCR has always made clear that temporary protection should not undermine the rights of those so protected to seek asylum under Geneva Convention status. This involves the individual determination of a case, but with the war over in Bosnia or Kosovo it was assumed by many host nations that the well-founded fear of persecution had been removed. But this may not be the case. Political differences within the Albanian Kosovar community may endanger the lives of temporarily protected refugees from the same community who sought refuge in a host nation. Furthermore, the return of refugees to Bosnia, may and has largely meant (at least until well into 2000), that they will be swooping the status of temporarily protected refugee for internally displaced person. Most of the voluntarily and forcibly repatriated have ended up living in ethnically homogenous zones not in their former homes.[38] UNHCR, of course has over the years, attempted to assist in reconciliation and rebuilding.[39] However, from the broader perspective, in terms of the future of the Geneva Convention, the policies concerning return in temporary protection has further undermined its vitality. The experience of temporary protection cannot be understood outside the narrowing of the legal and geographical routes open into Europe for potential claimants of Geneva Convention status. I will now turn my attention to the role of restrictionist policymaking.

From the late 1980s to the Treaty of Amsterdam in 1997 and beyond, the aim policy in all member states of the EU has been the restriction of flows of asylum-seekers and refugees through a variety of legal instruments. But these instruments were controlled by the member states themselves and, will not really be threatened by the supranationalism of the Treaty of Amsterdam until at least 2004, if even then. Until then, these instruments are under the jurisdictions of their national courts and it remains to be seen what role the European Court of Justice will really play. In any case the aims of the intergovernmental Schengen and Dublin Conventions was to generalize certain principles of restrictionism:[40]

1. the principle that refugees and asylum-seekers should be dealt with in the first "safe country" they have entered and not be allowed to claim asylum in another "safe country" once their case has been dismissed;[41]

2. the concept that airline carriers will incur liability if they allow passengers on their planes from outside Europe who do not carry adequate documentation;

3. the coordination of immigration information by police forces and home offices of Europe.

By 1996–1997 most member states of the EU were dissatisfied with the effects of Schengen and Dublin because they either lacked sufficient clarity or teeth, and the very process of ratification through intergovernmental treaty was time-consuming.

In 1997 (indeed in 2002) policies in the member states of the EU varied enormously. There were wild inconsistencies in the nature of detention of asylum-seekers before status was arrived at and in the adjudication and determination systems of the asylum-seekers.[42] The Treaty of Amsterdam was supposed to remedy these problems.

The Treaty of Amsterdam came into effect on 1 May 1999. This meant that the EU could, in the future, negotiate readmission agreements with third countries. Secondly, it established a High Level Working Group on Asylum and Migration in December 1998 that essentially tried to monitor the movements of third-country nationals from refugee-producing countries. The major turning point was the Tampere Council held at the end of 1999. It laid the way forward after the meeting at Cardiff in June 1998 and Vienna of the same year.[43] At Tampere the European Council affirmed the goal of creating a Common European Asylum System in the long term. This was important because according to the timetable of the Treaty of Amsterdam the EU was supposed to define the basic parameters for a common refugee and asylum system by May 2001.[44] By the time of the Inter-Governmental Conference at Nice in December 2000, the EU had succeeded in issuing ("soft law") resolutions on the minimum standards for the granting or withdrawing of refugee status and for the reception of asylum-seekers, as well as creating a pilot refugee fund.

How has the UNHCR reacted to the intergovernmental and supranational legislation from the middle 1990s? First of all, Dublin, Schengen, and Amsterdam have all made it nearly impossible for individual asylum-seekers to get to a European country to claim asylum without breaking the law. The controversies concerning the granting or not of asylum to the victims of non-state agent persecution has exercised the UNHCR on several occasions.[45] The UNHCR argues that the Geneva Convention should be read more broadly as do Denmark and Sweden. The concept of the safe third country has also been a continual source of argument because it may undermine the fundamental right of *non-refoulement*. Like Belgium, the UNHCR does not agree that a resident of one of the member states of the EU cannot in certain cases seek asylum in another.[46] Readmission agreements have been under withering criticism because they undermine the concept of the fair determination of a case. The UNHCR argues a claimant may be shunted from an EU member state to the first safe country he or she had traversed without getting a proper hearing in either place.[47] The UNHCR has also examined closely the draft resolution on the minimum standards for the reception of asylum-seekers. It has been particularly disturbed by the widespread practice of the detention of asylum-seekers throughout the EU. While UNHCR seems pleased by harmonization because it will allow it to "work more closely and systematically with the institutions of the EU, including the European Commission,"[48] the general tenor of negotiations on the intergovernmental and supranational level has not been too comforting for its hopes. The UNHCR "has endorsed these efforts (harmonization) where they have been aimed at making asylum systems fairer, more efficient, and more predictable, not only for the benefit of governments but also for refugee asylum-seekers themselves." However, this recent statement by the guardian of the Geneva Convention also expresses worries that in many cases the standard of the lowest common denominator has prevailed, and thus "resulting in diminished rather than enhanced protection for refugees."[49] In any case, the attempt to create a buffer zone has not prevented illegal migration of forced and economic migrants into the EU. Much energy has been expended on combating the organizers of the lucrative and dangerous business of trafficking. UNHCR has intervened by arguing that the EU's policy of concentric buffer zones has merely driven both forced migration and economic migration underground and into the hands of the traffickers.[50] Thus, leading to the tragic deaths of forty-six Chinese migrants in a lorry crossing to Dover in 2000,[51] or the countless hundreds if not thousands drowned or murdered crossing the Straits of Gibraltar or in the Adriatic.[52]

But continued argument between UNHCR and the member states of the EU puts the guardian of the Geneva Convention at a disadvantage. As long as the member states can stay within the spirit of the convention, there is little that can be done. In the past two years, however, the very existence of the Geneva Convention has been called into question by a variety of voices in the EU. I will conclude with a discussion of these events and query what significance they have for the future of the Geneva Convention.

THE NEW RESTRICTIONISM

The UNHCR has always insisted that adherence to the Geneva Convention is not determined by a given nation's policy on immigration. I have already noted that for the historical or social scientific analysis of the past fifty years of international refugee law, this is nonsense. On the other hand, if one wants to retain the Geneva Convention, the only internationally recognized law that orients refugee policy and defends the bedrock principle of *non-refoulement*, then in terms of policymaking this polite fiction should be defended with the greatest vigor.

In 1998 and 1999 the debates over the Austrian presidency's contentious paper and the lobbying by academics and NGOs that led up to the meeting at Tampere set the scene for the first high-level questioning of the future of the Geneva Convention seen in recent memory.

The Austrian "Strategy Paper on Migration and Asylum Policy" led a rather eventful life. First submitted on 1 July 1998, it met with such consternation it had to be resubmitted twice on 29 September and 19 November.[53] The report was widely reported in the quality press throughout Europe. The UN-HCR, NGOs, and MEPs were outraged. Drafted by the head of Austria's Aliens Department of the Ministry of Interior, Manfred Matzka, it apparently was not read by the Austrian Minister of the Interior, Karl Schlögl, but approved by his assistant who dealt with immigration and asylum policy.[54] Once the storm broke Schlögl distanced himself from Matzka's paper, but Matzka insisted that the minister has always had full knowledge of its content. UN high commissioner for refugees, Sadako Ogata, expressed her grave concerns and the Austrian federal president, T. Klestil, stepped in, claiming that it was the mere "draft of a civil servant."[55] In fact, the revisions of this document did not alter its content.

Essentially the civil servant argued that the Geneva Convention was outmoded and needed amendments or to be complemented by provisions that returned international law to its condition before 1951. The right of asylum was not an international binding duty upon the community of nation-states but a gift that nation-states could subjectively impart. He also wanted to change the UNCHR's mandate "to favor repatriation and protection and assistance in the countries of origin."[56]

The Austrian civil servant was bound to get an outraged response. However, there may have been some guilty consciences among the heads of state and government. His rather opaque passages concerning "Fortress Europe" were not very far from the actual effects of the European policy of "safe third countries" and intergovernmental and, in the future, supranational readmission agreements with third countries. His suggestion that the EU tie aid to the "outer rim" countries with their ability to control flows of migration towards Europe was not dissimilar to unsuccessful attempts by the EU during the negotiations for the Fiji Convention.

However, this cynicism can be excessive. At an informal meeting at Turku on 16–17 September 1999, just before the Tampere Council meeting, the German Federal Minister of Interior, Otto Schily, and his French partner, Jean-Pierre Chevènement, addressed the future of EU policy on asylum and immigration. The Austrian paper was looming in the background. Their document argued that "asylum is not immigration and in spite of the confusion kept up by applicants, the control of migratory movements ought not undermine the EU's capacity of offering reception to those persecuted."[57] And the Franco-German document also reiterated the sanctity of *non-refoulement*. For all intents and purposes this statement formed a draft for the reaffirmation of the values of the Geneva Convention found in the conclusions of the Tampere Council.

Another intervention that preceded the Tampere Council came from a group of distinguished academics and lawyers, Academic Group on (Im)migration-Tampere (AGIT).[58] Though their first premises were distant from Matzka's, unlike the Schily/Chevènement document, this group too refused to disconnect immigration from asylum. They acknowledged that even if the Geneva Convention had to be defended, the issue of temporary protection, which had been the major issue during the crisis in Kosovo that spring, had to be addressed with an open mind. They proposed a European Asylum Agency to oversee the standards of reception in member states of the EU. They also believed that a new status—conditional protection, limited to a few years—would be applied before unlimited protection, convention status, came into operation. In other words, they suggested that a time dimension be added to article 1C of the Geneva Convention. AGIT's proposals, concerning the refinement of temporary protection, might be listened to by policymakers in the EU.[59] In a certain respect it is rather similar to Sweden's Aliens Act that dispenses with a de facto status and gives refugees a temporary status of two to four years that may lead to full convention status.[60]

However, in the spring of 2000, the debate took a further turn with the intervention of Jack Straw at the European Conference on Asylum, sponsored by the then current Portuguese presidency of the EU.[61] Straw called for a redraft of the 1951 convention. He suggested that an international quota system under which European countries would share asylum-seekers from countries recognized as violators of human rights. If this were a mere supplement to the treaty this would be fine. However, it appeared that Straw had used an unhelpful analogy that muddled his reasoning. And the mechanisms of his proposed system were worrying, if not downright alarming.[62] First, he suggested that the Council of Ministers of the EU, advised by the commission, with the help of UNHCR, would identify countries and ethnic groups within them facing a high level of persecution. They would agree on "quotas for each EU state to consider applications for asylum made outside the receiving state." This might help those genuine refugees who could no longer penetrate the concentric barriers in Europe, which Straw and his fellow Home Ministers had crafted and honed down in the 1990s. But the analogy was taken directly from the case of the cooperation over the crisis in Kosovo the year earlier. Straw seemed to be confusing temporary protection with the Geneva Convention system of individual determination of cases. And furthermore, he would also create a worldwide system of safe countries (that the Belgians had already objected to in the more geographically limited EU), which would include all EU states, the United States, Canada, Australia, and "many others" from which applications would not be considered. There would also be a third intermediate group where there would be a "general presumption of safety." How this system would be maintained was not explained. It certainly would wound the universal concept of fair determination of cases and perhaps also *non-refoulement*.

CONCLUSION

The future of the Geneva Convention is under threat. Most refugees in Europe do not receive convention status and the era of temporary status is certainly here to stay. Perhaps the demand for labor will lessen the pressure on refugees and a new enlightened form of temporary protection will become the universal standard in this century, but whatever does happen, it is important to fight for the principle of *non-refoulement*. Without this bedrock concept we will return to the years, when as is now admitted by Swiss historians, thousands of Jews and Roma were turned back at the border of Switzerland and sent to their deaths in Nazi Germany. It was those guilty memories that hovered over Geneva in 1951. They should not be forgotten, nor the more recent but equally shameful ones of Srebrenica or the African Great Lakes region.

NOTES

1. Selm, J. van (ed.)., *Kosovo's Refugees in the EU,* (London: Continuum, 2000).

2. Levy, C., "European Asylum and Refugee Policy after the Treaty of Amsterdam: the Birth of a New Regime?," in *Refugees, Citizenship and Social Policy in Europe,* A. Bloch, and C. Levy, eds. (Basingstoke: Macmillan, 1999), 12–50.

3. Levy, C., "Asylum Seekers, Refugees and the Future of Citizenship in the European Union," in Ibid., 211–231.

4. Levy, C. "After Amsterdam and Kosovo," ECPR Workshop 14, "Beyond Fortress Europe? New Responses to Migration in Europe: Dual Nationality, Co-Development and the Effects of EU Enlargement," Copenhagen, 14–19 April 2000.

5. Noll, G. and Vedsted-Hansen, J. "Non-Communitarians: Refugee and Asylum Policy," in *The EU and Human Rights,* ed. P. Alston (Oxford: Oxford University Press, 1999), 359–410.

6. Joly, D., *Haven or Hell? Asylum Policies and Refugees in Europe* (Basingstoke: Macmillan, 1996), 46.

7. Hargeaves, D. "Brussels Eyes Immigration Targets," *Financial Times,* 22 November 2000, 1.

8. Loescher, G. *The UNHCR and World Politics. A Perilous Path* (Oxford: Oxford University Press, 2001).

9. Ibid., 176, 183, 185, 230–233, 238.

10. Bloch and Levy, op. cit., Bommes, M. and Geddes, A. (eds.), *Immigration and Welfare: Challenging the Boundaries of the Welfare State* (London: Routledge, 2000).

11. Schuster, L. "A Composite Analysis of the Asylum Policy of Seven European Governments," *Journal of Refugee Studies* 13, No. 1: (2000) 118–132.

12. Millbank, A. "The Problem with the 1951 Refugee Convention," (Parliament of Australia: Social Policy Group, 2000), 5.

13. Marsh, V. "Canberra in Hot Water over Refugee 'Crisis,'" *Financial Times*, 12 December 2001, 12.

14. Loescher, op. cit., 184–185, 231–235.

15. "Workshop on Temporary Protection Organized by the International Association for the Study of Forced Migration," ESKOM Centre, South Africa, 7 January 2001.

16. Millbank, op. cit., 4, 9–10.

17. Lavanex, S. "Migration and the EU's New Eastern Border: Between Realism and Liberalism," *Journal of European Public Policy* 8, No. 1: (2001), pp. 24–42.

18. See chapter 8 of this volume, K. Kirşci, "Turkey, UNHCR, and the 1951 Convention on the Status of Refugees: Problems and Prospects of Cooperation."

19. Vicenzi, S. "Italy: A Newcomer with a Positive Attitude?," *Journal of Refugee Studies* 13, No. 1 (2000): 91–104.

20. An excellent review of the state of play of EU legislation was summarized in a paper given at the IRAP Conference in South Africa. See, A. Hurwitz, "The European Union and the Refugee Convention."

21. Hailbronner, K. *Immigration and Asylum Law and Policy of the European Union* (The Hague: Kluwer, 2000).

22. Suhrke, A. "Burden-Sharing during Refugee Emergencies. The Logic of Collective versus National Action," *Journal of Refugee Studies* 11, No. 4 (1998): 396–415.

23. Selm-Thorburn, J. van. *Refugee Protection in Europe: Lessons of the Yugoslav Crisis* (Dordrecht: Martinus Nijhoff, 1998).

24. Koser, K. "Germany: Protection *for* Refugees or Protection *from* Refugees?," in van Selm, op. cit., 24–42.

25. UNHCR, *Statistics. Asylum Applications in Europe in 1999* (Geneva: UNHCR, 2000), 1–4.

26. UNHCR, *The State of the World's Refugees. Fifty Years of Humanitarian Action* (Oxford: Oxford University Press, 2000), 171.

27. UNHCR, *Statistics. Applications in Europe in 1999. (Table 2), Applications and Total Population, Europe 1998 and 1999*, www.unhcr, 2000.

28. Billings, P. "The Influence of Human Rights Law on the Procedural Formalities of the Asylum Determination Process," *International Journal of Human Rights* 2, No. 1 (1998): 32–61.

29. Plender, R. QC and Mole, N. "Beyond the Geneva Convention: Constructing a *de facto* Right of Asylum from International Human Rights Instruments," in F. Nicolson, and P. Twomey (eds.), *Refugee Rights and Realities: Evolving International Concepts and Regimes* (Cambridge: Cambridge University Press, 1999) 336–356.

30. Loescher, op. cit., 199, 211, 281–293, 311–313, 318, 338.

31. Cunliffe, A. and Pugh, M. "The politicisation of the UNHCR in the former Yugoslavia," *Journal of Refugee Studies* 10, No. 2 (1997): 134–55.

32. Barutciski, M. and. Suhrke, A "Lessons From the Kosovo Refugee Crisis: Innovations in Protection and Burden-Sharing," *Journal of Refugee Studies* 14, No. 2 (2001): 95– 133.

33. UNHCR, *The State*, op. cit., 243.

34. Joly, D. "Temporary Protection Within the Framework of a New European Asylum Regime," *International Journal of Human Rights* 2, No. 3 (1998): 49–76.

35. For IDPs in general see, E. D. Mooney, "In-Country Protection: Out of Bounds for the UNHCR?" in F. Nicolson, and P. Twomey (eds.), op. cit., 200–219.

36. UNHCR, *The State*, op. cit., 243.

37. Koser, K. M., Walsh, M., and Black, R. "Temporary Protection and the Assisted Return of Refugees from the European Union," *International Journal of Refugee Law* 10, No. 3 (1998): 444–461.

38. Phuong, C. "Freely to Return: Reversing Ethnic Cleansing in Bosnia-Herzegovina," *Journal of Refugee Studies* 13, No. 2 (2000): 165–183.

39. Ito, A. "Return to Prejedor: Politics and UNHCR," *Forced Migration* 10, April (2000): 35–37.

40. Joly, D. "A New Asylum Regime in Europe," F. Nicolson, and Twomey P. (eds.), op. cit., 336–356.

41. Abell, N. A. "The Compatibility of Readmission Agreements with the 1951 Convention Relating to the Status of Refugees," *International Journal of Refugee Law* 11, No. 1 (1999): 60–83.

42. Levy, C. "European Asylum," op. cit., 31–34.

43. Geddes, A. *Immigration and European Integration: Towards a Fortress Europe?* (Manchester: Manchester University Press, 2000) 126–129.

44. Ibid., 128.

45. UNHCR, *The State*, op. cit., 163.

46. Levy, C. "European Asylum," op. cit., 44.

47. UNHCR, *Reception Standards for Asylum Seekers in the European Union* (Geneva: UNHCR, 2000), 9–11.

48. UNHCR, *The State*, op. cit., 169.

49. Ibid., 165.

50. Morrison, J. and Crosland, B. *The Trafficking and Smuggling of Refugees: The End Game in European Asylum Policy?* (Geneva: UNHCR, 2000).

51. Ward, A. "Journey of Hope that Ended in Tragedy," *Financial Times*, 20 June 2000, 3.

52.. Harding, J. *The Uninvited: Refugees at the Rich Man's Gate* (London: Profile Books and the London Review of Books, 2000).

53. *Migration News Sheet*, December 1998, 3.

54. Ibid., October 1998, 1.

55. Ibid., November 1998, 1.

56. Ibid.

57. Ibid., December 1999, p. 1.

58. AGIT (Academic Group on (Im)migration—Tampere), "Efficient, Effective and Encompassing Approaches to a European Immigration and Asylum Policy (9 June 1999)," *International Journal of Refugee Law* 11, No. 2 (1999): 330–374.

59. Geddes, op. cit., 131–151.

60. Hammar, T. "Closing the Doors of the Swedish Welfare State," in G. Brochmann, and T. Hammar (eds.), *Mechanisms of Immigration Control: A Comparative Analysis of European Regulation Policies* (Oxford and New York: Berg, 1999).

61. Straw, J. "Towards a Common Asylum Procedure, European Conference on Asylum," Lisbon, 16 June 2000; A. Travis. and I. Black, "EU Looks at Straw's Idea to Curb Migrants," *The Guardian*, 7 February 2001, 7.

62. Travis, A. and Black, I. "EU Looks at Straw's Idea to Curb Migrants," *The Guardian*, 7 February 2001, 7.

11

Roma Asylum Applicants in the United Kingdom: "Scroungers" or "Scapegoats"?

Dallal Stevens

This chapter is about the Roma of central and eastern Europe. Yet it is not entirely clear who the Roma are. The currently held view is that the Roma came from the northwest region of the Indian subcontinent, since linguistic experts have traced the origin of the Romani language to Sanskrit.[1] Today, there are numerous Romani communities employing a wide range of dialects, and though there may be a common origin, as well as some shared language and culture, these communities often differ markedly. While outsiders felt able, in the past, to identify "gypsies," "Roma," or "Romani communities," the Roma themselves appeared unsure of the indices of their identity.[2] For some, it rested primarily on an ability to speak the Romani language. Historically, however, each group seemed to regard the others as not being quite the genuine item.[3] How then did these groups, which did not perceive themselves to share an identity, become designated collectively as Roma? Istvan Pogany puts it thus: "In view of the diversity of communities involved, displaying sharply divergent incomes, customs, and lifestyles, only one thing could be said to have united them—the fact that they 'looked the same,' or 'seemed the same,' to those who were labeling them. But they did not seem the same to one another."[4]

The issue of Roma or gypsies traveling to the United Kingdom is not new. Historical accounts record their arrival in sixteeth-century England, where they soon encountered local hostility. Henry VIII passed an act in 1530 refusing them entry and ordering any who had entered to leave

within fifteen days threatening imprisonment.[5] Some were forcibly removed, while others found themselves the object of a further abortive
piece of legislation in 1545.[6] It may be presumed that some of these gypsies had made their way to England because of persecution suffered elsewhere in Europe and that they were therefore asylum-seekers in the sense
understood today. Henry VIII's reaction to them reveals an ingrained prejudice against the gypsies as a group and a lack of sympathy for any maltreatment they may already have encountered. It is clear that, in his view,
they should become some other country's problem, not England's.

Despite the passing of fifty years since the signing of the 1951 Convention
Relating to the Status of the Refugee, the protection afforded to certain
groups of asylum-seekers can appear limited. The Roma are one such group.
They provide an ideal case study of the difficulties associated with the search
for and the granting of asylum in the late twentieth and early twent-first centuries. This chapter will examine recent migration of Roma to the United
Kingdom, a migration that started in earnest in 1997 and continues today. It
will consider public perceptions of the Roma during the period 1997–2000
and will assess the extent to which the Roma are receiving protection under
United Kingdom refugee law. Though over four hundred years divide the
reign of Henry VIII and the incumbent Labor government, similarities in the
treatment of the Roma are striking. While generalizations have their risks, it
is undeniable that Roma have continued to be the victims of prejudice and
intolerance. Unwanted by Henry VIII, there are clear indications that they remain unwanted in today's Britain.

The chapter will be divided into three parts. First, it will describe the background to the recent arrival of Roma from central Europe, and the reaction of
the media and government; second, it will consider the conditions faced by the
Roma in two of the main countries of migration—the Czech Republic and Slovakia; and third, it will discuss legal developments in the courts in Roma cases.

THE EVENTS OF 1997 AND MEDIA HYSTERIA

In the summer of 1997, just months after the election of a Labor government
to power, an unexpected event occurred at the port of Dover on the south
coast of England. Hundreds of Roma arrived over the course of a few weeks
and lodged claims for asylum. While the United Kingdom was becoming ac-
customed to substantially higher numbers of asylum applications during the
1990s (excluding dependents, 44,870 in 1991; 24,605 in 1992; 22,370 in 1993;
32,830 in 1994; 43,965 in 1995; 29,640 in 1996),[7] applications from Roma were
not remarkable. Claims from countries with significant Roma populations had
remained relatively low: in 1996, 55 (Czech Republic), 455 (Romania), and 900
(Poland).[8] Nor can one even determine from Home Office statistics how many

of these were actually Roma, since ethnicity is not specified. Between 1997 and 1999, applications by Czech Republic nationals rose from 240 to 1,790; by Romanian nationals from 605 to 1,985; and by Poles from 565 to 1,860.[9] Again, how many were Roma is unclear. Yet according to media reports at the time, the Roma were arriving in "hordes": at a rate of about fifty to seventy per week.[10] In October 1997, *The Daily Telegraph* reported that "an estimated 800 gypsies have landed at Dover and Ramsgate in the past three months. The total includes up to 200 children."[11] The paper went on to state that Kent police were trying to play down claims that as many as 3,000 gypsies could be on their way across Europe, while one expert predicted that "the exodus could be joined by gypsies from Poland, Rumania, Hungary, and Bulgaria."[12]

Throughout the summer and autumn of 1997, the headlines screamed animosity: "Bounce the Giro Czechs"; "Refugees Czech in by the coachload"; "Britain not 'soft touch' for Czech gypsies"; "A calculated abuse of our hospitality."[13] While such might be expected of the tabloid press, the broadsheets were equally unsparing in their antagonism towards the Roma asylum-seekers, referring to "floods" and advocating increased use of detention.[14] It was suggested that an immigration racket was being orchestrated by the Czech and Slovak "immigrants" who "in letters back home . . . tell their friends how to get into Britain."[15] Even Labor M.P.s seemed to agree. The member of Parliament for Dover, one of the worst affected towns, claimed that there was "a whole raft of people" who were being brought to the country in search of a better standard of living and "to plug themselves into the benefit system."[16] Some inhabitants of Dover went further in their denunciations. "We should dump them in the English Channel" was one suggestion,[17] while another local advocated "shoot[ing] them all."[18] Prejudice and fear were reinforced when Kent County Council threatened cuts to normal services as a consequence of the estimated £1 million extra incurred in housing and feeding the new asylum-seekers.[19]

GOVERNMENT RESPONSES

The government did not remain idle in the face of the Roma issue. In September 1997, an alarmed Minister for Immigration, Mike O'Brien, quickly sided with the perceived majority view. In a press notice, he claimed that there was clear evidence that many asylum applicants were, in fact, economic migrants and he went on to single out the claims from eastern Europe.[20] In fact, before the home office had examined all claims on their individual merits, he had suggested that they were unfounded—an extraordinary position to adopt, both in view of the right of each claimant to have his or her claim individually assessed in accordance with the requirements of the 1951 convention, and in light of the increasing recognition by OSCE (Organisation for Security and Co-operation in Europe) countries that Roma did indeed face discrimination and violence in their home countries. The Czech Ministry, for its part, maintained that Roma asylum claims were "purely economically motivated."[21]

Concerned about reports that the influx from the Czech Republic and Slovakia had been sparked by a television program praising the United Kingdom's generous asylum and benefit policies, Mike O'Brien gave interviews in October 1997 to Czech and Slovak broadcast media in an attempt to halt the arrival of Roma.[22] He was assisted by the foreign secretary, Robin Cook, who informed the then president of the Czech Republic, Vaclav Havel, that the Roma should be made to feel that they had a future in their own country and that they should not expect to be granted asylum.[23] He sent a clear message that "Britain does not have an open-door policy to those who may allege persecution and cannot then prove it."[24] While no connection was made between the Czech Republic's application to join the EU and its alleged treatment of the Roma, President Havel could have been under no illusion as to the wider political implications of the Roma issue.

Although the opposition Conservative Party advocated immediate imposition of visa requirements on all Czech and Slovak citizens (the usual course of action adopted when a non visa country starts to produce increasing numbers of asylum-seekers), the government demurred, claiming that such a move had caused a rush of entrants in the past. This stance was somewhat surprising since even Canada, that bastion of liberal asylum policy, had chosen to introduce visas for citizens of the Czech Republic. Under pressure to show that it would be tough on "bogus asylum-seekers," the home office decided to try a new approach. The shipping carriers, P&O and Stena, were threatened with sanctions under carriers' liability legislation, which entitles the secretary of state to fine any carrier transporting an asylum-seeker not in possession of correct documentation.[25] Mike O'Brien also called upon carriers to pay for the cost of repatriating failed Roma claimants. As France refused to allow them to be returned overland, the carriers faced hefty costs: one estimate stood at £3,000 for three families.[26] In addition, the home secretary, Jack Straw, announced that asylum determination procedures would be accelerated. Under the previous system, asylum-seekers who applied for asylum at United Kingdom ports had twenty-eight days in which to provide supplementary evidence to support their cases; in October 1997, the time limit was reduced with immediate effect from twenty-eight to five days for cases considered "abusive."

Many male members of Roma families were placed in detention. As the numbers detained grew, suspicions were raised that the Home Office was employing detention as a policy of deterrence rather than for its intended use: as a last resort and to prevent asylum-seekers from absconding.[27] The normal decision is to grant temporary admission. At the time, there was no presumption in favor of bail[28] and free representation at any bail hearing was limited to two organizations, the Refugee Legal Centre and Immigration Advisory Service, which were unable to cope with the demand.[29] The reason provided by the Home Office for the wide-scale detention of Roma was their inability or unwillingness to comply with residence conditions attached to admission "because, as Roma, 'they would move and travel around.'"[30] The Refugee Legal Centre condemned this claim: "Such a statement, stereotypical if not outright offensive, indicated the poverty of arguments for maintaining detention."[31]

Part of the government's difficulty arose as a result of the Dublin Convention, which had come into force in September 1997. This convention, signed in 1990 between member states of the EU, was designed to determine which country would assume responsibility for particular asylum-seekers. Prior to enforcement, the United Kingdom had relied on bilateral agreements with its neighbors, in particular France. Under these agreements, the United Kingdom had been able to return a number of claimants to France through the application of the so-called "safe third-country rule."[32] However, the requirement in the Dublin Convention that the country to which the applicant was to be sent should agree worked against the interests of the United Kingdom in the case of the Roma: France declined to take responsibility, as the United Kingdom was unable to prove that undocumented individuals had first entered the EU through France.

Surprisingly, in view of all the attention focused on the Roma, Home Office figures for 1997 revealed that only 240 claims for asylum were in fact lodged by nationals of the Czech Republic.[33] The threat of thousands proved unfounded. Of the decisions taken in 1997, no applicant from the Czech Republic was granted refugee status or exceptional leave to remain (ELR).[34] By contrast, 210 refusals were issued.[35] While these may not all refer to the applications lodged in 1997, it is clear that the Home Office did, as promised, rush through refusals in the case of the Roma, some taking only a few months where the norm had become several years. All refusals declared the Roma claims to be "manifestly unfounded."

POST-1997: INCREASING ROMA CLAIMS

Despite the government's hard-line on Roma applications, the problem did not cease at the end of 1997. Roma have continued to arrive in the United Kingdom from a range of countries, more recently from Slovakia and Romania. The tabloid press has continued to lambast them, and the government to experiment with a variety of schemes and changes in the law. For example, following the arrival at Heathrow airport of some seven hundred Roma from the Slovak Republic in August 1998, Jack Straw announced an inquiry into the sudden influx.[36] It was reported that they turned to the United Kingdom having been refused asylum in Canada and that the majority of them were "street criminals and

gypsies" who operated together "in crimes such as pick-pocketing, intimidation, and theft."[37] By October, visas were imposed on Slovakian citizens, in contrast to the government's earlier approach towards the Czech Republic. It was
clear that the new visa requirement was introduced specifically to stem the flow
of Slovakian Roma claiming asylum in the United Kingdom. 'We are imposing
this visa regime because of the abuse of the visa-free arrangements by some
passengers from the Slovak Republic," declared the home secretary.[38] Some
Slovakians complained of double standards and political motivations behind
the differing treatment between the two countries. The British Embassy in
Prague denied this and asserted that visas were imposed purely on account of
the numbers: if numbers continued to rise from the Czech Republic, it too could
face a visa requirement.[39] The Slovakian government responded by imposing a
reciprocal visa requirement on British citizens. In the ten days following the visa
order, not one Roma claim from Slovakia was lodged in the United Kingdom[40]

CONDITIONS FACED BY THE ROMA IN THE
CZECH REPUBLIC AND SLOVAKIA

Both media and government succeeded in projecting the Roma as a group
with no genuine claim to asylum, who were attracted to the United Kingdom
purely in order to take advantage of its generosity and humanitarianism. The
actual conditions and treatment of the Roma in their countries of origin received relatively little discussion. While the more liberal broadsheets offered
some insight into the anti-Roma culture in central and eastern European
countries, the popular press remained silent on this. More surprising was the
silence of the Home Office, since OSCE members had long been aware of violence and discrimination against the Roma in their own countries.

Since 1995, Roma issues have been on the agenda of the OSCE Office for
Democratic Institutions and Human Rights (ODIHR), and there is regular
monitoring of compliance with the OSCE's commitments by participating
states.[41] A report in 1995 stated:

> Awareness of the vulnerable situation of Roma and Sinti[42] has increased, but in-
> tolerance, discrimination and racial violence against them continue to exist. A
> low level of education, high illiteracy rates, economic hardship and a low de-
> gree of participation in political life were noted.[43]

Yet four years later, little seemed to have improved:

> In some countries, the situation of Roma and Sinti had deteriorated to the extent
> that they were faced with violence, even murder, and persecution. Their
> socio-economic conditions were often deplorable. Many States and NGOs
> stressed that further consideration needed to be given to ways to secure the hu-

man rights of the Roma and Sinti people. . . . NGOs pointed to the negative response of some of these receiving States, such as strengthening migration control or imposing sudden visa requirements for the countries the Roma and Sinti were emanating from.[44]

While the situation of the Roma in Europe was sufficiently serious to warrant attention by a specific ODIHR body, the Contact Point for Roma and Sinti Issues, and while special high commissioner Max van der Stoel was appointed to deal with national minorities, words were not matched by actions. Thus, van der Stoel commented in 1999 that, "despite the seriousness of the problems now confronting Roma, neither the OSCE nor its participating states have devoted the attention or resources to this issue that are plainly warranted."[45]

THE CZECH REPUBLIC

The United Kingdom Home Office prepares country assessments for use in its refugee determination procedures.[46] In the country assessment on the Czech Republic, a special section is provided for the Roma, covering a wide range of issues from history and law to employment, education, and housing.[47] A summary of conditions is provided in one section of the report:

> The Czech authorities and the representatives of non-governmental organisations and Roma community associations admit that Roma continue to be the victims of intolerance and discrimination in various forms, particularly in employment, education, housing and access to public places. They are also exposed to the violence perpetrated by members of extreme right-wing organisations, or skinheads. Roma also suffer disproportionately from poverty, illiteracy and disease.[48]

The Home Office acknowledges that employers are often prejudiced against Roma and reject them on the grounds of ethnic origin alone.[49] Their unemployment rate is consequently as high as 90 percent in certain areas, and is rising. Many survive on government support or "earnings from illegal activities."[50] The Czech government admits that the education of Roma children is a serious problem and Roma children are often sent to schools for children with special educational needs.[51] The UNHCR reports that the level of education among Roma is very low, with many leaving school prior to the ninth grade.[52] Housing is also an acute problem for the Roma and they are frequently ghettoized outside the main centers with limited access to public services, power, and water supplies.[53]

The Czech Roma have also faced a change in the citizenship law that has resulted in many becoming "stateless." From 1993, when Czechoslovakia returned to the Czech and Slovak Republics, anyone designated earlier as Slovak was required to apply for Czech citizenship.[54] The Roma, who had moved from Slovakia to the Czech lands following the end of World War II, largely held Slovak citizenship, and were therefore expected to apply for Czech citizenship. They were required, however, to fulfill certain preconditions: two years' continuous permanent residence in the Czech Republic,[55] and a clean criminal record of five years' standing. Both provisions proved problematic for the Roma: many possessed low levels of literacy and were unaware of the new requirements; many had never registered as permanent residents; and Roma had been convicted for a large number of petty crimes.[56] The OSCE's high commissioner on national minorities, the UNHCR, the Council of Europe, and various NGOs expressed concern about the disproportionate impact of the legislation on the Roma. In response, two amendments emerged in 1999, somewhat improving the position.[57] The first allowed the minister of the interior to waive the clean-record requirement on a discretionary basis;[58] the second altered the 1993 law and enabled all persons who were citizens of Czechoslovakia, and who had permanent residence on Czech territory at the time of the breakup of the federation, to apply for Czech citizenship.[59] Although this was an advance, Roma, who have for some time lived in the Czech territory but have never registered, continue to face difficulties. Such difficulties are exacerbated by the fact that Slovakia does not want them either.

While a degree of institutionalized discrimination is evident from the foregoing discussion, the most serious issue relates to racial prejudice and violence. It is often on the grounds of such violence that the Roma base their asylum claims. The Czech Republic, Slovakia, and Bulgaria have had the highest recorded number of skinhead attacks.[60] The European Roma Rights Center (ERRC) documents such attacks together with positive steps taken to address the violence.[61] For example, the Czech Republic instituted a new policy for the integration of Roma[62] and promised training for judges and magistrates on racism and the Roma.[63]

The Roma have consistently argued that, when they are attacked, there is no point in reporting the matter to the police, since they will undertake a limited investigation at best, and that court sentences, where they are handed down, are derisory. There is evidence to support their claims.[64] The ERRC reports that the police may themselves be a source of violence.[65] However, in a recent Czech decision, the Supreme Court in Brno overturned the district court's decision in relation to a racially motivated attack against a Rom by six skinheads. The district court judge was criticized for acquitting four of the accused on the basis of an individual assessment rather than examining the question of a joint racial attack.[66] The case was returned to the district court for reassessment, suggesting a new judicial sensitivity in these matters.

SLOVAKIA

The general position of the Roma in Slovakia is very similar to that in the Czech Republic. The UN and Council of Europe recently published reports expressing serious concerns about the conditions faced by Roma in Slovakia in relation to: violence, poor protection by police and the courts, segregation and discrimination in housing and schooling, discrimination in employment, and health care.[67] The UN Committee on the Elimination of Racial Discrimination raised specific concerns about:

- the persistence of acts of violence by groups, particularly "skinheads," directed towards Roma and other ethnic minorities;
- the disproportionate number of Roma children not enrolled in schools, their high drop-out rates, their segregation, and their placement in schools for the mentally challenged;
- the poor nutrition levels, low levels of maternal and child health, and high mortality rate of the Roma.[68]

The second report of the European Commission against Racism and Intolerance (ECRI), published in December 1999, stated that a "pressing problem in Slovakia is posed by racial violence and harassment, often perpetrated by skinheads against members of the Roma/Gypsy community." "More alarming still," the report continued, was, "the apparent lack of police response to such incidents: in fact, several cases of reported violence against the Roma/Gypsy community have allegedly been carried out by police officers themselves."[69] Unemployment was again extraordinarily high: between 80 and 100 percent, depending on the location. As in the case of the Czech Republic, the ERRC and ECRI have monitored events in Slovakia and have reported on serious violence suffered by Roma in police custody or at the hands of racists.[70] Among ECRI's specific recommendations to the Slovak authorities were the need to ensure that an antiracist law was fully implemented, to adopt a range of measures to combat discrimination and racism against the Roma/Gypsy community in all fields, and to empower the community to participate as an equal component of society.[71]

THE ASSESSMENT OF THE ROMA CASE IN UNITED KINGDOM LAW

Following these brief summaries of the situation of the Roma in the Czech and Slovak Republics, the chapter will now consider the extent to which the Roma have succeeded in persuading the United Kingdom authorities and courts that they have a well-founded fear of persecution for the purposes of article 1(A)(2) of the 1951 convention.

As previously indicated, despite the acceptance that serious discrimination and even violence were being perpetrated against the Roma, particularly in the former Czechoslovakia, the Home Office consistently found their claims to be "manifestly unfounded." The effect of such a certification had two consequences for the Roma asylum-seekers: their cases were "fast-tracked" through the appeals process, and they were only permitted one appeal to a "Special Adjudicator." Any further recourse to the courts had to be made on the grounds of judicial review by which claimants may question, inter alia, the reasonableness of the home secretary's decision. The Refugee Legal Centre, which was able to represent clients at appeal without charge, decided at the end of 1997 to run a test case on the Roma, in view of the large number of refusals and consequent appeals. Four cases were selected for combined consideration: "the Slovak Roma Test Case."[72] After considering evidence presented by counsel for the appellants, the Adjudicator found in favor of the four families. He declared that:

> at the present time, given the recent political developments in Slovakia and the deteriorating climate for Roma there . . . there is a reasonable likelihood that what they will face is serious, and persistent, ill treatment—the definition of persecution given by Lord Justice Staughton in the case of Ravichandran and Sandralingham—because of their social group and that their fear of persecution on return to Slovakia is well-founded.[73]

According to the Refugee Legal Centre, following this decision, the Home Office denied that there had ever been a test case and argued that each Roma case still had to be decided on its merits.[74] Nonetheless, the impact of the decision was significant, as increasing numbers of Roma appeals were upheld by the Immigration Appellate Authorities.[75]

Most of the Roma cases dealt with harassment, discrimination, or maltreatment by neofascist groups or skinheads. As they started to come to the Immigration Appeal Tribunal (IAT) and higher courts, the judiciary were forced to decide whether there was, in fact, a justifiable claim for refugee status. First, was the maltreatment or discrimination sufficiently serious to constitute persecution? Second, should the United Kingdom provide protection or was the country of origin able to do so? Through the late 1990s, the IAT, in considering appeals from the adjudicators, swayed between positive and negative decisions as it sought a suitable legal formula.

By way of example of a positive decision, the Tribunal in the case of *Peter Balaz*, in 1999, upheld the finding of the special adjudicator that the respondent did have a subjective and objective fear of persecution if returned to Slovakia.[76] Counsel for the respondent cited in particular Amnesty International and Human Rights Reports on Slovakia:

> In general, recourse to protection from the police is not considered by Roma or Roma experts to be a plausible alternative: police are perceived—correctly in

some instances—to at least passively and even actively co-operate with hatred groups such as skinheads, and use counter charges to pressure Roma victims of police brutality to drop their complaints. Roma experience unequal treatment before the law as well as disproportionate abuse and discrimination by authority. In any case, the police have failed to protect the Roma community adequately.

The secretary of state's lawyers were unable to provide evidence to counter this claim, or to demonstrate that conditions in Slovakia had changed. The IAT had no alternative but to agree with the special adjudicator's finding.

Not all decisions were so positive. In a string of cases in the 1990s,[77] the Tribunal considered in some detail the question of "sufficiency of protection" provided by the country of origin. A test finally emerged, mainly championed by the then president of the IAT, Judge Pearl:

> Is there in place in the country a sufficiency of protection? One needs to enquire into the various steps which have been taken by the country to see whether this protection is in place. If this sufficiency of protection is in place, then the need for protection is not required. Thus it is not the test simply to ask whether the country "knowingly tolerates" persecutory acts by its agents or by sections of the community. Neither is it the test to ask whether the protection is effective . . . we believe that it is indeed the responsibility of the decision maker to ascertain whether the systems of domestic protection which are in place are sufficient from the perspective of international law.[78]

With this in mind, some Tribunal panels were able to dismiss appeals by Roma with relative ease. Thus, for example, in *Jaworski*[79] and in *Mojka and Mojka*,[80] members of the Tribunal decided, after considering the documentary evidence, that there was "in place now in Poland a sufficiency of protection against any racial persecution, which may be directed against [the appellant] or other Roma by some sections of the Polish community."[81] With regard to the Czech Republic, the Tribunal found in *Karel Levai*

> that, while the police are seen to be inefficient and ineffective by the Roma, that it is the case that they very rarely seek police protection, and that there is some evidence that the police have been slow to deal with complaints, nevertheless, there is also evidence that there have been prosecutions, that the police have intervened to provide protection, when asked to do so, . . ., and that the prosecuting authorities have taken action to have inadequate sentences for racially-motivated crimes enhanced by the Courts.[82]

While the Tribunal decisions are not binding,[83] a recent case, which reached the House of Lords, has provided the definitive judgment on the sufficiency of protection criterion. In July 2000, the House of Lords handed down the landmark decision of *Horvath v. Secretary of State for the Home Department*.[84] There it was held that where persecution by nonstate agents was alleged, the failure of the state to provide protection was an essential element in confirming refugee status. In fact, the court confirmed that the definition of "persecution" under the convention implied a failure by the state to make protection available against the ill-treatment or violence suffered.[85] What was expected of sufficient protection was spelled out: "There must be in place a system of domestic protection and machinery for the detection, prosecution, and punishment of actings contrary to the purposes that the convention requires to have protected. More importantly there must be an ability and a readiness to operate that machinery."[86] Although the tribunal found the appellant in the case to have a genuine and well-founded fear of *discrimination*, and while it accepted reports of violence and maltreatment of the Roma, it was not prepared to acknowledge that the line between discrimination and persecution had been crossed; the reason given was that there was sufficient protection provided by the state. The House of Lords concurred with the reasoning.

CONCLUSION

If one is looking for a measure of current practice in relation to the 1951 convention in its fiftieth year, there is arguably no better case than that of the Roma. All the issues are contained therein: xenophobia, the politics of asylum, a culture of disbelief by those entrusted with status determination, the question of economic migration, the narrow interpretation of article 1(A)(2) of the convention, and the strong affirmation of the surrogacy principle.[87]

The consequences for the Roma are serious. While they may suffer extreme forms of discrimination and even violence, they face return whenever it is deemed that the country of origin is providing protection. The decision in *Horvath* by the House of Lords was criticized abroad. In New Zealand, for example, Roger Haines, QC, expressed surprise at the Lords' readiness to measure the sufficiency of state protection "not against the absence of a real risk of persecution, but against the availability of a system for the protection of the citizen and a reasonable willingness by the state to operate that system."[88] Haines feared that such an interpretation would lead to *refoulement*.

This must surely be right. As has been shown in this paper, there is ample evidence supporting the view that the Roma are systematically subjected, at the least, to discrimination in central and eastern European countries; violence, too, appears to be increasing in some areas. Yet the view of the United Kingdom authorities has been that the Roma are primarily economic migrants who have abused the asylum system by making manifestly unfounded claims. The appellate authorities and courts, while acknowledging the unacceptable conditions faced by many Roma, have chosen to impose the burden of protection on the originating rather than host countries. Such an approach was evident in a recent finding where the tribunal took issue with an expert witness. Dr. Thomas Acton, who was at the time a reader in Romani studies at the University of Greenwich, provided the following statement as evidence:

> I applaud the courage of those Roma who are campaigning in Poland against this [discrimination], but that is a long way from believing it right to enforce such courage on isolated and less well-educated families with small children. Not to offer refuge to those under attack would be to repeat the error of not offering refuge to Jews and Gypsies under similar attack in Germany and Poland in the 1930s.[89]

The tribunal was not impressed; it referred to Dr. Acton's bias and "extravagant language," and rejected outright "any comparison between the democratically elected government of the Republic of Poland . . . and the National Socialist administration of Herr Hitler." It spoke of the "real and genuine efforts . . . being made in Poland to get to grips with the problem of discrimination" and expressed its "hope that there [would] be no further instances of discrimination" on the appellant's return. Whether such confident hope can be vested in the treatment of Roma elsewhere remains seriously open to question.

NOTES

I should like to thank the British Academy and the Legal Research Institute, University of Warwick, for their generous financial support.

1. OSCE High Commissioner on National Minorities, *Report on the Situation of Roma and Sinti in the OSCE Area*, March 2000, 19.

2. Pogany, I. "Accommodating an Emergent National Identity: The Roma of Central and Eastern Europe," *International Journal of Minority and Group Rights* 6 (1999): 149, 153, citing Stewart, *The Time of the Gypsies* (Boulder, Colorado: Westview Press), 59.

3. Fraser, A. *The Gypsies* (Oxford: Blackwells, 1992), 8.

4. Pogany, op. cit., 153.

5. Fraser, op. cit., 113–114; Kenrick and Puxon, *The Destiny of Europe's Gypsies* (London: Heinemann, 1972).

6. Fraser, op. cit., 115.

7. Home Office, *Asylum Statistics United Kingdom 1999*, 12 October 2000.

8. Ibid, table 2.1. These figures exclude dependents.

9. Ibid.

10. Doughty, S. "Towns Buckle under Burden of Refugees," *The Daily Mail*, 19 September 1997.

11. Walmsley, D. "Minister Tries to Halt Flood of Gypsies," *The Daily Telegraph*, 22 October 1997.

12. Professor Aubrey Newman from the Centre for Holocaust Studies at Leicester University. See Williams and Field, "Script for a Scam," *The Daily Mail*, 24 October 1997.

13. *The Daily Star*, 14 November 1997; *The Daily Telegraph*, 28 November 1997; The *Daily Mail*, 24 October 1997.

14. See, for example, D. Walmsley, "Minister Tries to Halt Flood of Gypsies," *The Daily Telegraph*, 22 October 1997.

15. Williams and Field, "Script for a Scam," *The Daily Mail*, 24 October 1997.

16. Ibid.

17. Utley, "Town's Tolerance Snaps under Gypsy 'Invasion,'" *The Daily Telegraph*, 23 October 1997.

18. Mills, "No Gypsies Please, We're British," *The Observer*, 26 October 1997.

19. Bridge, "They Steal—Not that I've Met Any Myself," *Independent on Sunday*, 26 October 1997.

20. Home Office Press Notice 030/97, 19 September 1997.

21. "Warning Over New Influx of Gypsies," *The Daily Mail*, 23 October 1997.

22. Walmsley, "Minister Tries to Halt Flood of gypsies," *The Daily Telegraph*, 22 October 1997.

23. Black, "Cook Warns Off Gypsies," *The Guardian*, 28 November 1997.

24. Ibid.

25. Immigration (Carriers' Liability) Act 1987; now replaced by Immigration and Asylum Act 1999, Part II.

26. Millward, "P&O Men Face Jail Threat for Gypsy Ban," *The Daily Telegraph,* 19 November 1997.

27. Refugee Legal Centre, *Annual Report 1997–1998,* 10.

28. A presumption in favor of bail was introduced by the Immigration and Asylum Act 1999, section 46, but this has never been implemented and is to be revoked under new legislation currently passing through Parliament: the Nationality, Immigration, and Asylum Bill 2002.

29. The RLC and IAS received government funding under Immigration Act 1971, section 23 and, unlike private solicitors, were able to provide representation at certain hearings; section 88 of the Immigration and Asylum Act 1999 largely reflects section 23.

30. Refugee Legal Centre, *Annual Report 1997–1998,* 11.

31. Ibid.

32. The safe third-country rule allows a state in which an application is lodged (the second country) to send the applicant to another country deemed safe and where the application will be considered (the third country).

33. The figure excludes dependents.

34. ELR is a secondary status of leave to enter or remain granted outside the immigration rules.

35. Home Office, *Asylum Statistics United Kingdom 1999,* 12 October 2000, tables 3.1, 3.2, 3.3.

36. Smith, "Straw Inquiry into Influx of Gypsies," *The Daily Telegraph*, 28 August 1998.

37. Williams, "The Refugee Robbers," *The Daily Mail*.

38. Millward, "Straw Acts to Curb Bogus Slovakian Refugees," *The Daily Telegraph*, 8 October 1998.

39. Connolly, "Indignation Builds in Visa War," *The Guardian*, 19 October 1998.

40. Travis, "British Ban Ends Romany Claims," *The Guardian*, 19 October 1998.

41. www.osce.org/odihr/cprsi/i_exce.htm

42. The German term for Roma.

43. Rapporteurs Report, ODIHR, 1995 Warsaw Human Dimension Implementation Meeting: www.osce.org/odihr/cprsi/i_exce.htm

44. Rapporteurs Report, ODIHR, 1999 Vienna Review Conference: www.osce.org/odihr/cprsi/i_exce.htm

45. Max van der Stoel, Address to the Supplementary Human Dimension Meeting on Roma and Sinti Issues, Vienna, 6 September 1999: www.osce.org/hcnm/speeches/1999/06sep99.htm

46. In a relatively recent attempt at transparency, these have been made available on the Home Office website: www.ind.homeoffice.gov.uk/default.asp?PageId=88. Note: the country assessments cited in this paper refer to the pre-April 2002 versions.

47. www.ind.homeoffice.gov.uk/default.asp?PageId=406

48. Ibid., par. 7.18.

49. Ibid., par. 7.24.

50. Ibid., par. 7.22.

51. Ibid., par. 7.33.

52. Ibid., par. 7.35.

53. Ibid., par. 7.50.

54. Law on Acquisition and Loss of Citizenship, Law No. 40/1993.

55. Increased to five years in June 1994 following the end of preferential treatment for Slovaks.

56. See, for a further discussion, Helen O'Nions, "Bonafide or Bogus? Roma Asylum Seekers from the Czech Republic," [1999] 3 Web JCLI.

57. Law No. 159/1999.

58. OSCE High Commissioner on National Minorities, *Report on the Situation of Roma and Sinti in the OSCE Area*, March 2000, 158.

59. Ibid.

60. Ibid., 39.

61. See errc.org

62. "Ground Concepts of Government Policy Towards Members of the Roma Community with a View to Facilitating their Integration into Society: www.ind.homeoffice.gov.uk/default.asp?PageId=406, par. 7.78.

63. Ibid, par. 7.84.

64. OSCE High Commissioner on National Minorities, *Report on the Situation of Roma and Sinti in the OSCE Area*, March 2000, 37.

65. See, for example, ERRC, "Romani Youth Attacked by Police in Czech Republic," *Roma Rights*, No. 4, 2000: www.errc.org/rr_nr4_2000/snap13.shtml

66. ERRC, "Prosecuting Racist Criminals in the Czech Republic," *Roma Rights*, No. 3, 2000: www.errc.org/rr_nr3_2000/snap21.shtml

67. ERRC, "UN and Council of Europe Express Concern about Roma Rights in Slovakia," *Roma Rights*, No. 3, 2000: www.errc.org/rr_nr3_2000/snap3.shtml

68. UN Doc: A/55/18, par. 252–270.

69. CRI (2000) 35, 11.

70. See, for example, ERRC, "More Disturbing Events in Slovak Police Custody," *Roma Rights*, No. 3, 2000: www.errc.org/rr_nr3_2000/snap18.shtml and ERRC, "Romani Woman in Slovakia Dies after Beating," *Roma Rights*, No. 3, 2000: www.errc.org/rr_nr3_2000/snap2.shtml

71. CRI (2000) 35, 4.

72. Refugee Legal Centre, *Annual Report 1997–1998,* 13.

73. Ibid., 15.

74. Ibid.,

75. Ibid.,

76. *Peter Balaz* (19294).

77. *Jaworski* (17152), *Debrah* (17606) [1998] INLR 383, *Chinder Singh* (BILS 2E [701](G0055), *Mojka* (18265), *Dymiter* (18467).

78. *Debrah* (17606) [1998] INLR 383.

79. *Jaworski* (17152).

80. *Mojka* (18265).

81. *Jaworski* (17152).

82. *Karel Levai* (18807).

83. A recent innovation is the introduction of the "starred" decision of the IAT which is made by a legally-constituted panel and will be expected to be followed.

84. [2000] INLR 239.

85. [2000] INLR 239, Lord Hope, 246.

86. [2000] INLR 239, Lord Clyde, 259.

87. The surrogacy principle provides that only where a person no longer enjoys protection for a convention reason in his or her own country may he or she turn for protection to the international community.

88. Roger Haines, QC, Decision 71472/99, cited in Mark Symes, *Caselaw on the Refugee Convention—The UK's Interpretation in the Light of the International Authorities* (London: The Refugee Legal Centre, 2000), 236.

89. *Zofia Huczko* (00TH00403).

12

Human Smuggling and Refugee Protection in the European Union: Myths and Realities

Aninia Nadig and John Morrison

European states today are faced with a seemingly irresolvable dilemma between controlling immigration and fulfilling their international obligations to offer protection to refugees. States clearly have an interest in determining to whom they want to grant access to their territory. As Europe has involuntarily evolved into a continent of immigration, border control has become of increasing concern to national authorities, particularly in connection with the harmonization process of the EU.

This chapter is a synthesis of four conference presentations on human smuggling. Each paper had a very distinct approach to the topic, but they all agree on several key issues, the most important being the ability for refugees to seek international protection upon European territory.[1] Furthermore, they emphasize the lack of reliable data concerning human smuggling, which leads to a misinterpretation of the phenomenon, in the public domain.

After describing some of the realities of human smuggling in Europe, including the description of restrictive policy measures, the article will elaborate on the myths that surround human smuggling in relation to the unresolved policy conundrums faced by states. In the last part of the chapter, the authors briefly expound on the alternatives to current research and policy-making on human smuggling, as proposed in the four original presentations.

The chapter focuses on national and regional policy measures pertaining to Europe only. Yet, as it is often stated, European approaches toward asylum and migration issues tend to influence measures taken in other parts of the world, particularly in developing countries. Therefore, we believe that Europe serves as a good example to illustrate the complex issues at stake in the smuggling and trafficking debate.

THE REALITIES OF HUMAN SMUGGLING IN EUROPE

Just as human migration is a phenomenon that has occurred since the beginning of time, so has the need of humans to defend a territory they regard as theirs. Since the seventeenth century, territorial sovereignty has been one of the fundamental characteristics of modern nation-states and managing migration in terms of cultural and political diversity, and change has become one of their major challenges.

The emergence of the welfare state in the second half of the nineteenth century has been a particularly important factor in understanding some of the tensions built up in the context of migration movements to Europe in the twentieth century (Nadig). New forms of social contracts guaranteed citizens' security and prosperity, while guaranteeing state stability and the competence to implement necessary social policies. The concepts of citizenship and rights are now intrinsically linked. This means that immigrants are faced with questions of undeservingly taking advantage of social benefits originally only appertaining to citizens of their host state.

Over the last 100 years, Europe has been a region of immigration. With the exception of large-scale emigration and refugee flight during and after World War II, it was mainly the northern European and, in the last few decades southern European countries, that have attracted increasing numbers of migrant workers and refugees.

In order to highlight the relationship between migration, asylum, and human smuggling, we can roughly distinguish three phases over the last fifty years (Koser, Nadig). After World War II, the reconstruction of western Europe, combined with greatly expanding production, demanded large numbers of low-skilled foreign labor. At the same time, refugee flows to Europe were relatively low; most refugees were accepted on the basis of "quota" systems. Therefore, during the 1960s and 1970s, and particularly before the oil crisis of 1973, there were two distinct legal migration channels into western Europe, one for labor migrants and another for refugees.

Profound economic changes in the mid-1970s, in connection with the oil crisis, focused attention on the question of economic growth and social welfare, and the improvement of technology put large sectors of the labor market out of work. The attempts of European states to follow a policy of "zero immigration" failed: guestworkers stayed and brought their families. At the same time, policies restricting labor migration had the unintended consequence of forcing migrants into the asylum channel: asylum applications in the EU grew steadily through the late 1980s, reaching a peak in 1992.

In those years, along with greater economic and social tensions, national policymaking became less consensual in most western European states because the underlying social contract had lost some of its cohesive influence on society. At the same time, and as a direct result of the social malaise, migration became an important issue of political confrontation, contributing to the rise of right-wing anti-immigrant parties. One part of the public policy responses adopted in the 1990s in most European countries was to restrict access to asylum for so-called "economic migrants." Those measures, some of which will be discussed in greater detail later, seemed to have the desired impact, as the number of asylum applications decreased dramatically after 1992 to less than half in 1996, only to rebound thereafter to almost the same level as at the beginning of the decade (Koser).

One possible interpretation of these changes in numbers of asylum applications is that, just as closing down the labor migration channel forced economic migrants into the asylum channel, increasing restrictions upon this asylum channel are now forcing asylum-seekers into a new, illegal channel. And the indications are that this channel is increasingly monopolized by smugglers and traffickers (Koser, Nadig).

It may be misleading, however, to conclude from the above that opening up labor markets would diminish smuggling. Even during active recruitment by the more industrialized northern European countries, illegal entries from countries in which active recruitment was taking place were not uncommon, as the legal labor market could not absorb as many people as were looking for a job. Also, a vibrant economy and slow administration can cause irregular migration (Black).

The term "irregular" migration—"intercountry movements that take place in defiance of national laws and regulations"[2]—is sometimes debated. Confusion can arise when distinguishing between "irregular" and "illegal." These two terms do not necessarily coincide. For example, according to article 31.1 of the 1951 Refugee Convention,[3] a refugee may not be punished for the use of false documents or illegal border crossing. Asylum-seekers may thus be entering the country of destination irregularly without becoming illegal. Also, an illegal entry may not always be recognized as such.[4] We have chosen to use the term "irregular" migration because in our opinion it best reflects the complexity of human smuggling. On occasion the authors use the terms legal and illegal, in place of regular and irregular, in order to emphasize the domestic legal situation in a specific country.

Human smuggling and trafficking are old phenomena that were given relatively little international attention until the late 1980s. Since then, a growing number of reports have dealt with the subject. Whereas the topic of study was not clear from the outset and the phenomena themselves continue to evolve, commonly accepted definitions for smuggling and trafficking now have a legal basis in the UN Convention against Transnational Organized Crime, signed in Palermo in December 2000 and soon to enter into international law.

—Smuggling of migrants shall mean the procurement, in order to obtain, directly or indirectly, a financial or other material benefit, of the illegal entry of a person into a state party of which the person is not a national or a permanent resident.[5]

—Trafficking in persons shall mean the recruitment, transportation, transfer, and harboring or receipt of persons, by means of a threat or use of force or other forms of coercion, of abduction, of fraud, of deception, of the abuse of power, or of a position of vulnerability, or of giving or receiving payments or benefits to achieve the consent of a person having control over another person, for the purpose of exploitation.[6]

Such definitions have benefits as well as limitations. Both Morrison and Koser stress the fact that by clearly separating smuggling and trafficking, the victimization of the trafficked persons is widely accepted, whereas smuggled migrants' human rights, and especially the right to protection of smuggled refugees receive too little attention. While states have a great interest in cracking down on human smuggling as an international crime, there is hardly any discussion on alternative options to smuggling for refugees in need of protection. "Herein lies a policy conundrum: How to protect asylumseekers from the insecurity associated with smuggling, without closing the door on what is one of the last possibilities for applying for asylum in western Europe."[7]

When studying public policy and security measures taken by European states to tackle the flow of irregular migration, it is interesting to note that practically all measures are intended to block entry into Europe. Only very few and hesitant attempts have been made to "attack" the root causes of migratory movements, for example, in part by the EU High Level Working Group on Asylum and Migration. The large majority of current policy measures are widely considered reactive and defensive but not contributing to the elimination of the problem itself (Morrison, Nadig). Most importantly, these measures were introduced to crack down on migrants "misusing" the asylum channel, yet they hurt refugees who rely on the same travel and asylum systems, just as much and more, as refugees are more vulnerable to begin with.

The most important restrictive measures are analyzed in detail by Morrison. He starts out by pointing out the very limited chances for refugees to make use of one of the few legal possibilities for traveling to Europe. Visa requirements imposed on refugee-generating countries are in fact a very effective way of denying refugees the possibility of legal migration, as such visa are not given to applicants suspected of being potential asylum-seekers. UNHCR resettlement from refugee-generating countries is only available to a handful of persons each year and leaves most refugees unprotected. Temporary protection programs so far have offered sketchy protection and many people from the former Republic of Yugoslavia were forced to enter illegally despite these programs.

There are a number of clearly restrictive measures. Carrier sanctions introduced Europe-wide in 1990 through the Schengen agreement, force airline and shipping companies to take strong measures to detect persons with false identities, thereby blocking another important (illegal) way of access for refugee protection. Since 1996, EU Airline Liaison Officers advise airline staff in certain countries about the authenticity of specific travel documents.

Carrier sanctions and Airline Liaison Officers rest on a platform of pre-existing intergovernmental cooperation on issues of Readmission Agreements and "safe third-country" definitions that prevent asylum-seekers from claiming asylum at the border. For example, Germany has such arrangements with all its neighboring countries, and this has had an effect in both limiting the growth of asylum claims as well as growing a market for irregular entry (Morrison). Since the conclusions of the Tampere European Council in October 1999, the EU High Level Working Group on Asylum and Immigration has focused the attention of both the foreign and interior ministries of member states on the migration from Somalia, Afghanistan, Iraq, Kosovo/Albania, Sri Lanka, and Morocco. The first five of these states are significant refugee-sending countries and while the "action plans" are concerned with fighting smuggling and trafficking with the blanket measures outlined above, the focus on refugee protection seems limited to only in-country solutions (Morrison, Nadig). A corresponding approach is taken by EU states in their national programs against smuggling, as Nadig's work in the Netherlands shows.

Furthermore, a number of grounds for refusing an asylum claim are detrimental to smuggled asylum-seekers, such as "manifesting false" evidence (false or nonexistent identification), or short time limits for lodging an asylum claim (Black).

Within the context of migration policies in Europe, all four authors agree that governments view human smuggling as a growing problem that must be solved by policymaking both at the pan-European level and with transnational agreements between the EU and countries of origin and transit. At the same time, however, we currently witness the development of national policy measures proving counterproductive to the development of common asylum and migration policies. It is therefore not clear how national and international commitments to refugee protection, such as the 1951 Refugee Convention, can flourish in an environment focused on national border control and combating transnational organized crime.

THE MYTHS OF REFUGEE PROTECTION IN EUROPE

A growing body of the literature on human smuggling recognizes the dilemma states face between fulfilling their obligations under international human rights and refugee treaties, and their interest in controlling their national borders. Instead of coming up with answers to this dilemma, Koser proposes to explain just why it is so difficult to solve. He breaks down the whole conundrum into three distinct policy dilemmas, each of which, he argues, arise from a set of new characteristics of contemporary human smuggling.

One dilemma arises from the complex composition of smuggled persons, in connection with the restrictions of access points to European states mentioned above. Today, people with very different motivations to move—from refugees to economic migrants—all are using the same channels of human smuggling, leaving the states with the well-known dilemma of migration control versus refugee protection.

The second dilemma identified by Koser is the vicious circle states and smuggling rings are engaged in: with smugglers always seeming to find ways to circumvent new restrictive asylum and migration policies. States are slowly starting to recognize this dilemma.

The third policy dilemma is also connected to the sophistication of today's smuggling rings. As human smuggling has turned into a very lucrative business, even actively recruiting migrants, it will be difficult to break up smuggling processes, without thereby depriving refugees from the only way they may have to leave their country and reach a safe destination.

Nadig mentions a fourth dilemma: the active recruitment of persons who often give up a small but secure income for the glossy pictures painted in the smugglers' sales pitches. So, arguably, restricting access may actually, in itself, increase human smuggling and certainly act to increase the clandestine nature of the process and the risks and costs involved. Morrison cites European government reports that chart the growth of "clandestine" entry when compared to "deceptive" entry through regular immigration channels and how some governments have attributed the rise of "criminal involvement" as partly the result of their success in enforcing controls at the border.

There are no "quick wins" for European governments looking at resolving the policy dilemmas outlined above. Therefore, before suggesting a number of areas where policy might be improved, we should at this point examine the question of the real interest of states in migration issues, driven often by short-term electoral considerations, and by the way these issues are discussed publicly.

Black, Nadig, and Morrison point out that governments are often not actually as concerned with irregular migration as the impression might be. Many of their resources are invested in fighting crime, etc., whereas human smuggling does not actually have the same social and economic cost as do other sorts of criminal activities. Black goes further by pointing out possible advantages states may have by tacitly condoning illegal residents who are cheap (no social rights) and easily exploited in a growing informal market in many European states.

In contrast, however, politicians and the media hype up the phenomenon of human smuggling, often presenting irregular migration as a national security threat (Black, Nadig, Koser). Often, official ciphers are extrapolated arbitrarily from the meager existing empirical data, possibly inflating figures and thereby leading to xenophobia or misused for stirring xenophobic tendencies (Black). Much of this hype may have to do with the wish of governments to present problems inherent to their own society and policy structure as originating in the presence of too many illegal immigrants and asylum-seekers.

With regard to the way human smuggling is approached publicly, Morrison urges European governments, UNHCR, and NGOs to acknowledge that, when speaking about specific nationalities such as Iraqis, Somalis, or Afghans, between one-third and two-thirds of those asylum-seekers smuggled to the EU end up with some sort of refugee or other protective status. It does nothing to serve the public debate, if politicians claim that a 5–10 percent refugee recognition rate, across all nationalities, justifies blanket border restrictions that will affect known refugee-producing countries or regions. This is where policy-related initiatives that do look at specific countries of origin, such as the action plans of the High Level Working Group, are driven by the generalized myth of the "bogus asylum-seeker" even though this is not supported by the data for the country in question. If "antismuggling" measures are brought to bear on a migration route where no other routes to protection are available to asylum-seekers, then it would be more honest of governments to call these "antirefugee" policies, too.

Koser and Nadig both conclude that national and EU immigration and asylum policies must take into account the complexities of human smuggling, lest they only respond to a "growing public clamor" (Koser), without proper regard to the consequences for the refugees involved. Nadig, furthermore, suggests that one important step toward convincing European governments to revise their approach toward human smuggling is to indicate the potential benefits of such a revision for their own societies. She points out that governments hardly ever really discuss the complexities of irregular migration publicly and that they refuse to acknowledge the potential benefits of a multicultural society.

Persons in need of protection are placed in a very difficult position by restricted access possibilities to Western countries (see above, Morrison): they often have virtually no other choice than to revert to a smuggler. The very fact that their safety is apparently of no concern to Western states, confronts refugees, to an even greater extent than migrants, with a set of insecurities additional to those that prompted them to leave their country.

Koser develops three particular insecurities: political, economic, and social. After repatriation, rejected asylum-seekers may face political insecurity just for having lodged an asylum claim at all. According to Koser, the fact that an asylum-seeker was smuggled may possibly reduce his or her chance of getting accepted as a refugee or even be allowed to enter the asylum procedure. Also, a growing number of readmission agreements with "safe third-countries" make deportation to those countries more likely. Economic insecurity stems mainly from the financial obligations imposed on the smuggled person by the smuggler. Such insecurity and dependency can drag on for many years after having reached the country of destination. Social insecurity can arise where the smuggler chooses a country of destination where the smuggled person cannot rely on a preexisting social network. Black also points to such insecurities, but puts equal emphasis on the opportunities given to migrants and refugees.

The atomistic approach to refugee protection across the EU is clearly part of the problem, with the failure to implement the Dublin Convention, widely different recognition rates for the same nationalities in different EU states, and profile of the asylum issue in domestic party politics and populist and short-term policymaking (Morrison). It seems most likely that any EU approach to protecting refugees in Europe, or outside, will only be successful if it is truly holistic in embodying both the right of asylum upon European territory as well as programs for refugee resettlement and that the European Commission is empowered to set a medium to long-term policy agenda that goes beyond any short-term political or national interests of member states.

REFUGEE PROTECTION BASED ON REALITIES?

In this last section, we want to lay out the concerns common to all four authors and their approaches and suggestions regarding future research and policymaking on human smuggling.

Human smuggling as a security concern to states is a relatively new phenomenon. Accordingly, and also due to the clandestine nature of the phenomenon, reliable data, both quantitative and qualitative, are sparse. Moreover, there still seems to be a lack of consensus concerning definitions and terminology. This lack of clarity is potentially detrimental for refugees: as we have seen, the phenomenon of human smuggling occupies a definite place in the perceptions of receiving societies and can easily be manipulated as long as it is based on myths.

Recognizing the lack of knowledge concerning human smuggling, all four authors direct the focus of their recommendations on the need for a better understanding of the phenomenon, and of the interaction between human smuggling and Western policy responses.

Morrison emphasizes the need for accuracy and consistency in language and terminology, on opening up the border enforcement and organized crime debate that to this day remain closed and inaccessible to many specialists in refugee rights and to NGO participation. He also urges broader thinking by European refugee and human rights agencies, which mostly neglected to follow the Vienna process that culminated in the adoption of the Palermo Protocols and Convention in December 2000. Morrison asks European governments actively to adopt the right to asylum as a core European value and to adopt a regional approach to refugee protection that supports refugee protection in other regions but allows spontaneous asylum in Europe. He sees the real risk of asylum losing its legal significance as an unalienable and universal human right and EU governments replacing it with a more administrative ad hoc procedure more reminiscent of the world before the 1951 Refugee Convention.

Morrison puts great emphasis on the immediate need for good research and accurate data on the different phases of smuggling and on the risks involved for refugees. Here again, much could be improved if national and European governments shared their data on human smuggling and trafficking with academics and NGOs.

As for the few existing empirical studies on human smuggling, Koser conducted one of them in 1996–1997, interviewing thirty-two Iranian asylum-seekers in the Netherlands. Based on his findings, he approached the issue of human smuggling from a migration perspective and as a human rights issue. Of the thirty-two respondents, twenty-nine admitted to having being smuggled at some stage on the journey from Iran. What clearly emerged was the complexity of motives and methods of irregular migration. There were a range of "exit," "migration," and "entry" strategies—with the smugglers often playing the decisive role in choosing which strategies to use at which stages of the journey. Similar findings have been found in other interview-based studies from other European countries, such as in the United Kingdom [8]

Black again stresses the need for more research in this area but challenges whether such work can ever be "value neutral." He notes that conceptualizing irregular migration as "illegal migration" and outside of the law, there is a strong tendency for research to seek to assign "blame" for this (seemingly) abnormal state of affairs. Recognizing the fact that irregular migration is an area in which human activity is increasingly becoming criminalized, we should shift the research agenda (at least in part) to one that attempts to challenge the assertions of the powerful and respond to discrimination. Although there are possible dangers in undermining the position of the powerless still further, the evidence of harm implicit in the smuggling and trafficking processes means there is a "values" basis for considering such research:[9]

Of course, it could be argued that research on illegal migration is not necessary or desirable at all. By revealing migrants' or asylum-seekers strategies that lie outside of defined legal limits, research might simply assist States in the process of controlling both individuals and groups, and thus breach the acceptable ethical guideline of doing no harm to those being researched. However, the widespread evidence of harm—and vulnerability to harm—that characterises both the use of illegal migration channels, and failure to access such channels, seems reason enough for research to be at least considered. The potential for research to benefit asylum-seekers and other migrants is worth exploring.

Much of the research that has been done, Black states, has focused mainly on the receiving countries and not the countries of origin. There is a growing recognition that a "transnational" approach to understanding the social fields of refugees, as well as other migrants, can yield a better understanding of motivations, choices, and methods.

In her paper, Nadig also examines human smuggling to the EU in 1990, arguing that the increase in human smuggling and the development of restrictive access policies to EU states, are interlinked and reinforce each other. Human smuggling is widely described as a threat to the national and societal security of a receiving country.

Observing a sort of stalemate in the fight against irregular migration, the author makes a theory-based argument for approaching irregular migration in a radically different way by taking it off the national security agenda. Whereas states cling to their national sovereignty when migration and asylum are concerned, such a move would pave the way for a more long-term and Europe-wide approach toward irregular migration, while refugees' rights of access to protection could be respected. Nadig also points to the possible advantages of such an approach for receiving societies that would experience the presence of foreigners among them as less stressful than they do now. The responsibility for such a change of attitude must be placed mostly with politicians who, up to now, have not taken on their task of dealing with migration issues openly.

Nadig reaches her conclusions by examining human smuggling through the lens of three international relations theories: realism, critical security studies, and pluralism. Realism best reflects today's perception of human smuggling as a threat to a state, and that state's self-interest to protect itself; "state" and "self-interest" are its central concepts. Critical security studies recognize that "danger" and "threat" are constructs of each society, reflected in the government. The theory thus includes societal factors in its analysis, while accepting a nation's interest in protecting itself from perceived threats. Pluralism, finally, identifies the state as pluralist and integrative of sub- and supranational forces, best capable to respond to a complex and multilayered problem like human smuggling.

CONCLUSIONS

The authors call for a European migration policy that is driven by reality more than myth and call for a more empirical study relating to how human smuggling and antismuggling policies affect refugee protection. There is nothing new about human smuggling in Europe, but there is everything new about the level of governmental concern that it is attracting, as well as the border enforcement and anticriminal resources it attracts. Unlike the Europe of the early 1950s, there is no vision that places refugee protection high on the agenda of states other than when it coincides with foreign policy interests and does not aggravate public perception in the host communities. Unless governments sponsor and publish the necessary research and then lead an informed public debate, there is a real risk that the myths will have an ever-increasing hold on policy.

NOTES

1. Richard Black (2000) Breaking the Convention: The Study of 'Illegal Migration,'" Khalid Koser (2000) "The Smuggling of Asylum Seekers into Western Europe: Contradictions, Conundrums and Dilemmas," John Morrison (2000) "The Smuggling and Trafficking of Refugees into Europe: The Endgame in European Asylum Policy," Aninia Nadig (2000) "Human Smuggling Seen Through the Lens of International Relations Theories." References in parentheses throughout this chapter refer to these four papers.

2. Ghosh B., *Huddled Masses, Uncertain Shores* (Den Haag: Martinus Nijhoff Publishers, 1998) preface.

3. Article 31.1 of the 1951 Geneva Refugee Convention reads: "The Contracting States shall not impose penalties, on account of their illegal entry or presence, on refugees who, coming directly from a territory where their life or freedom was threatened in the sense of Article 1, or are present in their territory without authorization, provided they present themselves without delay to the authorities and show good cause for their illegal entry or presence. (Text: 189 *UNTS* 150)

4. There is, for example, the "legal" entry with a falsified passport.

5. UN Convention against Transnational Organized Crime, annex III, Protocol against the Smuggling of Migrants by Land, Sea, and Air, Article 3. www.uncjin.org/Documents/Conventions/dcatoc/final_documents_2/convention_eng.pdf

6. UN Convention against Transnational Organized Crime, annex II, Protocol to Prevent, Suppress, and Punish Trafficking in Persons, Especially Women and Children, Article 3.

7. Koser paper at note 1.

8. Morrison, John. "The Cost of Survival: The Trafficking of Refugees to the UK," British Refugee Council, London, (1998).

9. Black paper at note 1.

13

The Fight against Migrant Smuggling: Migration Containment over Refugee Protection

François Crépeau

This chapter intends to demonstrate, using the 2000 Palermo Protocol against the smuggling of migrants and Canadian examples, that the fight against migrant smuggling uses essentially repressive means, which shows a simplistic understanding of the phenomenon, can prove dangerous for the migrants, and completely disregards the protection needs of the refugees.

In Palermo, in December 2000, states adopted the United Nations Convention against Transnational Organized Crime.[1] Two protocols supplement this new instrument: one on the trafficking in persons, especially women and children[2] (signed by eighty-one countries), and one on the smuggling of migrants[3] (signed by seventy-eight countries). The negotiation of the convention and protocols took less than two years, which shows that countries were generally in agreement on the objectives, principles, and means to be adopted.[4] The will to have the adoption of such Convention and Protocols coincide with the "Millennium Assembly" demonstrated the symbolic weight these instruments carry.

The protocol against the smuggling of migrants is aimed at combating what all countries (including all refugee-receiving countries) qualify as a plague: uncontrolled immigration that is not dictated by the needs and interests of the receiving state and can put at risk its security and stability. If the preoccupation is very legitimate, the means provided for are illustrative of the very paradoxical situation we are in. Canada is illustrative of this paradox.

The paradox is the following:

—Canadians pride themselves on their humanitarian tradition and the number of refugees who have become part of the fabric of Canadian society;
—at the same time, Canada closes each and every crack through which refugees may arrive in the country on their own to find protection.

This paradox was not, at least until (last) 11 September 2001, readily acknowledged. As a refugee-receiving country, Canada's officials would not publicly say that they were actively trying to prevent refugees from coming to Canada. They would argue that all the government wanted was to curb illegal migrations, not mentioning the fact that a good part of this migration is made up of refugees (i.e., persons in need of protection who cannot find any regular means of obtaining this protection).

It is remarkable that half the asylum applicants in Canada are recognized as refugees. In Europe, this rate is lower, often because the definition of a refugee is interpreted very narrowly, excluding, for example, refugees from countries torn by civil war. But, in most European countries, if one adds up all recognized refugees with those who are not so recognized but are still granted temporary protection or humanitarian status (like the Bosnians in Germany) and those who are not given any status but are not *refouled* (such as many Algerians in France), one comes up with a quite similar percentage: between 40 and 60 percent of all asylum-seekers are effectively deemed worthy of some protection. One out of two: a remarkable rate of success in judicial terms, one that many tax or criminal or civil litigation lawyers would envy.

States in the West have established all the barriers they could think of to prevent refugees from coming: imposition of visas for all refugee-producing countries, carrier sanctions, "short stop operations," training of airport or border police personnel, lists of "safe third countries," lists of "safe countries of origin," readmission agreements with neighboring countries forming a "buffer zone," immigration intelligence sharing, reinforced border controls, armed interventions on the high seas (such as that of the Americans against Haitian boats, or, more recently, that of the Australians against boats coming from Indonesia), military intervention (such as the sealing of the Turkish border implicitly authorized by Security Council Resolution 688 to prevent the spill over of Iraqi Kurds into Turkey after the Gulf War in April 1991), etc.[5]

Despite all these barriers, the refugees are still coming, because they need to come. Canadians, like everyone worldwide, would do the same if they were in the same situation—as indeed many of our own forefathers have done.

THE PROTOCOL AGAINST THE SMUGGLING OF MIGRANTS IS ESSENTIALLY REPRESSIVE

Most asylum-seekers entering Europe do so nowadays with the help of smuggling rings.[6] The same seems to be true for Canada[7]. It would not be surprising that this was true also in many other parts of the world. Most other doors are closed to refugees.

We can decide to ignore the situation and treat all the asylum-seekers as frauds, as a Canadian immigration official did, a few years ago, stating publicly at a conference of the Canadian Council on International Law, said publicly that not 10 percent of all "self-selected migrants" in Canada need protection, and not 10 percent of that 10 percent need the protection of Canada. The 1 percent result flies in the face of the decade-long work of the Immigration and Refugee Board.[8]

We can also take the cynical approach and wish that the Supreme Court would reverse the "wrong-headed Singh decision," whereby "the judges went so far . . . as to extend Charter protection to refugee claimants upon their arrival in Canada,"[9] as if "human" rights, were meant to be restricted to certain categories of human beings only.

The Palermo Protocol deals with illegal migration in a more hypocritical way. The drafters portray the smuggled migrants as potential "victims," in order to obtain the consent of public opinion to a major crackdown on the smugglers. The fact that this protocol is parallel to the one on trafficking in persons enhances this profile. However, the facts do not seem to sustain this approach, as, in most cases, the smuggling is a service handled very "professionally," without violence, and to the satisfaction of the "client":

> With simple delivery the OC group's role ends with the delivery of the individual safely within the target country or the successful attainment of whatever stage of the journey they are handling. The vast majority of migrant trafficking transactions are understood to involve simple delivery.[10]

This confusion has been largely amplified since 11 September 2001, when national security considerations were added to the debate and suggestions were made that all these smugglers and their "cargo" could be terrorists.[11]

The real objective of the international cooperation to combat migrant smuggling, which has been formalized through the Protocol, can quite clearly be read between the lines of the instrument. I would argue that the refugee-receiving countries are trying to strengthen their strategy of migration containment, more than they are trying to incriminate the individuals who actually commit the acts, which are now heavily criminalized. The protection and the assistance of the victims was not the first objective, except where it can contribute to the main objective (i.e., to deter the smugglers to even try to illegally introduce migrants across western/northern borders).

This can be seen in that, in paragraph E of the initial draft preamble of the protocol,[12] states did not hide that their central preoccupation is the reduction of the pressure that illegal migrations create on the refugee determination systems:

> Concerned that the smuggling of migrants may lead to the misuse of established procedures for immigration, including those for seeking asylum.

The disappearance of this sentence in the final text of the protocol as adopted seems quite significant of what the states do not want to reveal as to the motives of their endeavor.

On the other hand, guarantees in favor of the smuggled migrants have been included in the protocol. Article 5 states that:

> Migrants shall not become liable to criminal prosecution under this Protocol for the fact of having been the object of conduct set forth in article 6 of this Protocol.

Article 19 provides that

> Nothing in this Protocol shall affect the other rights, obligations and responsibilities of states and individuals under international law, including international humanitarian law and international human rights law and, in particular, the 1951 Convention and the 1967 Protocol Relating to the Status of Refugees and the principle of *non-refoulement* as contained therein.

However, these guarantees did not exist in the initial draft versions of the protocol and were only added at the ninth negotiating session, thanks to a forceful joint intervention by UNHCHR, IOM, UNHCR, and UNICEF.[13] In effect, the protection of the migrant was not initially the essential preoccupation of the negotiators.

There are no other meaningful measures of protection specific to the migrant in this protocol, apart from a general rule of protection of the rights of and assistance to the migrants and of consideration for the special needs of women and children (article 16), which simply state the obvious obligation to protect the human rights of these persons. If one compares it to the protocol against trafficking in persons, especially women and children, the difference is striking, in that the latter contains numerous clauses dedicated to protection issues. It is clear that, even if the drafters of the protocol against the smuggling of migrants rhetorically said that the migrant is a "victim" of the smugglers, he is not awarded the status of a victim, with meaningful protection and assistance measures. He is more the "object" of the smuggling than its "victim," as is clearly said in article 16 of the protocol, which precisely deals with protection issues and does not use the word "victim." When we compare the measures of the protocol aimed at containing migrations and those aimed at protecting migrants, as in the annexed table 13.1, we can clearly see the difference in the number of provisions and in their precision.

This absence of a real and effective protection objective is also exemplified by state practice following the adoption of the protocol. In effect, for example, Canada has not even incorporated the specific protective measures in its new Immigration and Refugee Protection Act,[14] that contains all the repressive apparatus provided for fighting migrant smuggling in the protocol.

Far from trying to protect "victims" of criminalized smugglers, the protocol really provides states with measures to combat illegal migration:

1. The criminalization of smuggling activities (article 6). Canada has included this in its new Immigration and Refugee Protection Act and provided for the possibility of imprisonment for a maximum of two years on summary conviction, or fourteen years on indictment for smuggling less than ten persons, and of imprisonment for life for smuggling a group of ten persons or more or for disembarking illegal migrants at sea.[15] When one compares sexual assault with a weapon, which triggers a maximum of fourteen years,[16] and the facilitation of the crossing of a border, without harm to persons or damage to property, which can trigger a life sentence, one may think that the latter is

Table 13.1. Comparison between the Measures of the Protocol Aimed at Containing Migrations and Those Aimed at Protecting Migrants

Measures Aimed at Containing Migrations	Measures Aimed at Protecting Migrants
• Criminalization of migrant smuggling (Article 6) • Measures against the smuggling of migrants by sea (Article 8) • Information exchange (Article 10) • Border measures (Article 11) — Strengthened controls — Obligations and sanctions for carriers — Denial of entry for smugglers — Strengthened cooperation between border control agencies • Security and control of documents (Article 12) • Training and technical cooperation (Article 14) • Prevention measures (Article 15) • Cooperation on repression (Article 17) • Return of smuggled migrants (Article 18)	• Protection and assistance measures (Article 16) — Measures to preserve and protect the rights of smuggled migrants — Measures against violence — Assistance to migrants whose life and safety is in danger — Measures to take into account the special needs of women and children

not proportionate to a reasonable scale of penalties. Even the solicitor general of Canada acknowledged that, among all organized crime activities, migrant smuggling did not have a significant violence generation impact, as can be seen from annexed table 13.2.

2. The universalization of the obligation of commercial carriers of persons to control the travel documents of passengers (article 11, paragraphs 3, 4). This measure, fairly common in national legislations, was only provided for, until then, in international law, in the Schengen Convention of 1990.[17]

3. The criminalization of the procuring, providing, possessing, but also the producing of "fraudulent travel or identity documents" (article 6). From the point of view of the protection of refugees, this is a real threat, since we know that, because of the visa requirements and carrier sanctions in place, refugees are obliged to consciously use false documents if they want to cross the border or board a plane, in order to escape. Canada has expressly included more precise provisions on this in the new Immigration and Refugee Protection Act,[18] specifying that it is forbidden to possess or use documents for the purpose of contravening the Act. This is especially troublesome when one considers the heavy sanctions provided for in case of smuggling. There is at least one case before Canadian courts where a permanent resident in Canada who used false documents to help his brother's wife and child escape and

Table 13.2.   Impact Ranking of Organized-Crime-Related Activities

OC Activity	Social-Political	Economic-Commercial	Health & Safety	Violence Generation	Environmental
Money Laundering	***	*	—	—	—
Illicit Drugs	***	***	**	***	*
Environmental Crime	*	***	***	—	***
Selected Contraband	***	**	**	*	—
Economic Crime	**	***	—	*	—
Migrant Trafficking	**	*	*	*	—
Counterfeit Products	*	**	*	*	—
Motor Vehicle Theft	—	**	—	*	—

Legend: —   Little or no impact
          *   Some impact
          **   Significant impact
          *** Very significant impact

Source: Samuel D. Porteous, *Organized Crime Impact Study*, Ottawa, Office of the Solicitor General of Canada, 1998. www.sgc.gc.ca/EPub/Pol/e1998orgcrim/e1998orgcrim.htm

Comment from the author of the chapter: in the report from which this table is extracted, it is clear from the context that the words "migrant trafficking" are used to mean what is called in this article "migrant smuggling" (corresponding to the definition of the protocol against the smuggling of migrants) and not what is called "migrant trafficking" (corresponding to the definition of the protocol against trafficking in persons, especially women and children).

enter the country is being prosecuted for possessing and procuring false documents, while the asylum application of the sister-in-law has not yet been adjudicated. In this case, the accused has been offered a plea bargain by the Crown: if he pleads guilty he will receive a suspended sentence. The Crown wants to secure a conviction, establishing its right to prosecute all persons who participate in the illegal introduction of a migrant, including those who help real refugees for humanitarian reasons.[19]

4. The *establishment as a criminal offense of the "participating as an accomplice"* in the smuggling activities (article 4.2.b). This language allows the state authorities to cast a wide net if necessary, and reinforces the possibility (mentioned immediately above) for state authorities to prosecute all "accomplices," even family members acting in good faith for humanitarian purposes, as any of us would do for a sister or a nephew.

5. The fact that the smuggling activities take place in circumstances (a) that endanger, or are likely to endanger, the lives or safety of the migrants concerned; or (b) that entail inhuman or degrading treatment, including for exploitation, of such migrants, are *simply aggravating circumstances* to the offenses already established (article 6, paragraph 3). The new Canadian Immigration and Refugee Protection Act includes these aggravating circumstances provisions. But the fact that the illegal entry is procured for profit is not part of the definition of the smuggling activity (see annexed table 13.3): it is also merely considered as an aggravating circumstance. Again, Canadian authorities want to ascertain that smuggling for humanitarian purposes by NGOs or family members can be and will be prosecuted.

6. The *sharing of immigration intelligence information* seems to be a key component of the protection scheme (article 10). This is very problematic in terms of privacy. We have seen the recent Canadian Act to Amend the Aeronautics Act (Bill C-44),[20] which was enacted in answer to a new American exigency and whereby Canada authorized the communication to foreign authorities of all passenger information, includ-

Table 13.3. Definition of Migrant Smuggling

Protocol against the smuggling of migrants, Article 3	Immigration and Refugee Protection Act, Article 117
"Smuggling in migrants" shall mean the procurement, in order to obtain, directly or indirectly, a financial or other material benefit, of the illegal entry of a person into a state party of which the person is not a national or permanent resident.	"Organizing entry into Canada": No person shall knowingly organize, induce, aid, or abet the coming into Canada of one or more persons who are not in possession of a visa, passport, or other document required by this Act.

ing that which it would be forbidden to divulge in Canada (for which it had to expressly derogate to the Personal Information Protection and Electronic Documents Act). The act limits the use of that information only by other Canadian departments if that information is reintroduced into Canada: foreign authorities to which they are communicated can use it as they please and retransmit it if necessary to yet other aeronautics authorities. If the example of the Schengen Information System (SIS) is to be followed, we can expect a huge database of personal information, that is very little supervised and virtually unchallengeable under domestic and international law.[21]

7. The *return "without undue or unreasonable delay" of the smuggled migrant* remains the ultimate objective (article 18). Not much protection is offered to the individual in the protocol itself to prevent this outcome. The logic seems to be that it should not be, since the objective of the protocol is not to protect individuals but to contain flows. A significant protection of the migrant would imply taking the time to know what his protection needs are, and this would run contrary to the speedy resolution of the case envisaged by the states in the protocol.

THE REPRESSIVE APPROACH IS SIMPLISTIC AND MAY BE DANGEROUS FOR MIGRANTS

Two distressing grey areas, which, to date, have not attracted much attention show that the repressive approach adopted by states in their fight against migrant smuggling is simplistic and may be dangerous for the migrants themselves.

Firstly, *how does one concretely distinguish a smuggled individual from a trafficked person?* Politically, it was important to associate the two protocols to make sure that the one against smuggling would benefit from the natural legitimacy of the one against trafficking, even if, in their texts, as we have mentioned, there is a huge difference in the measures of protection offered to the "clientele."

Even if we took this distinction as a clear one, nothing is provided in either of the two protocols, nor in the new Canadian legislation, to make sure that the two situations will effectively be distinguished in the field. The consequences, in terms of protection measures, are very significant: the trafficked will need specific protective measures if she is not to fall prey to the same (prostitution) ring when returned, the smuggled will need protection against the state of origin when there is a risk of persecution. In both situations, the real victims should be identified and effectively protected. In most cases, this will require time and energy: gaining the confidence of the person so as to allow her to tell her whole story will generally necessitate the intervention of an NGO, a social assistant or lawyer, and might not be effectuated "without unreasonable delay" (depending on the interpretation of what "unreasonable" means). If protection of the persons is the real objective, receiving states will have to put in place all the measures necessary to ensure it. Otherwise, it will be clear that the only protection at stake is that of the state against illegal migration.[22]

Secondly, *smugglers do save lives,* despite the fact that smuggling rings are effectively very often part of mafias, which control other types of illegal activities (prostitution, arms trafficking, drug trafficking, smuggling of goods, etc.). As the Canadian Council for Refugees said:

> People smuggling is undeniably a nasty business. It costs untold numbers of people their lives (drowned, suffocated, shot, frozen or crushed to death). Many others are raped or suffer violence and traumatic experiences. People are routinely cheated out of thousands of dollars. After a painful journey, some find themselves detained and deported back home. [...] People smuggling, despite its evils, has also been life-giving. It has made it possible for significant numbers of people to flee persecution and reach a place of asylum when no government was willing or able to offer an escape route. It has allowed them to exercise their human right to seek and to enjoy in other countries asylum from persecution (Article 14, Universal Declaration of Human Rights). For others, smugglers have offered a way out of a situation of misery and an opportunity for a new life of dignity. Even some of the people who are trafficked, knowing the wrongs of their situation of bondage, may still prefer it to what they left behind, either for themselves or for what it enables them to do for family members. This of course does not in any way justify the abuses perpetrated by the traffickers. But it is relevant to any discussion about solutions to the problem of trafficking.[23]

History abounds with situations where "smugglers" have allowed individuals to escape death or violence. In the recent past, many German Jews gave all they had to smugglers in order to escape the Nazi inferno, Spanish Republicans often did the same to cross the Pyrenees, French Resistance fighters crossed the demarcation line the same way, Eastern Europeans jumped the Iron Curtain with the help of paid smugglers, and most Indo-Chinese boatpeople were able to embark only after paying a heavy price to the boat owner. Most of them would never have made it, had the Protocol been in place and effectively applied.

Nothing in the protocol, apart from the affirmation that international obligations will be respected, provides for concrete measures that would allow those in need of protection, including refugees, to obtain this protection despite the antismuggling arsenal deployed by the states.

People smuggling has its roots in the border control measures of our states, inasmuch as alcohol smuggling stemmed out of the prohibition policies. The word "smuggling" is used to equate symbolically the smuggling of persons with the traditional smuggling of goods: as we have said, the smuggled migrants are said to be the "object" of the smuggling, not victims. This is precisely done to devoid the concept of its intricate human elements, in situations where we should insist on the vulnerability of persons who need to escape violence and have little other choice than to use the services of those who can, for a lot of money, take them where safety lies.

CONCLUSION

The reasons that set people on the go, with or without smugglers, are social, economic, and political. The differences in prosperity, peace, and respect for human rights are the driving force of these movements of persons, as they have been throughout history for our ancestors.

Smuggling is but a symptom that a demand for free movement of persons is mounting, as a companion to the free movement of goods, capital, and services. Treating these issues only through an escalation of repressive mechanisms, as is provided for in the 2000 Palermo Protocol against the smuggling of migrants, will not lower the pressure: as John Morrison has amply demonstrated,[24] it will only exacerbate the tensions, fuel international criminality and result in more rights violations for the migrants themselves, by the smugglers, as well as by our own national authorities.

Protection of the person should be the central objective of any migration control policy. Since we have, in article 13 of the Universal Declaration of Human Rights of 1946, proclaimed that it was a fundamental human right (and this goes for "them" as much as for "us"), allowing individuals to "seek" asylum should prevail.

NOTES

A version of this paper was presented at the Canadian Council for International Law, Ottawa, 20 October 2001, and will be published in the Proceedings of the meeting. The author thanks his excellent research assistants, Philippe Tremblay, LLB, LLM, member of the Quebec Bar, former Protection Officer for UNHCR in Rwanda, former Coordinator of *Centre d'études sur le droit international et la mondialisation* (CEDIM-UQAM), former ICRC delegate to Colombia, and Estibalitz Jimenez, PhD student at the School of Criminology at the University of Montreal, as well as Ms. Cecilia Thompson for her precious work on this version of the text.

1. United Nations Convention against Transnational Organized Crime, full text available on the web site of the United Nations Office for Drug Control and Crime Prevention (UNODCCP): www.uncjin.org/Documents/Conventions/dcatoc/final_documents_2/convention_eng.pdf

2. Protocol to Prevent, Suppress and Punish Trafficking in Persons, Especially Women and Children, supplementing the United Nations Convention against Transnational Organized Crime, full text available on the web site of the UNODCCP:

www.uncjin.org/Documents/Conventions/dcatoc/final_documents_2/convention_%20traff_eng.pdf

3. Protocol against the Smuggling of Migrants by Land, Air and Sea, supplementing the United Nations Convention against Transnational Organized Crime (hereafter called the "Protocol"), full text available on the web site of the UNODCCP: www.uncjin.org/Documents/Conventions/dcatoc/final_documents_2/convention_smug_eng.pdf.

4. See all the successive drafts of the Convention and Protocols on the website of the United Nations Crime and Justice Information Network at: www.uncjin.org/Documents/documents.html.

5. See, *inter alia*: Crépeau, F., and Tremblay, P. "Les stratégies nord-américaines en matière d'asile," in LEGOUX, Luc (dir.), *La place de l'asile politique dans l'immigration*, 2001 (to be published); Crépeau, F., Carlier, J. Y. "Intégration régionale et politique migratoir —Le 'modèle européen' entre coopération et communautarisation," *Journal du droit international*, no. 4, (1999), 953–1019; Crépeau, F. "International Cooperation on Interdiction of Asylum Seekers—A Global Perspective," in Canadian Council for Refugees, *Interdicting Refugees*, May 1998, 7–20; Crock, M. "Echoes of the Old Countries or Brave New Worlds? Legal Responses to Refugees and Asylum Seekers in Australia and New Zealand," *Revue québécoise de droit international* 14 (2001), pp. 55–89.

6. Morrison, J. *The Trafficking and Smuggling of Refugees—The End Game in European Asylum Policy?* Prepublication edition, July 2000, 104 pages. The full text is available on the UNHCR's Evaluation & Policy Analysis Unit website at: www.unhcr.ch/evaluate/reports/traffick.pdf

7. See, Porteous, S. D. *Organized Crime Impact Study*, Ottawa: Office of the Solicitor General of Canada, 1998. www.sgc.gc.ca/EPub/Pol/e1998orgcrim/e1998orgcrim.htm. The number of asylum-seekers having used the services of smugglers to enter Canada in 1996 was estimated at between 8,000 and 16,000, out of a total of 26,000. However, the basis for these calculations are rough, to say the least.

8. Grant, B. "Globalism and Regionalism: The Challenge of Population Movements," in Proceedings of the 1995 Conference of the Canadian Council of International Law, *Globalism and Regionalism: Options for the 21st Century*, Ottawa: Canadian Council on International Law, 161–167. Brian Grant was a senior policy advisor with Immigration Canada. This oral comment was somewhat watered down in the written version.

9. Simpson, J., "Finally, the Liberals wake up to the new reality," *Globe & Mail*, Toronto, 17 Oct. 2001, A15. The *Canadian Charter of Rights and Freedoms* is part of the Constitution Act 1982. It allows any person in Canada whose rights and freedoms are affected by any law to challenge the constitutionality of this law on the basis that it is inconsistent with the Charter and eventually have it declared, to the extent of the inconsistency, of no force or effect. In *Singh v. Canada (Minister of Employment and Immigration)*, [1985] 1 SCR 177, an asylum-seeker obtained that the asylum mechanism of the Canadian Immigration Act be declared unconstitutional on the basis that, in a proceeding that can affect such fundamental rights as the right to life, liberty, and security, it is essential that the individual be able to explain her case in a proper hearing. This judgment paved the way for the creation of the Immigration and Refugee Board in 1989.

10. See, Porteous, S. D., op. cit. Note that, in the report, the words "migrant trafficking" are used to mean "migrant smuggling." See annexed table 13.2.

11. "The Committee feels it is crucial that Canada work with other countries to continually develop new tools and methods for combating organized crime, especially people smuggling and trafficking. Clearly, this is a global issue requiring widespread cooperation as the proceeds of such activities are often used to finance terrorism in many countries. The new Immigration and Refugee Protection Act will assist in this respect through new offenses targeting the proceeds of crime, as well as significantly increased penalties for human smuggling and trafficking." (*Hands Across The Border: Working Together at our Shared Border and Abroad to Ensure Safety, Security and Efficiency*, Report of the Standing Committee on Citizenship and Immigration, Joe Fontana, M.P., Chair, December 2001).

12. This paragraph can still be found in the draft version submitted at the eleventh meeting (2–27 October 200) of the Ad Hoc Committee on the Elaboration of the Convention, but will disappear in its final report to the General Assembly dated 2 November 2000(A/55/383) and in the text adopted in Palermo.

13. Ad Hoc Committee on the Elaboration of a Convention against Transnational Organised Crime, Eighth Session, *Note by the United Nations High Commissioner for Human Rights, International Organization for Migration, United Nations High Commissioner for Refugees, and the United Nations Children's Fund on the Protocols Concerning Migrant Smuggling and Trafficking in Persons*, Vienna, 21 February–3 March, 2000. Text at: www.uncjin.org/Documents/Conventions/dcatoc/8session/27e.pdf

14. Immigration and Refugee Protection Act (Bill C-11), S.C. 2001, chapter 27, passed by the House of Commons on 13 June 2001, Royal Assent on 1 November 2001, entry into force expected in June 2002, Article 117ss. Text at: www.cic.gc.ca/english/pdffiles/pub/C-11_4.pdf

15. Immigration and Refugee Protection Act (Bill C-11), Article 117(3).

16. Criminal Code, R.S. 1985, chapter C-46, Article 271ss.

17. Schengen Convention, of 19 June 1990, Article 26. Text at: www.consilium.eu.int/ejn/data/vol_c/9_autres_textes/schengen/indexen.html

18. Immigration and Refugee Protection Act (Bill C-11), Article 122ss.

19. The author has been consulted on the case.

20. Act to Amend the Aeronautics Act (Bill C-44), S.C. 2001, chapter 38, passed by the House of Commons on 6 December 2001, Royal Assent on 18 December 2001. Text at: www.parl.gc.ca/37/1/parlbus/chambus/house/bills/government/C-44/C-44_4/90175bE.html

21. See our comments on the S.I.S. in: Crépeau, F. and Carlier, J. Y., op. cit., 972–977.

22. "Yet very little thought seems to have gone into how on the ground people who are being trafficked are to be identified. If the authorities have no means of determining among the intercepted or arrested who is being trafficked, how do they propose to grant them the measures of protection they are committing themselves to? Conversely, where states in fact use the fear of trafficking as a motivation for more punitive measures, it is those who are not being trafficked that have an interest in having the determination made. This is a real dilemma facing Chinese nationals in detention in Canada, where release is being denied based on the hypothesis that the individuals will disappear into the

hands of the presumed traffickers if released (despite the fact that there is no specific evidence that the individuals were being trafficked)" (Canadian Council for Refugees, *Migrant Smuggling and Trafficking in Persons*, 20 February 2000. Full text in the CCR website at: www.web.net/~ccr/traffick.htm).

23. Canadian Council for Refugees, Ibid.

24. Morrison, J., op. cit.

14

Medical Anthropology in the Service of Forcefully Migrating Populations: Current Boundaries, Future Horizons, and Possible Delusions

Sanja Špoljar-Vržina

Why medical anthropology? Why anthropology? Although anthropology has been proved, in the last decades, to be more than a useful conductor of articulating at least some of the problems of forced migrants,[1] I see these questions as being of continuing value and importance, if we are to focus upon the future benefits that our disciplines can bring to the challenging problems of forcefully migrating populations. Furthermore, it is especially worthwhile to pose them after having been reminded that anthropology has been one of the dominating disciplines of forced migration and refugee studies scholarship over the past twenty years.[2] A group of papers on medical anthropology presented at the conference from which this volume is derived were intended as a testing ground for this discipline and its capacity for interdisciplinarity. On reflection it seems that the papers[3] might also have, erroneously, been interpreted as a proclamation of the dominance of anthropology. This mistaken view should be rectified, and that is one aim of this chapter. Although the majority of examples presented in this paper refer to refugees from the former Yugoslavia, they portray a much wider problem. Today, more than ever, there is a need for comprehending anthropology as a discipline that provides more than simple translations and interpretations of cultures. Although my own work can testify to a decade of the "Balkan" misrepresentations, the strongest hallmark in that direction has been demonstrated through the process of questioning, self-critiquing, and introspection expressed within the anthropological discipline for the past twenty plus years. This *spiritus movens* of engaged anthropological thinking in forced migration studies has been best reflected and recognizable in papers confronting the methodologies of usage,[4] the policies that are to be sensitized,[5] in engendering the forced migration knowledge and practice,[6] or testifying of the ways in which the approach to the (mental) health problems can (and must) be interdisciplinary.[7] Overall, what is expressed through the mentioned work is a confirmation, in the best possible way, of what Keesing[8] discussed when warning that we must strive to gain a greater self-consciousness of the ways we address societies, their cultural meanings, and *real humans*[9] within them. Indeed, the quest to understand any problem of forced migrants encompasses the need to include ourselves in the *real humans,* being aware that we share knowledge that is *distributed and controlled.*

However, based on the experiences of past decades we must honestly conclude that the results of induced sensitivities frequently fell short of the enthusiastic leap that anthropology made towards other disciplines and vice versa. In a valuable evaluation of the current medical discourse regarding refugees Weinstein[10] gave an American case example and concluded that refugee health policy, being based on the policy of exclusion and protection (of the host population) is solidified in unchanged stereotypes about foreigners that have not changed over the last 200 years. In a situation of such restricted health care possibilities it is not surprising that little attention is paid towards knowledge of social and cultural factors about the refugees going beyond the basics. Not to mention the understanding of influences upon symptom presentations or care seeking.[11] Yet the seriousness of his presented data goes powerfully beyond the position of inactive despair and into a possibly constructive critique. Weinstein very clearly presents the unacknowledged *circulus vitiosus* expressed by those that should include the provision of social and health services into refugee protection. He warns:

> The Universal Declaration of Human Rights is based upon the concept of human dignity and I would suggest that the dignity of refugees is compromised along with their right to health when we provide limited access to health care and when we develop health programs based upon limited knowledge.

To further add to the possibilities of this contemplation we must return to Keesing[12] and ask ourselves about the faith of "the meanings we create together, the texts we write collectively" or the "social worlds in which we create them" that never cease to be "multiple, complex, open, and changing." How does the (anthropological) knowledge about cultural and social factors get distributed and controlled and at what point does this positioning bring us back to the basics of discussions that all disciplines should share—about the humanism that should prevail? The critical question is does it prevail?

HISTORICAL FLASHBACKS AND FUTURE RESPONSIBILITIES

When contemplating the kind of interdisciplinary action needed nowadays in forced migration and refugee studies it is apparent that a greater involvement of disciplines such as political science, economics, development, security studies, and law would be tremendously appreciated.[13] Certainly so, it is striking that these disciplines are so underrepresented and that many domains of refugee studies are, while being in need of reevaluation, left untouched by critical scientific implementations of these disciplines, that would lead to faster change. From the scientific point it was over three decades ago that Gjessing (1968)[14] wrote about the *Social Responsibility of the Social Scientist* and underlined the ambivalence with which the outcomes of politics and economy influence the problems of humanity. Of course, when inviting all to join and *"reapproach the humanities,"* Gjessing was heavily leaning on the confessions made by one of the greatest modern time intellectuals, Claude Levi-Strauss,[15] in his honest appraisal of the discipline he was a cofounder. Early on, he described the vices of anthropological thinking foreseeing the essence of nowadays-globalistic political and economical stances by remarking: "Anthropology is daughter to this era of violence: its capacity to assess more objectively the facts pertaining to the human condition reflects, on the epistemological level, a state of affairs in which one part of mankind treated the other as an object."

Four decades have passed since Levi-Strauss wrote this. The challenging question of what is the changing fate of the *other* in "our" time of violence remains. The debates over who is the *other* deepened. Questions that concerned scientists shared decades ago swirl our emotions in our numerous attempts to grasp our present (scientific) time. It is seemingly hard to differentiate the *era of violence,* mentioned by Levi-Strauss and the *violence* studied by Malkki,[16] Kleinman, Das and Lock,[17] or Scheper-Hughes.[18] In a very metaphorical sense of the word I am drawn to rephrase *Barth* in a much bolder way (given the strength of being an "insider") that indeed—"in such a perspective it becomes an empirical question what concepts and mental operations are used by a group of people to construct their world"[19]—and therefore why not apply this dictum to all our scientific endeavors, regardless of our "insiders" or "outsiders" positioning.

However, the problem of contesting, manipulating, and controlling anthropology's foundational categories is not only tied to the ongoing self-reflection and debates within the anthropological subdisciplines. The dangers that lie in simple translations of these concepts into other disciplines

go beyond being useful and ubiquitous, into widening the possibilities of
further misusage, manipulation, and creation of distorting reality portray-
als. This makes the work dedicated to the most vulnerable populations
even more endangered since its focus continuously creates new paradigms, not necessarily aimed at rectifying the distortions that materialize
in interdisciplinary efforts. The case in point to confirm this process is
connected to the refugees from former Yugoslavia and their shared identities through which they are not only categorized in a distinctive culture
pertaining to the "Balkan history," but are also classified into a "culture" of
postcommunist countries. The significance of the two is indisputable,
while their value and importance is never unified in the search of learning
the specific cultural meanings and contests that might endorse new un-
derstandings beneficial to the populations. The understanding that one
belongs to a country in transition to which one must return is detached
from one's belonging to a former Yugoslavian state from which one had
fled. The emotional processes are perceived to be isolated from the historical events. After a war in the heart of Europe we have entered into a
heartless process of stabilization and transition of the region, in which its
significance is only weighed by the *stability* it can bring to the EU.
Refugees and ex-refugees (in the return process) become important factors of this *stabilization* and are treated as carriers of the political decision
rather than individuals with a will of their own. Being a refugee from the
Balkans is painful—it encompasses the avoidance of being glued to the
many identities that are projected onto one's selfhood.

Significantly, the papers of both Fox[20] and Weinstein[21] gave a careful
analysis of how to counteract the consequences of knowing too much (in
the wrong way) or too little of one's cultural and social background. They
have both tried to go one step beyond the opinion of one of the leading
human rights activists, the late Jonathan Mann, in which health policies
and programs are seen as potentially discriminatory for marginalized or
stigmatized groups.[22] Weinstein argued that our knowledge of the impact
that the refugee experience has on health runs the risk of losing its momentum. Seldom is our focus adjusted towards grasping both—the physi-
ological and the social suffering of one's flight experience. We could conclude that this too joins the battlefield of reflective chaos. Again, Barth
describes these academic urges with a word of advice and cautions that
when grasping to access other "human conceptual worlds we end up in a
hall of mirrors when trying to represent categories and concepts different
from our own by means of our own language and concepts. . . . In a hall
of mirrors, one needs to move with considerable circumspection,"[23]—he
says, to which I wish to add that even if we do engage with the culture of
another in a realistic way, the restrictions of every discipline has it halls of
mirrors. Thus the levels on which misconceptions can occur are many and

nonetheless influenced by the *professional cultures* we come from, as well.

THE PROCESS OF NEGATIVE MIRRORING
AND THE ROLE OF MEDICAL ANTHROPOLOGY

What are the consequences of this mirroring of our social responsibilities as scientists? Superficially, the concern over responsibilities can be confirmed through a growing number of studies dedicated to suffering, violence, exploitation, force, and recovery.[24] Although these studies compensate for the negation of experience that previous general concepts (such as in the case of "culture contact" or "acculturation")[25] left unsaid, in order to be operable and useful they must also be tied to a better understanding of the on-the-ground politics, economics, history, and overall social interactions they strive to present. In the words of Eastmond,[26] "power and morality are, not unexpectedly, issues which are at the heart of the experience of people living in the shadow of violent and dramatic events of war and forced migration, sometimes also at the social margin of their hosts," and furthermore our caution should be focused at the fact that "the representations of suffering may also be a site for the workings of power relations; the representations of suffering and their moral force may be claimed or contested by different social actors or interests." Precisely, some of the general concepts that entered into forced migration studies through anthropology tend to be used whenever a reliable and easy to handle cognition map of the process of dramatic migrating is needed.[27] On the level of our own everyday work the very terms we use should repeatedly be recognized for the countermeanings they carry, as well as denounced for the fallacies they end up representing. Medical anthropology started the debate over the process of this kind of mirroring a long time ago. The state of the observer becoming the observed, in the quest to understand the many contextual layers we socially constitute, provides a safeguard of sorts against forcing individuals and populations into culturally expected roles. For instance, the IDP's/returnees within Croatia represent a very heterogeneous group, yet the best known IDP's/returnees are men from Vukovar since they are the ones that became a synonym for being the victims of PTSD. This type of categorization and recognition of the prolonged effects of war on only one level is (and was) further deepened through a lively interest that the international community shows for mental health problems. The feeling that this aroused (and still does) among local professionals is eloquently expressed by a Slovenian colleague, Mikuš-Kos[28]:

> The narrowing of the psychological effects of war on PTSD, the neglect of misery, humiliation, sorrow, social uprooting, loss of social supportive network and

many other processes connected with war and exile, started to irritate local mental health workers. Maybe the "PTSD madness" as we used to say sometimes in Former Yugoslavia territories contributed sometimes even to the unjust rejection of the PTSD concept.

Unfortunately, the mentioned irritation grew stronger together with the awakening knowledge about the budgets that were created around the whole process of international support, which demonstrated such an unbalanced relation between useful knowledge and irrational fund spending. It is also unfortunate that if asked today, many colleagues would agree that the period of awakening to these hallmarks of economic globality has never ended.

The joint formulation of learned lessons lies not only in implementing them within one's scientific acts, own discipline, and the conquest of interdisciplinary territory, but in stretching these towards dialogues that prevent further misunderstandings.[29] Again, these thoughts would be on the path of easy simplifications towards interdisciplinarity if not coupled with the need for acknowledging the confrontations on the level of one's discipline. Interestingly the trail of misused anthropological concepts is evident and easily recognizable. Through the reminiscing of a Croatian psychologist the expressed misunderstandings of her international colleagues can be divided into two domains of predominant approaches—that of the *politics of culture* and that of the *politics of suffering*. Her reactions are a direct response to a text that is part of a teaching module regarding the *refugee experience*, presented by a colleague she closely worked with in the Croatian War years.[30] The high tide of her *"local"* response is when she speaks about the problem of cultural sensitiveness and describes the feeling of being a victim of its deviated perceptions in the following way:

> When British or French experts complain that I am too Westernised, this concern is probably reflecting their own colonialism and regrets about not finding local tribes in the Former Yugoslavia to give them the opportunity to be "culturally sensitive." In fact their complaint is an example of a real lack of cultural sensitivity.

The mentioned examples help draw our attention towards the continuously negated fact that the implementation of psychosocial projects in the "Balkan" region (and worldwide) are not only met, as planned, by the suffering people, the local professionals are also "affected" by them and live to tell the tale in numerous academic forums. Paradoxically, while a project of any sort may reach its aim in protecting the sanity and dignity of communities and populations they assist,[31] it is questionable whether they can be successful without recognizing the missing link with field-level practitioners. Furthermore, even if the links are established, the misunderstandings should be taken into serious account and worked through. Maybe this also should be included in the reasons of nonexisting evaluations of conducted programs and the anecdotal level of presenting their successfulness. After the help has been given and the funds spent, the contacts with "locals" remain ruled by the forces of power (direction of funds)[32] and ideology (heavily politicized in the majority of cases).[33]

The stripping of contexts can be variable, multiple, unpredictable and, finally, prevent any kind of international collaboration. The surprise, with which foreign professionals discover national potentials for intellectual resources, ranging from psychotherapy to building bridges and dams, is the same and confirms the overall hierarchy of power. The needy, while remaining in need of benefactors, should testify to the benefits of the global economical establishment. It is obvious that in such a framework of activities interdisciplinarity benefiting any population is an illusion. The emotions of Croatian and regional professionals are not uncalled for and also repeat the painful reality in which the "Western" and "non-Western" produce the "non-sensitive" and "sensitive" worlds. However, conditioned funding has just recently become a factor of the unproductive politicization/depoliticization sways of the programs in the south eastern European context. The prelude to this state was the fascination with the "choreography" of ethnicities, and recently added varying democratization capabilities. An examinee of mine once asked me—"*What about us—the Romanians in Slavonija?*" (In contrast to the Croats, Muslims, and Serbs he was tired of constantly hearing about).

The cumulative effects of irritation caused by experts epitomizes what refugee studies are all about—the cultures, the suffering, the emotions—all of which are claimed by concepts of the last decade, uncritically put into action. The sphere of today's academic confrontations is wide and dangerously imbued with popular stigmatizing concepts, yet still uninformed of the influence of politics upon the whole plethora of culture-sensitive approaches. For me personally, the most troublesome part in the writings (and actions) of such kind are presented in texts where whole regions and ethnicities are being qualified as having "the lack of interpersonal and group communication skills," "little knowledge of the techniques of nonviolent conflict resolution," "lacking the skills, knowledge, and attitudes of democratization,"[34] and/or overall capable of being *"far less tolerant of alterity,"*[35] etc. The dialogue becomes a debate swirling down to the basics and becomes a test ground in which similar debates of critical medical anthropology are being conducted,[36] linked to crucial health issues and presented in a way that no ignorance or misusage of the cultural meanings could dismiss. Among others, anthropologists often remind us of the necessity of further dialogues. How often they succeed in conducting them is also a matter of power battles. To paraphrase Waldron,[37] we all belong to cultural communities, have knowledge, and are all fellow humans—just like refugees.

However, being aware of the hierarchies of power we belong to—is another matter and a step possibly beyond greater ignorance.

BEYOND THE RECOGNITION OF DISTORTED PRESENTATIONS OF SUFFERING

The essentialization of "culture" gave rise to its usage in debates that involve lay individuals, academics, and practitioners alike. It has also helped in demystifying the fact that the possibilities for understanding a foreign culture depend less on our willingness to do so and more on our preparedness to handle the misunderstanding. Seldom do we become conscious of the fact that in dealing with this type of misunderstanding we need to develop a flexibility in accommodating apologies—primarily our own. It is as offensive to be denounced as being incapable of understanding another's culture as it is to being designated as a representative of a culture that is salient due to its geographical location or the ongoing violence and suffering of its people. Interestingly, we have not moved beyond making these characterizations on the basis of one's national and ethnic denominations. Yet the rightful critique should include the question: Who gets emotional over whose wrong representation? Don't we each play to many roles to pinpoint any fixed position? A colleague from former Yugoslavia, who emigrated to Sweden in 1991, told a story of his ambivalent identifying with the groups he belonged to. He was especially upset in situations where he became the translator for other refugees from former Yugoslavia with whom he had arrived. While he could easily understand the reasons why the people were unhappy with the hosts, being a doctor he could also relate to the professionals in the host country and the heavy job they took upon themselves when providing care for demanding groups, to which he himself also belonged. However, even if burdened by the emotions of both sides, he did have an opportunity of developing a greater sense of what the whole process of refugeehood was and that it included all parties equally in terms of expectations and potential apologizing for misunderstandings.

There are many ways in which we become part of the painful experiences through which refugees go. The way in which we justify the knowledge we use in helping solve their problems and protect their dignity is and should be only one—always oriented towards the benefit of those we represent in our work, research, and practice. Anthropologists are not the only ones that become entangled in the quest for defining the meanings of words, culture, and cognitive representations, as though human lives are separable from social interactions, politics, and economics.[38] It is tempting to observe, and dangerous to mistake a grip on the key as being a sign of the awareness of one's only possession in exile (a hotel room).[39] It is equally tempting to position oneself outside the cognitive maps of which we are a part and invite approaches that create areas of dominance, low self-critique, and a space of illusionary interdisciplinarity of academics and practitioners. Refugee studies have not been saved from happenings of this kind.[40] There are many illusionary spaces of interdisciplinarity into which anthropologists are invited to further explain the cultural differences, national and ethnic boundaries, or any other social pecularity.[41] In doing so they have a chance to join the fight against the *vicious cycle* they themselves have stirred up by influencing the everyday contemporary talk with anthropological concepts, such as that of culture.[42]

The dominance of our ignorance about individuals, nations, ethnicities, professions, disciplines, and even areas of practiced interdisciplinary work— is overwhelming. In the context of international humanitarian and peace engagements, the number of international "peacekeepers," "conflict negotiators," and "human rights activists" that has recently been seen in the "Balkan" territories, has become a painful repeating irony, especially when equaled by a concomitant number of local experts ready to abuse the donated programs of democratization for their individual economic benefit. Again, we should ask ourselves about the role that an (medical) anthropologist can play in such circumstances. Based on the experience of Somalia, Waldron[43] sees part of this role as functioning as a bridge between two bodies of cultural information, acting as an antidote to rumor and relating ideas and materials from the foreign literature to the practitioners. In my own work in Croatia, I have experienced the need to equalize the importance of many confronted concepts and rectify the misunderstandings that arise through attempts of their negative reflecting from culture to culture. However, the creation of a space for dialogues needs to be constantly expanded by questions—that nobody wishes to ask—but are frequently posed by anthropologists.[44] In doing so we must make the assumption that even our eager circumspection, as recommended by Barth,[45] cannot remove the blind spots by which we have learned to live.

HARMONIZING THE PLURALISM OF DISCIPLINARIAN THINKERS AND THE POVERTY OF INTERDISCIPLINARIAN ACTORS—THE DISCIPLINE OF EMPATHY IN ACTION

It is apparent that, whether we address the problems of forcefully migrating populations or any other suffering population, there are rigid approaches located outside one's discipline, as well as within its boundaries. Furthermore, the fuzziness that lies ahead of our attempts to reach into an adequate and useful interdisciplinary weaving of engaged and ethical approaches are predominantly tied to the question of preserving humanity within our disciplines. Given all the theoretical debates within contemporary medical anthropology, as well as its attempts to bridge all the mentioned opposing tensions, it is no surprise that its greatest goal is to compassionately address the needs of those in situations of great adversities. Therefore, the conceptual frameworks and methodologies of medical anthropology provide new means of responding to the leading problems of the twenty-first-century humanity, among which the problems of forced migrants present a major challenge. Support for this statement can also be found in Barth's[46] reflections on contemporary cultural and social anthropology, where he recognizes the very different and unique position of medical anthropology:

> But why should love come across so weakly: love for people, for the problems, and wonder and love for the various forms of "otherness" with which we engage? I believe this reflects the narrowing of focus, and the limited uses to which cultural "otherness" (or alterity) is currently put in anthropological theorizing. When the sub field of medical anthropology attracts so many young people today, it may be because it somehow escapes this stricture: it allows compassionate empathy and cultivates a concern for the other which is furthered, not hindered, by sophisticated attention to her alterity.

In the course of my very first engagements with the problems of forced migrants and displaced persons within Croatia one of the texts that I found to resonate with all the ongoing experiences of my colleagues and myself was that of Muecke on the "New Paradigms for Refugee Health Problems."[47] Apart from being part of the basic literature for my research it enhanced my empathy by reminding me of how easy it was to become a refugee or displaced within Croatia. Yet, the path from realizing that the paradigm of disease and pathology needs to be alternated with recognizing the many voiced experiences, recognition of resilient capacities and cultivating basic human understanding is long and hard to achieve.[48] In today's postgraduate course of medical anthropology that I teach (mainly to medical students)— the barrier of understanding and questioning—"Why are refugee health issues so important in contemporary Croatia?"(!)—get dissolved only after the recognition that at one time we were all in the position of becoming refugees, displaced or, as today, in the position of being their doctors. In fact many colleagues have a wide range of specific returnee problems to handle within the communities they treat, yet do not perceive it as related to prior exile experiences. They tend to belittle the health problems of an overwhelming number of returnees and their specific health status. However great their interdisciplinary eagerness to enroll in a postgraduate course in anthropology is, they are prepared to study the matters of many cultures, yet detached from challenges of empathy. Paradoxically so, the more culturally-sensitive, cross-culturally oriented and interested in the minute symbolist/interpretive modes of cultural articulation we are urged to be, the more scotomizations we seem to develop in our bereavement of the most intense human experiences.

We can continue in the manner of the provocative critical anthropological kind, and pose still more challenging questions: How are we to proceed in complementing policies that aim at adequate medical assistance, provide long-term healthcare, recognize the complexity of sociocultural aspects of forced migration, as well as avoid labeling and pathologicalization of any kind? Is it enough to address only the psychosocial issues, or any other detached (medical) issue? To answer these questions in practice we will need frameworks of research and action that, coincidentally, are rooted within the history of medical anthropology itself, through its critical recognition of its strengths and weaknesses and provision of space for correction. If anthropology is to be characterized as being one of the prior dominating disciplines within the forced migration studies, it should also be recognized for developing a subdiscipline of pioneer attempts to strive towards practicing its "inherent humanity."[49] The crucial stretch that our future academic consciousness should be capable of investing in is being able to join in "unmasking the structural roots of suffering and ill health."[50] Furthermore, what chances are there for informed and effective critical praxis to redirect gained knowledge back to the levels of individuals and populations? The past decade has marked an acceleration of the will for enabling this process in the subdiscipline of medical anthropology. Much of the work within it is aimed at attaining the mentioned critical reflexiveness necessary to not only understand the suffering, distressed, and in pain, but address their needs in a much more engaged manner. The aim is to create effective blueprints for changing the policies based on an increasingly homogenized medico-psychiatric knowledge.[51] Unfortunately, the same type of critical approach is needed for a wide range of human conditions, of which not lastly that of experienced exile and reconstructed living. From the times of Hansen's and Oliver-Smith's[52] visionary and pioneer writing the problems changed from bad to worse, and unfortunately, we still need to be reminded that migratory processes cannot be viewed as simple passive reactions to events. Evermore, a space for ongoing discussions needs to be created if we are to resolve the many problems that lie within the forgotten triangle of health, culture, and politics—a challenge for disciplines in the decades to come.

CONCLUSION

There are no easy blueprints, yet possibly medical anthropology, at this time and due to its own historical development, can help in making a step forward. We should be able to step out of the endless processes of mirroring, regardless of the fact that the sway from pure ethnographic to pure anamnestic/ catamnestic[53] presentations and back is a long one. Anthropologists have done tremendously engaged work and are prepared as always to share self-criticism about it.[54] However, the crucial question remains—how do we change the lives of those we address with our research? Is our work articulated well enough to reach policymakers, administrations, planners, and local community leaders alike. However critical of our work we may be, the favorable answer is not solely within our reach. The stretching of interdisciplinary efforts should be done on all sides and regardless of dominating interests of disciplines. After all, it is the act of individual empathy that bridges the gap of ignorance.

In contemplating the significance of medical anthropology it must not be forgotten that, although anthropologists are famous for "knowing" the culture and enhancing multidisciplinary thinking, the decades to come will witness a greater engagement of this significant subdiscipline. The hallmarks of its conduct are constituted through the capacity to embody a large quantity of self-critique, provide a ground for critical transdisciplinary questioning, and support constructively the creative enhancements of all present interdisciplinary efforts. I believe this triple act is the missing stepping-stone toward reaching the "insiders" with empathy—such as the suffering migrants of the whole region, the global suffering society, and the "local" practitioners (such as myself) of these *lost worlds*[55] of ours.

NOTES

1. Harrell-Bond, B., *Imposing Aid* (Oxford University Press: Oxford, 1986); Kleinman, A., *Rethinking Psychiatry* (The Free Press: New York, 1988), 159; for a valuable historical perspective see, Indra, D., "Interview with Barbara Harrell-Bond," in Indra, D. (ed.), *Engendering Forced Migration* (New York and Oxford: Berghan Books, 1999), 343–349.

2. Wilde, R., "The Refugee Convention at 50: Forced Migration Policy at the Turn of the Century," *Journal of Refugee Studies* 14, No. 2. (2001).

3. *The Need for Integration, Not Fragmentation* (Fox, Steven H., USA); *North Eastern Internal Migrants in São Paulo: a Challenging Experience in Promoting Community Participation* (Szymanski, Heloisa, Brazil); *Refugees and The Social Representations of Suffering* (Eastmond, M., Sweden); *Refugee Health, Human Suffering and Human Rights* (Weinstein, Harvey M., USA); and my own—*A Study of the Families in Exile Through the Use of a Genogram, an Example of Methodological Flexibility*.

4. Camino, A. L. and Krulfeld, R. M., *Reconstructing Lives, Recapturing Meaning* (Amsterdam: Gordon and Breach Publishers, 1994).

5. Harrell-Bond, B., op. cit., 343; Voutira, E., *A Strategic Action Plan for Making WFP'S Policy and Practice More Gender Sensitive: Recommendations for Operational Policy Development* (Oxford: Refugee Studies Programme, 1995).

6. Indra, D., op.cit. 1–349.

7. Eastmond, M., "Refugees and Health: Ethnographic Approaches," in Ahearn, F. L., Jr. (ed.), *Psychosocial Wellness of Refugees: Issues in Qualitative and Quantitative Research* (Berghan Books: New York and Oxford, 2000), 67–87.

8. Keesing, R. M., "Anthropology as Interpretive Quest," *Current Anthropology* 28, No. 2 (1987).

9. Ibid., 169—concerned over the fact that anthropological knowledge invites us to depict "culture" as a coherent system and translates another people's language into a view of its world, Keesing warns that the focus of anthropology should be situated more wisely, and connected more clearly and carefully to the *real humans*—living their lives through those depicted and interpreted cultural meanings. Although the introjections of Keesing's thoughts started decades ago and are imbedded in the codes of action, as well as nicely articulated by anthropologists within the forced migration studies, the confusion over culture translating is still ongoing.

10. Weinstein, H. M., *Refugee Health, Human Suffering and Human Rights,* Paper presented at the 7th IRAP Conference, January 2001, Johannesburg, South Africa. Cited with permission.

11. Weinstein, H. M., Sarnoff, R. H., Gladstone, E., and Lipson, J., "Physical and Psychological Health Issues of Resettled Refugees in the United States." *Journal of Refugee Studies* 13, No. 3 (2000): 1–25.

12. Keesing, R. M., op. cit., 175.

13. Wilde, R., op. cit., p. 140.

14. Gjessing, G., "The Social Responsibility of the Social Scientist," *Current Anthropology* 9, No. 5 (1968): 397–407.

15. Levi-Strauss, C., "Anthropology: Its Achievements and Future," *Current Anthropology* 7, No. 2 (1966): 126.

16. Malkki, L. H., *Purity and Exile: Violence, Memory, and National Cosmology among Hutu Refugees in Tanzania* (Chicago: Chicago University Press, 1995).

17. Kleinman, A., Das, V., and Lock, M., (eds.) *Social Suffering* (Berkeley: University of California Press, 1997).

18. Scheper-Hughes, N. and Sargent, C. (eds.), *Small Wars, the Cultural Politics of Childhood* (Berkeley: University of California Press, 1998).

19. Barth, F., "Boundaries and Connections," in Cohen, A. (ed.), *Signifying Identities* (London and New York: Routledge, 2000), 17–36.

20. Fox, S., *The Need for Integration, Not Fragmentation,* Paper presented at the 7th IRAP Conference, January 2001, Johannesburg, South Africa.

21. Weinstein, H. M., op.cit.

22. Mann, J. M., Gostin, L., Gruskin, S., Brennan, T., Lazzarinii, Z., and Fineberg, H. V., "Health and Human Rights," *Health and Human Rights* 1 (1994): 7–23.

23. Barth, F., op. cit.

24. Das, V., Kleinman, A., Lock, M., Mamphela, M. R., and Reynolds, P., *Remaking a World* (Berkeley: University of California Press, 2001).

25. Gjessing, G., op. cit., 405.

26. Eastmond, M., *Refugees and the Social Representations of Suffering,* Paper presented at the 7th IRAP Conference, January 2001, Johannesburg, South Africa. Cited with permission.

27. Gupta, A., "Beyond 'Culture': Space, Identity, and the Politics of Difference," *Cultural Anthropology* 7, No. 1. (1992); Malkki, L., "Refugees and Exile: From 'Refugee Studies' to the National Order of Things." *Annual Review of Anthropology,* 24 (1995).

28. Mikuš-Kos, A., "Changing explanatory models, changing mental health practice," in van Willigen, L. (ed.), *Health Hazards of Organized Violence in Children, Coping and Protective Factors (II)* (Stichting Pharos: Utrecht, 2000), 139–149.

29. Špoljar-Vržina, S. M., "Exile and the Undestroyable Perpetuity of Stigmatizations—Some Critical (Medical) Anthropological Reflections," *Collegium Antropologicum*, 24, No. 1 (2000), 35–46.

30. See Agger, I., *The Problem of the Wool: A Response,* and Mimica, J., *The Politics of Culture and Suffering in the Refugee Experience,* www.forcedmigration.org/rfgexp

31. Eyber, C., "The Refugee Experience: a Resource for Aid Workers," *Humanitarian Exchange* 20 (2002), 31–32.

32. See the site www.worldbank.org./html, and compare the projects designated for the health systems transitions of the Eastern European countries—there are little differences to be found. The projects are not concordant to actual needs, yet all present the expansion of the unified market of monetary dependency.

33. Furthermore, see the *Stability Pact for South Eastern Europe* (Conference of Ministers, Cologne, 1999) and compare its goals with those expressed by Susan Woodward about the conditionality of the World Bank and IMF programs and the role that returning refugees should play in the multiethnic scenario of post-Dayton former Yugoslav countries (Woodward, S., *Implementing Peace in Bosnia and Herzegovina: A Post-Dayton Primer and Memorandum of Warning* (The Brookings Institution, Brookings Discussion Papers: Washington, D.C., 1996).

34. See the site of *Coalition for Work with Psychotrauma and Peace, Philosophy and Mandate,* 18th May 2001, www.zamir.hr/cwwpp

35. Bowman, G., "The Violence in Identity," in Schmidt, B. E. and Schroder, I. W. (eds.), *Anthropology of Violence and Conflict* (London: Routledge, 2001), 25–46 (esp.41).

36. Singer, M., "Beyond the Ivory Tower: Critical Praxis in Medical Anthropology," *Medical Anthropology Quarterly* 9, No. 1 (1995): 80–106.

37. Waldron, S., "Anthropologists as Expert Witnesses," in Indra, D. (ed.), *Engendering Forced Migration* (Berghan Books: New York and Oxford, 1999), 343–349 (esp. 347).

38. Barth, F., op. cit., p. 31.

39. Agger, I., op. cit.,—In presenting one of the international NGO programs and its process of psychotherapeutical meetings that were motivated through knitting activities and the distribution of wool, she describes the women in the circle and their clutching of their hotel keys as a sign of taking good care not to lose the only possession they have—a hotel room. Why not interpret the clutching as a sign of anxiety; ambivalence raised from the fact that the women are part of a meeting they do not wish to attend and/or are embarrassed that they are there just to get the wool?

40. Špoljar-Vržina, S. M., "Towards Further Analyzing the Methodology in the Displaced Person and Refugee Research—An Example from the Island of Hvar, Croatia." *Collegium Antropologicum* 20, No. 2 (1996), 159–168.

41. Waldron, S., op. cit., 347.

42. Keesing, R. H., "Theories of Culture Revisted," in Borofsky, R. (ed.), *Assessing Cultural Anthropology* (New York: McGraw-Hill, 1994), 301–312, esp. 303).

43. Waldron, S., op. cit., 345.

44. Scheper-Hughes, N., "Demography Without Numbers," in Kertzer, I. D. and Fricke, T. (eds.), *Anthropological Demography: Towards a New Synthesis* (Chicago: University of Chicago Press, 1997), 201–222; Harrell-Bond, B., "Are Refugee Camps Good for Children?" www.jha.ac/articles/2000.

45. Barth, F., op. cit., 35

46. Barth, F., "A Personal View of Present Tasks and Priorities in Cultural and Social Anthropology," in Borofsky, R. (ed.), *Assessing Cultural Anthropology* (New York: McGraw-Hill, 1994), 301–312.

47. Muecke, M., "New Paradigms for Refugee Health Problems," *Soc. Sci. Med.* 35, No. 4. (1992): 515–523.

48. Ibid., 520–521.

49. Walker, S., "Health Interventions: A Focus for Applied Medical Anthropology," *Nexus* 13, No. 1 (1998).

50. Singer, M., op. cit., 80–106.

51. See the excellent programmatic text based on the initiative to build on the cooperative jointly undertaken by biomedical experts and social scientists in the aim of upgrading the services to those suffering in mental health domains—*"Modernity, Suffering and Psychopathology,"* Canadian Institutes of Health Research (CIHR), www.chrf.ca/docs/finalpsrts/HIDG/bibeau.pdf.

52. Hansen, A., and Oliver-Smith, A. (eds.), *Involuntary Migration and Resettlement: The Problems and Responses of Dislocated People* (Westview Press: Boulder, Colorado, 1982).

53. Both terms pertain to the basic medical documents about a patient's history/follow-up history. In my research with the refugees and displaced I learned that according to their experience they often classify their interviewers. Once such classification was into the types that *"wish to know about our bowels and its functioning"* and the type that *"wish to find out where this takes place."*

54. Indra, D., op. cit., "Interview with Barbara Harrell-Bond," 343–349; Van Arsdale, P. W., *"The International refugee situation: Reflections on Anthropology's Contributions,"* www.du.edu/gsis/gi/past/19991/interfug.htm

55. Špoljar-Vržina, S. M., "Genograms of Exile and Return Families in Croatia—A Medical Anthropological Approach," *Collegium Antropologicum* 24, No. 2 (2000): 565.—a metaphor used by an examinee presented in the paper, describing the seventh year of his life as a displaced person (in a hotel room in the center of Zagreb).

15

The Refugee Convention and Practice in South Asia: A Marriage of Inconvenience?

Sumit Sen

The partition of India in 1947 and the emergence of modern India and Pakistan was accompanied by the largest transfer of population in recorded history. Since then, states of south Asia have hosted several million refugees.[1] However, states have been wary of ratifying the 1951 Refugee Convention or instituting domestic legislations for the protection of refugees. This chapter will identity the diverse situations in which refugees find themselves in the territory of the host state, and seek to understand the dichotomy of practice in south Asia. This dichotomy is evidenced in the grant of asylum for various groups of refugees, and in assuring protection to refugees as a consequence of their international status. The chapter will explore issues relating to the minimum standard of treatment for refugees and the question of access of UNHCR. An oft forgotten issue in south Asia is the case of the Bihari refugees, whose status has seldom been recognized and remained in a protracted uncertain situation for the past thirty years.[2]

In this overall context, the chapter will discuss the role of UNHCR vis-à-vis host states, the process of the formulation of the model national law for future domestic legislations for refugees, and whether the ratification and incorporation of the 1951 Refugee Convention by states of south Asia would indeed be a marriage of inconvenience.

WHAT CONSTITUTES INTERNATIONAL REFUGEE LAW
AND PRACTICE IN SOUTH ASIA?

To answer the above question, the practice of the grant of asylum and the protection of refugees merit assessment.

The Grant of Asylum

Asylum in south Asia has been granted to persons fleeing their country of origin because of a well-founded fear of persecution due to reasons of race, religion, nationality, political opinion[3] due to events seriously disturbing public order in their country of origin[4] and/or due to gross violations of individual human rights, and escape from generalized violence. The grant of asylum is essentially based on humanitarian considerations during the mass influx of asylum-seekers, though the grant of refugee status is based on political and strategic considerations.

Though states of south Asia are not parties to the 1951/1967 convention and have not instituted national legislations for the protection of refugees, they have agreed to respect the provisions of the "Principles Concerning Treatment of Refugees," signed under the auspicies of the Asian African Legal Consultative Committee (AALCC).[5] While article III of the principles reaffirmed the discretion of states in providing for a "sovereign right to grant or refuse asylum,"[6] article III(4) provided for the "grant (of) provisional asylum . . .", thereby urging states to grant temporary refuge and therefore protection, to asylum-seekers fleeing a well-founded fear of persecution.

Asylum in south Asia has comprised a grant of permanent and temporary asylum to various refugee groups in south Asia. In most cases, refugee movements have resulted in the mass influx of asylum-seekers and status has been granted on a prima facie group basis. Though this grant of asylum is treated as a temporary national obligation, it constitutes an acknowledgment by states of existing international obligations in practice. Interestingly, while permanent asylum was granted to Tibetan refugees from 1959 onwards and to Chakma refugees resettled in the Indian state of Arunachal Pradesh in 1964, since the 1970s, all refugees in south Asia have been granted asylum on a temporary basis.

The practice of temporary asylum in south Asia began with the massive influx of 10 million Bengali refugees from East Pakistan (now Bangladesh) into India in 1971. Since then, the Rohingya refugees from Myanmar have sought asylum in Bangladesh; the animosity between the Sinhalese and the Tamil communities in postindependent Sri Lanka have resulted in the flight of Sri Lankan Tamil refugees into the Indian state of Tamil Nadu; the hiatus between the ruling Buddhist Drupka in northern Bhutan and Hindu Nepali-sepaking Lotshampa in southern Bhutan resulted in the forcible expulsion of about 100,000 Lotshampa to India and then to Nepal; the persecution and discrimination of the Chakma community in the Chittagong Hill Tracts led them to seek refuge in India, and the severe human rights violations by the Myanmar military has resulted in a number of minority communities seeking asylum in India.

While the grant of asylum in south Asia to those persons fleeing persecution in other south Asian states or states contiguous to south Asia has been on a generous scale, asylum-seekers are granted asylum on a prima facie basis and through the promulgation of administrative measures. In the absence of procedures for the determination of refugee status, there remains an anomaly in the practice of states with regard to the grant of refugee status to those asylum-seekers who come from noncontiguous states of south Asia. These asylum-seekers are merely tolerated by the host state, but they are not granted refugee status as determined by procedures established in law.

It is for such individual asylum-seekers that the determination of refugee status by UNHCR assumes importance. The role of UNHCR in south Asia had commenced with the provision of assistance for the consolidation of Tibetan refugee settlements in the 1960s. Its role expanded considerably when it served as the UN focal point coordinating relief during the mass influx of Bengali refugees from East Pakistan in 1971.[7] However, it was in 1981, when a significant number of refugees came from Afghanistan and Iran, that India requested UNHCR to begin the process of determination of mandate status for individual asylum-seekers. At this stage, India made a clear distinction between asylum-seekers: those who were recognized as refugees and provided with assistance, and others for whom UNHCR was expected to exercise its mandate. For over two decades, UNHCR has extended the individual determination process to Afghan, Iranian, Somali, Sudanese, Iraqi, Palestinian, Ethiopian, Liberian, Laotian, Croatian, Burmese, Chin, Tibetan, Rohingya, and Lotshampa refugees in south Asia.

Over the years, and in the absence of international and national legislations for refugees, UNHCR has used diverse approaches in applying the eligibility criteria in determining status of refugees from different nationalities, where most asylum-seekers enter the territory of the host state with valid travel documents. It has sometimes been claimed that if an asylum-seeker is in possession of a national passport, he would not be persecuted in his country of origin. However, while the individual may possess a passport and may not have said anything against the country of origin, his very act of leaving his own country illustrated his political opinion,[8] thus implicating fear. Though, individual asylum-seekers have generally entered India on passports with valid visas, it is on the basis of well-founded fear that UNHCR grants them mandate status, in the form of a Refugee Certificate.

In south Asia, for the individual asylum-seeker, the grant of asylum does not always translate into a grant of international status for all refugees. What is needed is a greater level of cooperation between states of south Asia and UNHCR. This would in fact improve the domestic asylum mechanisms, where UNHCR will be able to assess risk, rather than actual persecution faced by the refugees in the country of origin. In the future, when states institute national procedures for the determination of refugee status, the role of UNHCR would be required to independently monitor formal procedures of appeal in cases of rejection, in order to protect refugees from involuntary *refoulement.*

The Protection of Refugees

The states of south Asia have provided temporary protection to a large number of refugees and have generally demonstrated their support for the basic principles of protection. While states have granted refuge to asylum-seekers from certain states on a prima facie basis, other asylum-seekers are tolerated at the request of UNHCR. In the absence of international ratification and national legislation on refugees, protection is dependent on the policy of the successive governments of the host state. In such cases, protection based on the complete discretion of governments often becomes inconsistent, with its attendant risks and uncertainty. In this section, I will briefly discuss the standard of treatment granted by states to Tibetan, Tamil, and Rohingya refugees, and the function of international protection of UNHCR for those refugees who are treated under the immigration laws of the host state.

Since 1959, Tibetan refugees have rarely faced protection problems in India.[9] The integration of the Tibetan refugees has been extensively carried out in various parts of India,[10] and "[t]here (are) no known reports of any antagonism between the local people and the refugees. Hence they live in India as comfortably as any other Indian and enjoy all social security privileges available to an Indian."[11] The Tibetan refugees have acknowledged their assimilation and successful integration in India. As a token of gratitude to the government and the people of India, Tibetan refugees all over India observed 31 March 1995 as "Thank You India Day."[12] The role of UNHCR for the Tibetan refugees in the 1960s related to specific programs for their rehabilitation in the host state, and UNHCR was never required to assume its function of providing international protection to the Tibetan refugees in India.

On 23 April 1994, after an Indian youth was alleged to have been stabbed to death by a Tibetan refugee, some miscreants attacked and burnt Tibetan offices in Dharamshala. Though this has been an isolated and singular case of strife between the Indians and Tibetans, a major confrontation was averted by Tibetan restraint. Fearful of further problems and a possible threat to the security of the Dalai Lama in the host state, Tibetan refugees requested the then Indian Prime Minister Rao for urgent action for their protection.[13]

For its part, India exercised its sovereign responsibility by protecting the Tibetan refugees and contained the situation.[14] In fact, an authoritative Tibetan scholar has confirmed that "actual cases of host-refugee conflict have been rare in India."[15]

The practice of protection and the grant of a supervisory mechanism to UNHCR has varied considerably in south Asia, as is exemplified in the case of the Sri Lankan Tamil refugees in India. Not having ratified the 1951/1967 convention, states have acted in a way where the protection mandate of the UNHCR has either been restricted or completely curtailed. After inviting UNHCR to assist in the repatriation of Tamil refugees, India denied UNHCR access to the refugee camps.[16] In the absence of adequate protection of UNHCR, many Tamil refugees complained of "constant harassment and intimidation" by the Q-Branch of the Tamil Nadu police.

The state of the Tamil refugee camps has been a protection concern over the years. While the refugees were not demanding and seemed to understand that the lack of facilities in the camps were due to paucity of government funds, the conditions of asylum and level of protection have been described by numerous human rights organizations:[17]

> Camp sites were (situated in) a yard, a marketplace, rice godowns or even open air toilets. Hutment put up for a month in 1990, continue to shelter some 58,000 Sri Lankan Tamils in 100 camps in Tamil Nadu. Physical conditions in the camps are deplorable. The extensive damage to the physical surroundings has reduced the camps to a culture of slums. Housed in temporary hutment made of tar sheets, the scorching heat makes life in the camps intolerable.

This view has been corroborated by local NGOs,[18] and through research conducted by the South Asia Human Rights Documentation Centre (SAHRDC) in 1997–1998.[19] The lack of sufficient Indian government funding could have been alleviated by UNHCR, but the Indian government has maintained a policy of not accepting any international assistance for the Sri Lankan Tamil refugees.

The independence of Bangladesh from Pakistan affected the Bihari community on a massive scale. After Bangladesh gained independence in December 1971, the Biharis were under continual persecution for a period of one year and the state of Pakistan was unable to protect her own citizens. It has been claimed that several thousands of Biharis were killed by pro-Bengali supporters of secession *prior* to the Pakistani army's ruthless intervention on 25 March 1971 and a large number moved into camps all over the country.

Although their movement into the camps began in March 1971 and continued until the end of the year, the Biharis, until December 1971, were internally displaced persons in East Pakistan. The retention of effective nationality of Pakistan in the sovereign territory of Bangladesh changed their status into refugees. In this regard, the existence of persecution prior to the dismemberment of Pakistan in 1971 has been argued to favor the claim for refugee status on the basis of the "well-founded fear of persecution for reasons of race, . . . nationality (and) political opinion" of the entire Urdu-speaking Bihari community in their country of origin.[20]

Under the New Delhi Agreement of 28 August 1973, Pakistan transferred a substantial number of "non-Bengalis" in Bangladesh who had opted for repatriation to Pakistan, in exchange for Bengalis in Pakistan and the return of POWs. However, evidencing her practice of denying nationality, Pakistan resorted to a categorization that was extremely limited in scope. While engaging the ICRC as the route for all applications for repatriation from Biharis to the government of Pakistan, the ICRC made it clear that "[r]egistration with the ICRC does not give a right to repatriation. The final acceptance . . . lies with (the) Pakistan and Bangladesh governments."

Pakistan began issuing clearances in favor of those "non-Bengalis" who were either (i) domiciled in former West Pakistan, (ii) employees of the central government and their families, or (iii) members of divided families, irrespective of their original domicile. Pakistan reiterated that all those who fell under these three categories would be received by Pakistan without limit. In respect of persons whose applications had been rejected, Pakistan agreed, upon request, to provide reasons why any particular case was rejected. Any aggrieved applicant could, at any time, seek a review of his application provided he was able to supply new facts to support his contention that he qualified in one of the three categories. The claims of such persons would not be time limited. In the event of a review, it was decided that Pakistan and Bangladesh would resolve it by mutual consultation.

However, lacunae remained, which stemmed from the fact that persons under the established categories remain to be repatriated. The process of review of a rejected applicant by Pakistan has been assessed, whereby the definitions of the central government employees and divided families merit a fresh assessment. All railway employees should have been included within the first category, since the decision to provincialize the railways was essentially administrative. The service tenure and conditions of these employees remained the same. To not accept railway employees within central government staff can be stated to be a violation of her own categorization by Pakistan. It can be argued that the category of divided family applied by Pakistan was unilaterally determined and was more restrictive than that identified by ICRC in their letter requesting options regarding repatriation. It is estimated that 75 percent of Bihari families stand divided because of the restrictive definition of the divided families, since grandparents, parents, and unmarried siblings were not considered part of the same family for the issuance of clearance documents. Bangladesh has asserted the need for the acceptance of a broader and Islamic definition of the family, since the present definition is narrow and restrictive, based on the western concept of the family. This argument upholds family reunification as one of the fundamental provisions of refugee law in any effective resolution procedure.

It had been agreed between Pakistan and Bangladesh that the antecedents of the person who returned to Pakistan as a hardship case would be examined. If it were to be established that she or he fell within the other two categories, then additional hardship cases would be included. At the outset, the definitional and numeric limits of the hardship cases have caused a legal anomaly, since it needs to be explained as to why Pakistan limited that number to 25,000. In reality, the hardship cases had essentially accepted Biharis who had been within the other two categories, and certainly not war victims, orphans, or disabled persons. Over the years, Pakistan has failed to give a breakdown of the number of persons who were listed under the categories and the vacancies in the hardship category.

It needs to firmly be established that the Bihari refugees renounced their homes in 1947 in order to make East Pakistan their country of nationality and residence. Bangladesh was not the country they had migrated or opted to. Before the birth of Bangladesh, they stood for the integrity of Pakistan, were Pakistani nationals, and up to this date have not renounced their Pakistani nationality.[21] It is amply evident that the state of Pakistan is in complete violation of the international norm that "(n)o one shall be arbitrarily deprived of his nationality or forced to renounce his nationality as a means of divesting him of the right to return to his country," since by a process of arbitrary and selective acceptance into its new (erstwhile West Pakistan) territory, the vast majority of the Bihari community was forced to be stateless refugees.

Weis opined that only nationals are included within the meaning of Article 12(4), although he adds that the article "include(s) the state whose nationality the person possessed and of which he has been arbitrarily deprived."[22] Using this paradigm, the Bihari refugee can safely be categorized to be the national of Pakistan since 1947, and the deprivation of the right to a nationality since 1972, for a period of three decades is a gross violation of human rights by Pakistan.

The relationship of the Bihari community with the state of Pakistan should be located within the paradigms of international law—the expansive interpretation of "one's own country" in order to include one's homeland to the state to which the individual has an identifiable connection. In this regard, it is appropriate to remember the decision of the ICJ in the *Nottebohm* case,[23] where the substance of the Nottebohm's link with the state of Liechtenstein was assessed. Applying the determinative criteria used by the Court of "tradition, his establishment, his interests, his activities, his family ties, his intentions for the near future" to the Bihari refugees, it would be clear that the Biharis succeed in qualifying for the links to nationality of Pakistan on all counts.

The broad interpretation advanced at the Uppsala Colloquium[24] suggested that the language "his own country" was purposely chosen to avoid accepting formal governmental determinations of nationality as the final arbiter of whether there existed a right to return. The decision of the ICJ in *Nottebohm* was further illustrated, whereby a ". . . person's 'country' is that to which he is connected by a reasonable combination of . . . race, religion, ancestry, birth, and prolonged domicile."[25] Although nationals of Pakistan, the Biharis are subject to the lack of the usual attributes of nationality, including effective protection. The absence of the attributes causes the need to assess the genuine effective link.[26] The crucial question of link is that of effective nationality, where the Biharis have illustrated the fact of attachment, complete with interests and sentiments. Pakistan, in fulfilling her responsibilities as a nation-state must recognize the norms of international law espoused in the *Nottebohm* case in granting effective nationality and rights to the Bihari refugees. The political move of Pakistan in forcing the Biharis as stateless refugees can firmly be attributed to be contrary to the general principle of nondiscrimination, which is said to have become entrenched as part of customary international law. The *Barcelona Traction* case (Second Phase)[27] referred to obligations *erga omnes*[28] in contemporary international law, including "principles and rules concerning the basic rights of the human person, including protection from . . . racial discrimination."[29] Pakistan has remained well short of protecting the human rights of the Bihari stateless refugees for thirty years.

The Rohingya refugees have sought asylum on five different occasions in south Asia in the last century—in 1939–1941, in 1942, in 1954, in June 1978, and in 1991–1992.[30] Since there is a paucity of research material regarding the first three refugee flows, this section will analyze protection concerns during the fourth and fifth influx of Rohingya refugees into Bangladesh, in 1978 and 1991–1992, respectively.

After the 1978 influx, the Bangladeshi government forced the Rohingya refugees to return to Burma. In the event of the nonexistence of protection mechanisms for the Rohingya refugees, an estimated "10,000 refugees died." It has been alleged that the deaths were a direct result of malnutrition and the reduction of food supplies below the level of subsistence. In fact, "reports by the head of the UNHCR suboffice in 1978 and a Food and Nutrition Advisor to the Food and Agriculture Organisation (FAO) alleged that the Bangladesh government purposely cut food supplies to compel the refugees to return to Burma."[31]

During the fifth influx of the Rohingya refugees in late 1991, Bangladesh granted them temporary asylum on a prima facie basis, but was against the involvement of UNHCR or other humanitarian NGOs. The nonaccess soon led to the deterioration of the relief operation and in health facilities for the 250,000 refugees, and in mid-February 1992, Bangladesh allowed UNHCR to take charge of the operation. However, disregarding the principles of protection and the minimum standard of treatment in 1992, Bangladesh continued a process of coercing the Rohingya refugees to agree to their imposed return. The lack of host state protection and the brutality of methods used led UNHCR to withdraw from the proposed repatriation in December 1992.

The protection of the Rohingya refugees remained a matter of grave concern. In order to make them agree to repatriate to their country of origin, camp officials and police "fostered an extreme climate of fear . . . camp officials have used this fear, as well as inflicting actual abuses, to compel refugees to present themselves to UNHCR as 'volunteers' for repatriation."[32] Rather than adhering to the minimum standards of treatment for the protection of refugees, Bangladesh used pressure and intimidation through "physical assault, verbal abuse, denial of food rations, and denial of basic human rights including the right to health and education facilities."[33] While the Bangladesh foreign secretary admitted to the application of an element of force by certain junior officials, a former camp administrator testified to the repeated use of force against the refugees.[34] The complete lack of any protection standard has been further evidenced by UNHCR officials and staff from international NGOs, namely, OXFAM and MSF.[35] According to them, "Bangladeshi officials made life in the transit camps purposefully difficult as a means of coercing the refugees to return. Human rights abuses were the most severe in the transit camps, including at times shed-to-shed beatings by camp officials."[36] The decrease in the camp population and return of Rohingya refugees was more as a result of the lack of protection and less as a consequence of individual choice.

It must be remembered that protection was never envisaged to be permanent or temporary in the context of the 1951/1967 convention. In fact, when refugee protection is perceived to be temporary, states are more likely to adopt a generous approach, and include asylum-seekers with a nonconvention harm. As is clear from the UNHCR *Handbook*, protection is "not . . . that a refugee remain a refugee forever, but to ensure the individual's renewed membership of a community and the restoration of national protection, either in the homeland or through integration elsewhere . . . the convention makes it clear that refugee status is a transitory condition."[37]

Though transitory, the conditions of asylum, the extent of access to UNHCR, and the effect of nonaccess of UNHCR to certain groups of refugees assume a pertinent and crucial issue relating to protection of refugees. Though it is beyond the realm of this chapter,[38] here it will suffice to state that the lack of humanitarian access has resulted in the lack of minimum standards of treatment for the Chakma, Hajong refugees in Arunachal Pradesh, Chakma refugees in Tripura, and Mizoram and Tibetan refugees in Nepal.

While the grant of asylum is widespread in south Asia, protection accorded by host states for most refugee groups remain ad hoc and unpredictable. In spite of hosting refugees for over five decades, south Asia suffers from a general lack of refugee policy. Treatment is primarily based on administrative directives and national discretion, rather than being based on the provisions of the 1951/1967 convention and principles of international law relating of the protection of the human rights of refugees.

In the absence of domestic legislation for refugees, the protection of refugees in south Asia has seen a differentiated practice. In general, states of south Asia have not adhered to principles of international law, have not accorded protection to all refugees consummate with their international status, and have not guaranteed the provision of minimum standards of treatment to the refugees. The relatively low standard of protection accorded by states was further compounded by the practice of discrimination in granting protection to individual and group refugees. Individual refugees continue to be treated as foreigners under the immigration laws of the host state and often face prosecution for not fulfilling the requirements of such laws.

The practice of host states to treat refugees on the basis of administrative policies rather than on the rule of law has given rise to problems in the functioning of UNHCR in south Asia. While the host states of south Asia have allowed UNHCR to establish their international presence, as a result of their political and strategic imperatives, in certain cases host states have ignored their international human rights obligations and have disregarded the mandate of UNHCR by not allowing international access to various groups of refugees. Refugees are faced with numerous protection issues, which include among others, being held in incommunicado detention, housed in subhuman conditions, a lack of freedom of movement, a denial of employment opportunities, facing problems relating to travel documents, and attacks by the local people. Since refugees are not assured the minimum standard of treatment, the protection function of UNHCR for such refugees assume critical importance in south Asia.

Protection in south Asia can be illustrated by a wide range of practices of states, which can be summed up by the Tibetan and Rohingya refugees. The Indian policy for Tibetan refugees is commendable practice, which has conformed to the acceptable international law principles for the effective protection of the rights of refugees. On the other hand, the practice of Bangladesh for the Rohingya refugees was undesirable and a violation of human rights standards. Rohingya refugees were assaulted and forced to return to their country of origin by the Bangladesh government even when the causes of the original flight of the refugees had still not been eliminated. The protection of Tibetan refugees by India provides the model of the standards of treatment for refugee protection in south Asia.

WILL SOUTH ASIA RATIFY THE REFUGEE CONVENTION?

The practices of states of south Asia have distinguished binding international legal obligations for refugees from the nonbinding somewhat vague "generally accepted moral and political principles of refugee protection."[39] To improve this differentiated practice, UNHCR has initiated a debate in south Asia for the ratification of the 1951/1967 convention and the institution of national legislation for refugees.[40]

In the past five decades, "[t]he 1951/1967 Convention has become a symbol by reason of its core content . . . (to) represent the essence of protection (and is) considered as an active endeavor on behalf of unknown, unknowable numbers."[41] However, with the institution of restrictive administrative mechanisms in some of the western states, the provisions of the 1951/1967 convention stand undermined, eroding the rule of law for the protection of refugees. Though UNHCR has expressed concern about this practice in the western states,[42] the Office is faced with the curious situation where it is promoting the accession to the 1951/1967 convention when some of the states are interested in restricting its scope.

The practice of restriction in the grant of asylum and refugee status in western states have led states of south Asia to question the need to accede to the 1951/1967 convention. States of south Asia have argued that since the 1951/1967 convention is being undermined through restrictive practices by states had framed the 1951/1967 convention, they do not see much reason in ratifying the convention. Although some western states have impaired the system of asylum and protection through restrictive immigration regulations, it should be emphasized that international consensus believes in protecting the system of asylum for refugees.

States in south Asia are urged to contribute to the consensus by strengthening the institution of asylum and protection of refugees. Further, it must be reiterated to states of south Asia that by emulating the bad practice of certain western states it would only do disservice to refugees fleeing a well-founded fear and persecution in their country of origin. Given the large number of refugees hosted in their territory since the partition of India, if states of south Asia "continue a humanitarian policy (for refugees), it can perhaps push the international regime towards a more humanitarian path, and in the process review its own policy and build more humane guidelines."[43]

States of south Asia have generally refused to accede to the 1951/1967 convention, since they feel they would be unable to undertake further international obligations and believe the rights contained are too wide for their present economic situation. Some maintain that they are implementing the provisions without a formal ratification.[44] However, as was illustrated by the practice of asylum and protection, the adherence to the basic provisions contained in the 1951/1967 convention would assure refugees a minimum standard of treatment and result in a predictable and uniform practice by states of south Asia.

A first step has been the adoption of the Model National Law in 1997. It includes a definition of a refugee based on article 1(A)(2) of the 1951/1967 convention, Article 1(2) of the 1969 OAU convention, and the 1984 Cartagena Declaration on Refugees. Drawing from these instruments, the Model National Law has provisions dealing with exclusion, the principle of *non-refoulement*, constitution of authorities to deal with the cases of asylum-seekers, procedures for the determination of refugee status, rights and duties of refugees, situations of mass influx, and voluntary repatriation.[45] Since 1997, in most of the states of south Asia, there has been a significant move in discussing the provisions of the Model National Law. However, even after five years, since its adoption in 1997, none of the states of south Asia have legislated a national refugee protection regime.

CONCLUSION: IS SOUTH ASIA A "FORTRESS REGION"?

The above analysis seems to suggest that in certain aspects, south Asia has remained a fortress region and in other senses, it is not. It is a fortress region to the extent that south Asia has been averse to international scrutiny, and political and strategic imperatives of host states has often taken precedence over the human rights of refugees. Thus, the process of ratifying the Refugee Convention, the international obligations arising thereof, and the institution of national mechanisms for refugees have been progressing at turtle speed. On the other hand, it is not a secure fortress region, because it is not possible to have an effective moat outside of that fortress. The borders are too long, often too remote to patrol, and population movement will always remain possible. Unlike much of the industrialized countries, and given the state of its development, south Asia still hosts large numbers of refugees.

In conclusion, up until now, the application of the Refugee Convention in south Asia and the practice of states has been a marriage of inconvenience. In order to prevent south Asia in traversing the course of other industrialized countries in becoming fortress regions, it is imperative that states ratify the Refugee Convention and institute national legislations in the near future.

NOTES

This paper represents the personal opinion of the author and does not represent the official views of the United Nations or UNHCR.

1. The states of south Asia comprise India, Pakistan, Bangladesh, Sri Lanka, Nepal, and Bhutan.

2. Sen, Sumit, "Stateless Refugees and the Right to Return: The Bihari Refugees of South Asia," *International Journal of Refugee Law* 11, No. 4 (1999): 625–645, and 12, No. 1 (2000): 41–70.

3. Art. 1, 1951/1967 Convention.

4. Art. I(2), 1969 OAU Convention.

5. AALCC, *Principles Concerning Treatment of Refugees*, in UNHCR, *Collection of International Instruments and other Legal Texts concerning Refugees and Displaced Persons*, Volumes I and II, Geneva, 1995.

6. Art. III(1), AALCC, *Principles Concerning Treatment of Refugees*, in UNHCR, *Collection of International Instruments and other Legal Texts concerning Refugees and Displaced Persons*, Volumes I and II, Geneva, 1995.

7. See chapter 3, "Rupture in South Asia," in UNHCR, *The State of the World's Refugees: Fifty Years of Humanitarian Action*, (Oxford: Oxford University Press), 2000.

8. Gilbert, Geoffrey S., *Right of Asylum: A Change of Direction*, *ICLQ* 32 (1983): 634, 644.

9. Perhaps the only significant instance was protection concerns arising from the withdrawal of food ration cards of the Tibetan refugees by the Arunachal Pradesh government in 1994.

10. Also see Box 3.1 in UNHCR, *The State of the World's Refugees: Fifty Years of Humanitarian Action* (Oxford: Oxford University Press, 2000), 63.

11. See UNHCR, *Tibetan Refugees*, New Delhi, August 1993, 3.

12. See *Tibetan Bulletin*, Dharamsala, May-June 1995, 8.

13. Reuter News Service, 30 April 1994.

14. It has been established "that the 1994 riot was clearly premediated, its agenda and route were too specific to have been a spontaneous event. One man reported that two (Indian) Himachal businessmen were offered bribes from (by) a Chinese diplomat to distribute anti-Tibetan literature in Dharansala." Moynihan, Maura, *Tibetan Refugees: 36 Years of Flight*, March 1995 (mimeo), 12.

15. Norbu, Dawa, *Tibetan Refugees in South Asia: A Case of Peaceful Adjustment*, in S. D. Muni and L. R. Baral (ed.), *Refugees and Regional Security in South Asia* (New Delhi: Konark Publishers 1996), 87–89 at 88.

16. "UNHCR Complains India is Denying Access to Camps in TN (Tamilnadu)," *The Asian Age*, 9 September 1994.

17. Raj, Fr. C. Amal, *Sri Lankan Tamil Refugees in India*, in T. K. Bose and R. Manchanda (eds.), *States, Citizens and Outsiders: The Uprooted Peoples of South Asia*, South Asia Forum for Human Rights, Kathmandu, 1997, 197.

18. See contents of detailed memorandum from the State Coordinating Committee of NGO's for Relief and Rehabilitation of Sri Lankan Refugees, Madras, to KA Nambiar, Chief Secretary, Government of Tamil Nadu, 26 October 1996. Appendix to UNHCR, *Sri Lankan Refugees in Camps in Tamil Nadu*, 96/OCM/IND/264, 5 November 1996.

19. "Having lost our homeland," *Seminar*, No. 463, New Delhi, March 1998, 28–33.

20. Sen, Sumit, "Stateless Refugees and the Right to Return: The Bihari Refugees of South Asia," *International Journal of Refugee Law* 11, No. 4, 625–645, and 12, No. 1 41–70.

21. In their opinion, the Bihari refugees' right of self-determination is evidenced in the fact that the basic principle of their being Pakistanis is not negotiable. This was

reiterated in interviews conducted in 1996–1997. The nonnegotiability of their nationality is evidenced in their continuous state of refugeehood.

22. Weis, Paul, *Nationality and Statelessness in International Law*, 2d ed. (Germantown, Md: Sijthoff & Noordhoff, 1979, 65.

23. *Nottebohm* case, International Court of Justice, *ICJ Reports* (1955).

24. See Vasak, K. and S. Liskofsky (eds.), *The Right to Leave and to Return: Papers and Recommendations of the International Colloquium held in Uppsala, Sweden, 19–21 June 1972*, American Jewish Committee, New York (1976).

25. Muzzawi, *Comment on the Middle East*, in Vasak, K. and S. Liskofsky (eds.), *The Right to Leave and to Return*, op. cit., 343.

26. The *Nottebohm* case enunciated that according to the practice of state, of judicial decisions, and the opinion of writers, nationality is the legal bond having as its basis a social fact of attachment, a genuine connection of existence, interests, and sentiments, together with reciprocal rights and duties.

27. *ICJ Reports* (1970), 512–515.

28. This refers to the binding nature to all states, in addition to having achieved the status of peremptory norms (*jus cogens*) of international law.

29. Art. 1 of the International Convention on the Elimination of All Forms of Racial Discrimination, 1966, states that "the term 'racial discrimination' shall mean any distinction, exclusion, restriction, or preference based on race, color, descent, or national or ethnic origin, which has the purpose or effect of nullifying or impairing the recognition, enjoyment, or exercise . . . of human rights and fundamental freedoms." In sum, Biharis have been discriminated against on all the classifying provisions of the term.

30. Sen, Sumit, *International Refugee Law in South Asia*, PhD thesis, Department of Law, The London School of Economics and Political Science, at section III.2.2.

31. U.S. Committee for Refugees, *The Return of the Rohingya Refugees to Burma: Voluntary Repatriation or Refoulement?* March 1995, 3.

32. Ibid., 5–6.

33. Human Rights Watch/Asia, *Burma: The Rohingya Muslims—Ending a Cycle of Exodus* 8, No. 9(C), September (1996), 13.

34. Author interview with the Bangladesh Foreign Secretary Farooq Sobhan and former camp-in-charge Shameem at the Bangladesh Ministry of Foreign Affairs and Ministry of Home Affairs, respectively, in Dhaka, December 1995–January 1996. However, despite repeated attempts to assess the protection of refugees by the host state, Bangladesh government officials administering the Rohingya refugee camps in Teknaf and those based at Cox's Bazar refused to be interviewed.

35. Author interviews were conducted in December 1995–January 1996 and February 1998.

36. U.S. Committee for Refugees, *The Return of the Rohingya Refugees to Burma: Voluntary Repatriation or Refoulement?* March 1995, 7.

37. See UNHCR, *Voluntary Repatriation: International Protection*, Geneva, 1996.

38. This issue has been extensively discussed in Sen, Sumit, *International Refugee Law in South Asia*, PhD thesis, Department of Law, The London School of Economics and Political Science, at section V.3.2.

39. Goodwin-Gill, G. *The Refugee in International Law* (Oxford: Oxford University Press, 1996), 132.

40. UNHCR, *Model National Law on Refugees*, Fourth Regional Consultation on Refugees and Migratory Movements in South Asia, Dhaka, 10–11 November 1997.

41. Goodwin-Gill, G. *Refugees: The Functions and Limits of the Existing Protection System*, in *Human Rights and the Protection of Refugee in International Law*, ed. Alan E. Nash, The Institute for Research on Public Policy, (1988), 166.

42. Note for the File, Department of International Protection and Regional Bureau for Europe, UNHCR, Geneva, 15 November 1995.

43. Hans, Asha, *Repatriation of the Sri Lankan Refugees from India*, 2 Bulletin of International Humanitarian Law and Refugee Law (1997), 118.

44. See *Refugees in the SAARC Region: Building a Legal Framework*, Seminar Report, SAARCLAW and UNHCR, New Delhi, 2–3 May 1997.

45. UNHCR, *Fourth Informal Consultation on Refugee and Migratory Movements in South Asia*, Dhaka, 10–11 November 1997, 67–72.

16

Closing Keynote Address

Jeff Crisp

Let me begin by thanking the conference organizers for the opportunity to address the closing plenary of what has proven to be a fascinating and stimulating event. Over the past few days, we have had an opportunity to participate in discussions on an extraordinarily wide variety of topics, and it is difficult for me to think of what I can really add to those discussions. Our very able rapporteur, Ralph Wilde, will identify some of the principal issues and concerns that have emerged from this conference.[1]

There are, however, one or two topics that have received relatively little attention from the conference, and it is to those topics that I would now like to turn.

First, I would like to take a very brief look at the origins and development of refugee studies as an area of academic inquiry, and to take stock of the current state of affairs in that area. More specifically, I would like to identify some of the key challenges that now confront researchers in the refugee studies community, not least that of building more effective linkages with practitioners in operational agencies. As someone who sits somewhere halfway between researcher and practitioner, I am not sure whether I am in the best or the worst position to undertake this task.

Let me begin, then, with a brief introduction to the development of refugee and forced migration studies.

There is, of course, a long history of research and writing on refugees, much of it originating in the first five or six decades of the twentieth century, when the international refugee regime, as we now describe it, began to take shape.

While I cannot go into any detail, I would refer you to works such as Sir John Hope Simpson's work on refugees for the Royal Institute of International Affairs, published in 1936; Jacque Vernant's book, *The Refugee in the Post–War World*, which appeared in 1953; the legal texts of Paul Weiss and Atle Grahl-Madsen, published in the 1960s; and Louise Holborn's 1975 study in two volumes, *Refugees: A Problem of Our Times*.

Following the publication of Holborn's book in 1975, there appears to have been a distinct upsurge of academic and intellectual interest in refugee issues, manifested in the writing of scholars such as Barry Stein and Art Hansen. Significantly, however, much of this work appeared in journals concerned with international migration in general, rather than with refugees and forced migrants per se.

It is difficult to identify the moment at which this growing interest in refugees coalesced into a self-conscious academic phenomenon known as "refugee studies." But perhaps the defining moment came at the beginning of the 1980s, when Dr. Barbara Harrell-Bond, an American social anthropologist, set her sights on the establishment of a Refugee Studies Programme at the University of Oxford in the United Kingdom.

What exactly provoked this initiative? To a significant degree, it can be ascribed to the energy, the vision, and the tenacity of Barbara Harrell-Bond herself. At the same time, the emergence of refugee studies as a field of academic inquiry must be seen in relation to changes in the size and scope of the refugee problem. For in the two years preceding the establishment of the Refugee Studies in Oxford, the global refugee population had doubled— from just over 5 million in 1978 to over 10 million in 1981. During the same period, aid agency spending on refugee assistance programs had also increased very sharply. In the late 1970s, UNHCR's annual budget was below $200 million a year. By 1980, that had increased to over $500 million.

What Barbara Harrell-Bond and others quickly realized was that aid agencies such as UNHCR were not being held accountable for their rapidly growing expenditure, and that they devoted very few of their resources to research and analysis.

To substantiate this statement, let me quote from "The Quality of Mercy," a seminal analysis of the Cambodian refugee crisis, published by William Shawcross in 1984. "Humanitarian agencies," he wrote, "do not often publish discussions of their work. They release lists of the assistance they have given, but rarely offer real analysis. As a result, mistakes are repeated again and again, from one disaster to another. Like all generalizations," Shawcross concluded, "this one has its exceptions. But generally it applies both to UN organizations and to private agencies, large and small."

As this quotation suggests, there was from the very beginning a fundamental tension between aid organizations providing protection and assistance to refugees and researchers working in the emerging field of Refugee Studies. Whether that tension is a healthy one that should be fostered, or an unhealthy one that should be eradicated, is a question that I will return to later.

Let me now say a few words about the growth of refugee and forced migration studies over the past twenty years. Looking back to the early 1980s, those of us involved in the emerging field of refugee studies often repeated, in an almost mantralike manner, that refugees and refugee issues had been unfairly neglected by the academic community. I think we probably protested a little too much on this point. But at the same time, there was more than a kernel of truth to this argument. In general, the level of academic interest in refugee issues was low, and it took someone with a personality like Barbara Harrell-Bond to put refugee issues on the social science research agenda.

During the past two decades, I would suggest, the scenario has changed enormously. In the early 1980s, there were just a handful of academics working on refugee issues, most of them based in the United Kingdom and United States. Today, as demonstrated by this conference, as well as the establishment and growth of the International Association for the Study of Forced Migration, there are very large numbers of researchers working in this area, in many different parts of the world.

Going back to the early 1980s, there were no specialized journals on refugee and forced migration issues. By way of contrast, there are now three such journals: the *Journal of Refugee Studies*, the *International Journal of Refugee Law*, and *Refugee Survey Quarterly*, all of them published by Oxford University Press. There are also more popular publications such as the *Forced Migration Review and Refuge*, as well as the working papers on refugee issues, a series published by the Refugee Studies Centre and by UNHCR.

Institutionally, refugee studies has also experienced a significant expansion over the past twenty years. The Refugee Studies Programme—now called the Refugee Studies Centre—in Oxford, has survived and prospered. The Centre for Refugee Studies at York University in Canada has, I think, had a more difficult history, but is now consolidating itself again. But perhaps the most remarkable and positive development of recent years has been the growth of Refugee Studies in developing countries, most notably at the University of Dar-es-Salaam in Tanzania; at Moi University in Kenya; at the American University in Cairo, Egypt; and at Witwatersrand University here in South Africa.

Refugee Studies has expanded in another important way over the past two decades, and that is in the scope of its subject matter. I think it quickly became clear in the early and mid-1980s that refugee studies could not concern itself simply with refugees in the classical, 1951 convention meaning of the concept. Other categories of forced migration also had to be taken into account. Thus in 1986, Nick Van Hear and I worked on a book together for the Independent Commission on International Humanitarian issues entitled *Refugees: The Dynamics of Displacement.* But the book was not solely concerned with refugees. It also included chapters on internally displaced populations, returnees, asylum-seekers, victims of mass expulsions, and involuntary relocation programs.

Since that book was published, the notion of refugee studies has been replaced by the notion of forced migration studies, and many more categories of people have been added to the list. In addition to those already mentioned, forced migration studies concerns itself with development induced displacement, disaster-induced displacement, conservation-induced displacement, environmental refugees, nomads, irregular and illegal migrants, stateless people, diasporas, transnational communities, war-affected populations, and "stayees." As this list suggests, the notion of forced migration now seems to encompass people who haven't migrated at all, as well as migrants who haven't been forced to move.

The field of refugee studies and forced migration has, I would argue, become even more fuzzy and diffuse as a result of its close relationship with other areas of academic inquiry. Many of the papers presented at this conference, for example, could equally well have been presented at conferences on international migration, on peace and conflict studies, on international law and human rights, and on development studies.

The question that this leads me to pose—and I am not sure what my own answer would be—is whether we should try to set some kind of boundary to refugee and forced migration studies, so as to limit its concerns and retain its distinct identity. Or should we actually move beyond the concept of forced migration and begin to talk of vulnerable groups, or people in difficult circumstances?

In the next part of my presentation, I would also like to identify a number of other issues and challenges associated with the field of forced migration studies, and which seem to have emerged from this conference.

First, I would like to suggest that there is a need for better disciplinary balance in the area of forced migration studies. While I cannot present any empirical evidence to substantiate my claim, forced migration studies seem to be increasingly dominated by lawyers and anthropologists—a curious phenomenon, as they would appear to speak a mutually unintelligible language!

By way of contrast, two disciplines that are conspicuously absent from the forced migration discourse are history and economics. And that, I think, is a cause for some concern.

Since its inception, I would argue, refugee studies has been notoriously ahistorical. Preoccupied with the latest emergency and with the plight of living people, researchers in this area of study have all too rarely looked into the past.

Intellectually, historical research into refugee issues requires no justification. As with any other area of human activity, there is an inherent interest in reconstructing the past. In more practical and instrumental terms, a greater use of historical methods also seem to be called for. We need historians to understand the genesis and evolution of contemporary refugee crises. We need historians if we are to learn lessons from past experience and to avoid reinventing the wheel when dealing with refugee problems. We also need historians if we are to understand the behavior, culture, capacities, and constraints of the many different actors now involved in the international refugee regime.

As far as economics is concerned, I think it is probably self-evident that many of the issues that are of current interest to refugee researchers and practitioners would benefit from the contribution that this discipline could make. Under what conditions are refugee-producing conflicts most likely to arise? What impact do food aid and other refugee assistance have on local markets? What forms of livelihood do refugees and other forced migrants establish to supplement any aid they receive? How are local people affected by the sudden arrival of displaced populations? What forms of support are most needed when displaced populations are able to return to their country and community of origin? These are all staple questions posed by researchers and practitioners working on forced migration issues. And yet to a significant extent, we have been trying to answer them without the expertise that economists can provide.

Second, I would like to suggest that we strive for better geographical coverage in the area of refugee and forced migration studies. And by that I mean two things. Despite the steady expansion of the field, refugee and forced migration studies continue to be dominated by English-speaking researchers, many of them from so-called donor states.

Fortunately that is changing, as the multinational nature of this conference demonstrates. It is particularly pleasing to see so many participants from other parts of Africa, although the western and francophone parts of the continent seem conspicuous by their absence. It is equally pleasing to see so many conference participants from south Asia, an area where refugee and forced migration studies really seem to be taking off. As an International Association for the Study of Forced Migration, however, I believe that we should, both individually and collectively, strive to attain an even broader representation of countries and regions at the next biennial conference.

In that connection, may I also propose that at our next conference we strive to involve or engage refugees themselves in some meaningful way. It can be done. Some of you may recall the 1984 conference in Oxford, "Assistance to Refugees: Alternative Viewpoints," which led to a memorable and rather stormy encounter between a group of senior UNHCR officials from Geneva and a group of Ugandan refugees who had been flown to the conference from their refugee camps in southern Sudan.

Of course it is difficult to imagine such a remarkable event happening today, since the British government's visa policy would never allow the entry of refugees from a country of first asylum. But wherever our next conference is held, it should not be too difficult to involve locally based refugees who wish to participate in our discussions.[2]

In speaking of the geographical coverage of refugee and forced migration studies, I am also referring to the locations that we cover in our research. Here again, the scope has broadened in recent years, due in large part to global changes in the pattern of forced migration. In the 1980s, much of the research on refugees was undertaken in the Horn and east of Africa, Pakistan, southeast Asia and Central America, where the largest populations of forced migrants were to be found. Today, the attention of researchers has naturally shifted to new areas of mass displacement: the Great Lakes region of Africa, west Africa, south Asia, the Balkans and, to some extent, the countries of the former Soviet Union.

But other areas remain neglected. The Middle East and the Islamic world in general, stretching from Mauretania and Western Sahara in the west to Indonesia in the east, does not seem to be adequately represented on the Refugee Studies research agenda. And within that region, the situation of the Palestinian refugees—more than 3.5 million people—seems to have been scandalously neglected.

For reasons of its mandate, UNHCR does not consider Palestinians in the Middle East to be of concern to the organization, and does not even include the Palestinians in its global refugee statistics. But why do academic researchers appear to accept this arbitrary distinction? Why does research on refugee issues so rarely focus on the Palestinians or refer to the Palestinian case for comparative purposes? Why was it that the only papers on the Palestinians at this conference were presented at a session devoted to the Palestinian issue? Is it really the case that nothing can be learned from the Palestinian situation in relation to the many other themes and topics we have discussed?

The third challenge I want to mention is that of balancing analysis with advocacy. I think it's fair to say that very few of us become involved in refugee and forced migration studies for intellectual reasons alone. As Art Hansen said during one of the panels yesterday, most of us have a moral and ethical commitment to the welfare of refugees and to the many other categories of people who form the subject of our research.

That commitment is clearly a strength. Going back to the early days of our field, it is evident that Barbara Harrell-Bond's determination to establish the refugee studies program was driven not only by intellectual curiosity, but also by a powerful sense of injustice concerning the situation and treatment of refugees. I am sure that many other people in this room have been motivated by a similar combination of sentiments.

But I think we also have to be careful to maintain a balance and a dividing line between analysis and advocacy, both as individuals and, more importantly, as a community of researchers. To give one example from this conference, I was a little disturbed that during our opening round table, we began to discuss the academic community's strategy—and strategy was the word that was used—in relation to temporary protection.

I feel that it is entirely appropriate for NGOs and human rights agencies to develop a strategy in relation to temporary protection. I also feel that it is entirely appropriate for individual researchers to lend their intellectual weight to the efforts of NGOs and human rights agencies. But as a community and association of researchers, I have serious reservations about the wisdom of taking a collective or institutional position on specific policy issues. Indeed, it was the association of the Refugee Studies Programme in Oxford with particular policy positions that did much to undermine its credibility—especially in the eyes of UNHCR—in the early days of its development.

Similarly, I would like to call on members of the association to maintain an open-minded attitude and to encourage an open debate on policy issues in the domain of refugees and forced migration. Perhaps I am oversensitive, but at times I have felt this conference to be characterized by a kind of liberal hegemony, which makes it difficult for anyone to say unpopular things: that states have a right to control immigration, that refugees can have negative effects on the countries where they settle, or that unsuccessful asylum-seekers can justifiably be detained and deported. Perhaps some dissenting voices on these and other issues would make our community a livelier one and force us all to sharpen the quality of our thinking.

Fourth and finally, I would like to address an issue raised earlier in my presentation, namely that of the relationship—and the alleged gap—between researchers and practitioners in the field of refugees and forced migration.

This question has been a perennial preoccupation of people involved in the field of refugee studies, for the very reason that I mentioned earlier. As individuals with a moral and ethical commitment to the welfare of the people they study, most if not all researchers in the field want to ensure that their work has some practical and positive human consequence.

Let me close my presentation by making a few observations about the so-called gap between researchers and practitioners.

First, I do not think that we can dispute that such a gap exists, in the sense that researchers and practitioners have different objectives, different working methods, different interests, and different terms of employment. The immediate preoccupations of researchers and practitioners are also likely to be at variance with each other.

I can illustrate that point with an anecdote. In April 1991, I was traveling by air to Turkey with Mrs. Ogata, the newly appointed high commissioner for refugees, at the height of the Kurdish refugee crisis. Trying to make some conversation, I innocently asked Mrs. Ogata, who had recently left Sofia University in Tokyo, whether she would pursue her research interests in her new position as high commissioner. She gave me a withering look (and nobody does that better than Mrs. Ogata) and said, "you don't think I've got time for research at a time like this do you?" I'm sure many other practitioners have made similar comments to you.

Second, I would like to suggest that the gap between researchers and practitioners is not a wholly negative phenomenon. Indeed, I would not like to see the field of refugee and forced migration studies become purely instrumental and practical in nature, geared towards the immediate needs of refugees and aid organizations.

Surely the whole spirit of academic inquiry is a noninstrumental one—based on a belief that knowledge is important in its own right, and an understanding that research findings and the uses to which they will be put cannot be predicted in advance. In that respect, I would fully respect the wishes of any researcher who wanted to undertake an apparently obscure piece of refugee-related research, with no apparent use as a means of improving the welfare of the refugees concerned.

Third, I would like to suggest that the researcher/practitioner gap is not quite as wide or as serious as it is sometimes made out to be. If you look at the mixture of people who attend conferences such as this. If you look at the authors who contribute to the refugee-related journals I mentioned earlier. If you look at the curricula vitae of refugee researchers and practitioners. And if you look at the people engaged by agencies such as UNHCR as consultants, advisors, and evaluators, then you will see that a considerable amount of interaction takes place between the world of the researcher and the world of the practitioner.

At the same time, I believe that the research undertaken by academics in the field of refugee and forced migration studies does play a role in shaping the understanding, the perceptions, the policies, and the programs of operational agencies such as UNHCR. Now I am not going to suggest that every UNHCR fieldworker goes around with a copy of Jim Hathaway's or Gil Loescher's latest book in their back pocket. But significant connections can be found between academic research and the way in which UNHCR does business.

Let me give you three examples: the work undertaken by Susan Martin and others on refugee women and gender issues; the research carried out by Mary Anderson and others on war economies and the unintended consequences of humanitarian assistance; and the research carried out under the leadership of Fred Cuny and Barry Stein on repatriation under conflict. In each of these cases, I would argue, research had an impact on policy and practice.

Let us not be too despondent therefore. While there is a gap between researchers and practitioners, it is perhaps smaller than it is believed to be and in any case it is not a wholly unhealthy phenomenon.

At the same time, however, let us not be complacent. Researchers and research findings do have the potential to contribute to the work of operational agencies and to the welfare of refugees and other people in need. It would be irresponsible of us not to maximize and to realize that potential. How exactly can that be done?

First, be constructive in your criticisms. Humanitarian organizations and practitioners are easy targets, and have been subjected to their fair share of criticism in recent years. And none more so than UNHCR. There is nothing wrong with that. Humanitarian organizations absorb considerable resources and yield considerable power over people's lives. They should therefore be held accountable for their actions.

In tactical terms, however, if you want your research to be taken seriously and if you want to influence policy and programs, don't be entirely negative. Do have practical suggestions as to how aid agency practice might be improved, and unless you have strong evidence to support your case, don't question the motivations and personal integrity of people working as practitioners. In other words, don't write a book like Alex de Waal's *Famine Crimes*.

Second, make sure that your research involves fieldwork and is not purely conceptual in nature. We cannot deny that some practitioners regard academic research as irrelevant or esoteric, and that problem is exacerbated when researchers insist on undertaking library-based studies that fail to engage with empirical reality.

Unfortunately, that seems to be increasingly the case. To give just one example, during the past year I have seen at least five graduate students who wanted to write dissertations on the question of organizational responsibility for IDPs in the UN system. I have not seen one graduate student who wanted to go to Angola, Sudan, Liberia, or Sri Lanka to research an IDP situation on the ground.

I think this is an important point, because there is some evidence to suggest that UNHCR is losing contact with the people it assists. Certainly, during my last few field missions, colleagues have complained that as an organization we seem to know less and less about the people and communities we work with.

I am not totally sure why this is happening, but I think it can be ascribed to the following factors: the growing insecurity of many refugee-populated areas, and the consequent tendency of UNHCR staff to live in secure urban areas, often a long way from the nearest camp or settlement; the reporting requirements made on UNHCR staff and offices in the field, something which keeps staff members tied to their computers rather than mixing with and talking to refugees; and the rapid turnover of UNHCR staff in remote locations, which makes it difficult to develop any institutional memory at the local level. Academics, I would like to suggest, could play a valuable role in helping us to address this problem by means of extensive field-based research.

Third, I would like to suggest that if you want to narrow the researcher/practitioner gap, and if you want to influence policy and practice, then you should present your findings in an accessible form. While I recognize the dangers of dumbing down, I would also like to remind you that many practitioners are very busy people; they may have finished their studies many years ago and be unaccustomed to the academic discourse; and they may well have English as their second or third language. Research that is written up at enormous length or in the esoteric language of postmodernism is unlikely to attract their attention. Or mine for that matter.

Fourth—and now I will become even more condescending to my friends in the academic community, please respect—and encourage your students to respect, some basic research protocol. If you want to narrow the gap between researchers and practitioners, don't send an e-mail to UNHCR saying, "I am writing a dissertation on Afghan refugees. Please send me all the information you have got on this topic." If you want to narrow the gap between researchers and practitioners, don't go to the field assuming that there will always be a free seat in the next UNHCR plane or Land Cruiser that is heading in the direction you want to go. And if you want to narrow the gap between researchers and practitioners, make sure that you send a copy of your research findings to individuals and organizations who have assisted you with your work. For on too many occasions, we simply don't receive copies of research reports that might have the potential to influence our work.

Finally, and a little more seriously, UNHCR and other humanitarian agencies also have an evident obligation to make more effective use of academic research.

To what extent do we actually commission research that might enhance our understanding of refugee situations and improve the quality of our programs? Do we give adequate access and support to researchers who are working on issues that are of concern and interest to us? Do we make an effort to examine new research and to identify its implications for our work? And do those of us who have access to such research make any effort to synthesize and summarize it and to ensure that it is properly disseminated within the organization?

NOTES

1. See report in *Journal of Refugee Studies* 14.2.

2. Editor's Note: The 8th Conference of the International Association for the Study of Forced Migration is to be held in January 2003 in Chiang Mai, Thailand—and plans are underway as this volume is completed (June 2002) for Burmese refugees to be involved in many ways in that meeting.

Appendix: Convention Relating to the Status of Refugees, Adopted on 28 July 1951 by the United Nations Conference of Plenipotentiaries on the Status of Refugees and Stateless Persons, Convened under General Assembly Resolution 429(v) of 14 December 1950

Text: 189 UNTS 150 entry into force 22 April 1954, in accordance with Article 43

PREAMBLE

The High Contracting Parties,

Considering that the Charter of the United Nations and the Universal Declaration of Human Rights approved on 10 December 1948 by the General Assembly have affirmed the principle that human beings shall enjoy fundamental rights and freedoms without discrimination,

Considering that the United Nations has, on various occasions, manifested its profound concern for refugees and endeavoured to assure refugees the widest possible exercise of these fundamental rights and freedoms,

Considering that it is desirable to revise and consolidate previous international agreements relating to the status of refugees and to extend the scope of and the protection accorded by such instruments by means of a new agreement,

Considering that the grant of asylum may place unduly heavy burdens on certain countries, and that a satisfactory solution of a problem of which the United Nations has recognized the international-scope and nature cannot therefore be achieved without international co-operation,

Expressing the wish that all States, recognizing the social and humanitarian nature of the problem of refugees, will do everything within their power to prevent this problem from becoming a cause of tension between States,

Noting that the United Nations High Commissioner for Refugees is charged with the task of supervising international conventions providing for the protection of refugees, and recognizing that the effective co-ordination of measures taken to deal with this problem will depend upon the co-operation of States with the High Commissioner,

Have agreed as follows:

CHAPTER I—GENERAL PROVISIONS

Article 1.—Definition of the term "refugee"

A. For the purposes of the present convention, the term "refugee" shall apply to any person who:

(1) Has been considered a refugee under the Arrangements of 12 May 1926 and 30 June 1928 or under the Conventions of 28 October 1933 and 10 February 1938, the Protocol of 14 September 1939 or the Constitution of the International Refugee Organization;

　　Decisions of non-eligibility taken by the International Refugee Organization during the period of its activities shall not prevent the status of refugee being accorded to persons who fulfil the conditions of paragraph 2 of this section;

(2) As a result of events occurring before 1 January 1951 and owing to well-founded fear of being persecuted for reasons of race, religion, nationality, membership of a particular social group or political opinion, is outside the country of his nationality and is unable, or owing to such fear, is unwilling to avail himself of the protection of that country; or who, not having a nationality and being outside the country of his former habitual residence as a result of such events, is unable or, owing to such fear, is unwilling to return to it.

　　In the case of a person who has more than one nationality, the term "the country of his nationality" shall mean each of the countries of which he is a national, and a person shall not be deemed to be lacking the protection of the country of his nationality if, without any valid reason based on well-founded fear, he has not availed himself of the protection of one of the countries of which he is a national.

B. (1) For the purposes of this Convention, the words "events occurring before 1 January 1951" in article 1, section A, shall be understood to mean either

   (a) "events occurring in Europe before 1 January 1951"; or

   (b) "events occurring in Europe or elsewhere before 1 January 1951"; and each contracting state shall make a declaration at the time of signature, ratification, or accession, specifying which of these meanings it applies for the purpose of its obligations under this Convention.

(2) Any Contracting State, which has adopted alternative (a) may at any time extend its obligations by adopting alternative (b) by means of a notification addressed to the Secretary-General of the United Nations.

C. This Convention shall cease to apply to any person falling under the terms of section A if:

   (1) He has voluntarily re-availed himself of the protection of the country of his nationality; or

   (2) Having lost his nationality, he has voluntarily reacquired it; or

   (3) He has acquired a new nationality, and enjoys the protection of the country of his new nationality; or

   (4) He has voluntarily re-established himself in the country that he left or outside which he remained owing to fear of persecution; or

   (5) He can no longer, because the circumstances in connection with which he has been recognized as a refugee have ceased to exist, continue to refuse to avail himself of the protection of the country of his nationality;

      Provided that this paragraph shall not apply to a refugee falling under section A (I) of this article who is able to invoke compelling reasons arising out of previous persecution for refusing to avail himself of the protection of the country of nationality;

   (6) Being a person who has no nationality he is, because the circumstances in connection with which he has been recognized as a refugee have ceased to exist, able to return to the country of his former habitual residence;

      Provided that this paragraph shall not apply to a refugee falling under section A (I) of this article who is able to invoke compelling reasons arising out of previous persecution for refusing to return to the country of his former habitual residence.

D. This Convention shall not apply to persons who are at present receiving from organs or agencies of the United Nations other than the United Nations High Commissioner for Refugees protection or assistance.

When such protection or assistance has ceased for any reason, without the position of such persons being definitively settled in accordance with the relevant resolutions adopted by the General Assembly of the United Nations, these persons shall ipso facto be entitled to the benefits of this Convention.

E. This Convention shall not apply to a person who is recognized by the competent authorities of the country in which he has taken residence as having the rights and obligations which are attached to the possession of the nationality of that country.

F. The provisions of this Convention shall not apply to any person with respect to whom there are serious reasons for considering that:
  (a) He has committed a crime against peace, a war crime, or a crime against humanity, as defined in the international instruments drawn up to make provision in respect of such crimes;
  (b) He has committed a serious non-political crime outside the country of refuge prior to his admission to that country as a refugee;
  (c) He has been guilty of acts contrary to the purposes and principles of the United Nations.

Article 2.—General obligations

Every refugee has duties to the country in which he finds himself, which require, in particular, that he conform to its laws and regulations as well as to measures taken for the maintenance of public order.

Article 3.—Non-discrimination

The Contracting States shall apply the provisions of this Convention to refugees without discrimination as to race, religion or country of origin.

Article 4.—Religion

The Contracting States shall accord to refugees within their territories treatment at least as favourable as that accorded to their nationals with respect to freedom to practise their religion and freedom as regards the religious education of their children.

Article 5.—Rights granted apart from this Convention

Nothing in this Convention shall be deemed to impair any rights and benefits granted by a Contracting State to refugees apart from this Convention.

Article 6.—The term "in the same circumstances"

For the purposes of this Convention, the term "in the same circumstances" implies that any requirements (including requirements as to length and conditions of sojourn or residence) which the particular individual would have to fulfil for the enjoyment of the right in question, if he were not a refugee, must be fulfilled by him, with the exception of requirements which by their nature a refugee is incapable of fulfilling.

Article 7.—Exemption from reciprocity

1. Except where this Convention contains more favourable provisions, a Contracting State shall accord to refugees the same treatment as is accorded to aliens generally.
2. After a period of three years' residence, all refugees shall enjoy exemption from legislative reciprocity in the territory of the Contracting States.
3. Each Contracting State shall continue to accord to refugees the rights and benefits to which they were already entitled, in the absence of reciprocity, at the date of entry into force of this Convention for that State.
4. The Contracting States shall consider favourably the possibility of according to refugees, in the absence of reciprocity, rights and benefits beyond those to which they are entitled according to paragraphs 2 and 3, and to extending exemption from reciprocity to refugees who do not fulfil the conditions provided for in paragraphs 2 and 3.
5. The provisions of paragraphs 2 and 3 apply both to the rights and benefits referred to in articles 13, 18, 19, 21 and 22 of this Convention and to rights and benefits for which this Convention does not provide.

Article 8.—Exemption from exceptional measures

With regard to exceptional measures which may be taken against the person, property or interests of nationals of a foreign State, the Contracting States shall not apply such measures to a refugee who is formally a national of the said State solely on account of such nationality. Contracting States which, under their legislation, are prevented from applying the general principle expressed in this article, shall, in appropriate cases, grant exemptions in favour of such refugees.

Article 9.—Provisional measures

Nothing in this convention shall prevent a Contracting State, in time of war or other grave and exceptional circumstances, from taking provisional measures which it considers to be essential to the national security in the case of a particular person, pending a determination by the Contracting State that that person is in fact a refugee and that the continuance of such measures is necessary in his case in the interests of national security.

Article 10.—Continuity of residence

1. Where a refugee has been forcibly displaced during the Second World War and removed to the territory of a Contracting State, and is resident there, the period of such enforced sojourn shall be considered to have been lawful residence within that territory.
2. Where a refugee has been forcibly displaced during the Second World War from the territory of a Contracting State and has, prior to the date of entry into force of this Convention, returned there for the purpose of taking up residence, the period of residence before and after such enforced displacement shall be regarded as one uninterrupted period for any purposes for which uninterrupted residence is required.

Article 11.—Refugee seamen

In the case of refugees regularly serving as crew members on board a ship flying the flag of a Contracting State, that State shall give sympathetic consideration to their establishment on its territory and the issue of travel documents to them or their temporary admission to its territory particularly with a view to facilitating their establishment in another country.

CHAPTER II—JURIDICAL STATUS

Article 12.—Personal status

1. The personal status of a refugee shall be governed by the law of the country of his domicile or, if he has no domicile, by the law of the country of his residence.
2. Rights previously acquired by a refugee and dependent on personal status, more particularly rights attaching to marriage, shall be respected by a Contracting State, subject to compliance, if this be necessary, with the formalities required by the law of that State, provided that the right in question is one which would have been recognized by the law of that State had he not become a refugee.

Article 13.—Movable and immovable property

The Contracting States shall accord to a refugee treatment as favourable as possible and, in any event, not less favourable than that accorded to aliens generally in the same circumstances, as regards the acquisition of movable and immovable property and other rights pertaining thereto, and to leases and other contracts relating to movable and immovable property.

Article 14.—Artistic rights and industrial property

In respect of the protection of industrial property, such as inventions, designs or models, trade marks, trade names, and of rights in literary, artistic, and scientific works, a refugee shall be accorded in the country in which he has his habitual residence the same protection as is accorded to nationals of that country. In the territory of any other Contracting States, he shall be accorded the same protection as is accorded in that territory to nationals of the country in which he has his habitual residence.

Article 15.—Right of association

As regards non-political and nonprofit-making associations and trade unions the Contracting States shall accord to refugees lawfully staying in their territory the most favourable treatment accorded to nationals of a foreign country, in the same circumstances.

Article 16.—Access to courts

1. A refugee shall have free access to the courts of law on the territory of all Contracting States.
2. A refugee shall enjoy in the Contracting State in which he has his habitual residence the same treatment as a national in matters pertaining to access to the courts, including legal assistance and exemption from cautio judicatum solvi.
3. A refugee shall be accorded in the matters referred to in paragraph 2 in countries other than that in which he has his habitual residence the treatment granted to a national of the country of his habitual residence.

CHAPTER III—GAINFUL EMPLOYMENT

Article 17.—Wage-earning employment

1. The Contracting States shall accord to refugees lawfully staying in their territory the most favourable treatment accorded to nationals of a foreign country in the same circumstances, as regards the right to engage in wage-earning employment.
2. In any case, restrictive measures imposed on aliens or the employment of aliens for the protection of the national labour market shall not be applied to a refugee who was already exempt from them at the date of entry into force of this Convention for the Contracting State concerned, or who fulfils one of the following conditions:
   (a) He has completed three years' residence in the country;

(b) He has a spouse possessing the nationality of the country of residence. A refugee may not invoke the benefit of this provision if he has abandoned his spouse;

(c) He has one or more children possessing the nationality of the country of residence.

3. The Contracting States shall give sympathetic consideration to assimilating the rights of all refugees with regard to wage-earning employment to those of nationals, and in particular of those refugees who have entered their territory pursuant to programmes of labour recruitment or under immigration schemes.

Article 18.—Self-employment

The Contracting States shall accord to a refugee lawfully in their territory treatment as favourable as possible and, in any event, not less favourable than that accorded to aliens generally in the same circumstances, as regards the right to engage on his own account in agriculture, industry, handicrafts and commerce and to establish commercial and industrial companies.

Article 19.—Liberal professions

1. Each Contracting State shall accord to refugees lawfully staying in their territory who hold diplomas recognized by the competent authorities of that State, and who are desirous of practising a liberal profession, treatment as favourable as possible and, in any event, not less favourable than that accorded to aliens generally in the same circumstances.

2. The Contracting States shall use their best endeavours consistently with their laws and constitutions to secure the settlement of such refugees in the territories, other than the metropolitan territory, for whose international relations they are responsible.

CHAPTER IV—WELFARE

Article 20.—Rationing

Where a rationing system exists, which applies to the population at large and regulates the general distribution of products in short supply, refugees shall be accorded the same treatment as nationals.

Article 21.—Housing

As regards housing, the Contracting States, in so far as the matter is regulated by laws or regulations or is subject to the control of public authorities, shall accord to refugees lawfully staying in their territory treatment as favourable as possible and, in any event, not less favourable than that accorded to aliens generally in the same circumstances.

Article 22.—Public education

1. The Contracting States shall accord to refugees the same treatment as is accorded to nationals with respect to elementary education.
2. The Contracting States shall accord to refugees treatment as favourable as possible, and, in any event, not less favourable than that accorded to aliens generally in the same circumstances, with respect to education other than elementary education and, in particular, as regards access to studies, the recognition of foreign school certificates, diplomas and degrees, the remission of fees and charges and the award of scholarships.

Article 23.—Public relief

The Contracting States shall accord to refugees lawfully staying in their territory the same treatment with respect to public relief and assistance as is accorded to their nationals.

Article 24.—Labour legislation and social security

1. The Contracting States shall accord to refugees lawfully staying in their territory the same treatment as is accorded to nationals in respect of the following matters:
   (a) In so far as such matters are governed by laws or regulations or are subject to the control of administrative authorities: remuneration, including family allowances where these form part of remuneration, hours of work, overtime arrangements, holidays with pay, restrictions on home work, minimum age of employment, apprenticeship and training, women's work and the work of young persons, and the enjoyment of the benefits of collective bargaining;
   (b) Social security (legal provisions in respect of employment injury, occupational diseases, maternity, sickness, disability, old age, death, unemployment, family responsibilities and any other contingency which, according to national laws or regulations, is covered by a social security scheme), subject to the following limitations:
      (i) There may be appropriate arrangements for the maintenance of acquired rights and rights in course of acquisition;
      (ii) National laws or regulations of the country of residence may prescribe special arrangements concerning benefits or portions

of benefits which are payable wholly out of public funds, and concerning allowances paid to persons who do not fulfil the contribution conditions prescribed for the award of a normal pension.

2. The right to compensation for the death of a refugee resulting from employment injury or from occupational disease shall not be affected by the fact that the residence of the beneficiary is outside the territory of the Contracting State.

3. The Contracting States shall extend to refugees the benefits of agreements concluded between them, or which may be concluded between them in the future, concerning the maintenance of acquired rights and rights in the process of acquisition in regard to social security, subject only to the conditions which apply to nationals of the States signatory to the agreements in question.

4. The Contracting States will give sympathetic consideration to extending to refugees so far as possible the benefits of similar agreements which may at any time be in force between such Contracting States and non-contracting States.

CHAPTER V—ADMINISTRATIVE MEASURES

Article 25.—Administrative assistance

1. When the exercise of a right by a refugee would normally require the assistance of authorities of a foreign country to whom he cannot have recourse, the Contracting States in whose territory he is residing shall arrange that such assistance be afforded to him by their own authorities or by an international authority.

2. The authority or authorities mentioned in paragraph 1 shall deliver or cause to be delivered under their supervision to refugees such documents or certifications as would normally be delivered to aliens by or through their national authorities.

3. Documents or certifications so delivered shall stand in the stead of the official instruments delivered to aliens by or through their national authorities, and shall be given credence in the absence of proof to the contrary.

4. Subject to such exceptional treatment as may be granted to indigent persons, fees may be charged for the services mentioned herein, but such fees shall be moderate and commensurate with those charged to nationals for similar services.

5 The provisions of this article shall be without prejudice to articles 27 and 28.

Article 26.—Freedom of movement

Each Contracting State shall accord to refugees lawfully in its territory the right to choose their place of residence and to move freely within its territory subject to any regulations applicable to aliens generally in the same circumstances.

Article 27.—Identity papers

The Contracting States shall issue identity papers to any refugee in their territory who does not possess a valid travel document.

Article 28.—Travel documents

1. The Contracting States shall issue to refugees lawfully staying in their territory travel documents for the purpose of travel outside their territory, unless compelling reasons of national security or public order otherwise require, and the provisions of the Schedule to this Convention shall apply with respect to such documents. The Contracting States may issue such a travel document to any other refugee in their territory; they shall in particular give sympathetic consideration to the issue of such a travel document to refugees in their territory who are unable to obtain a travel document from the country of their lawful residence.
2. Travel documents issued to refugees under previous international agreements by Parties thereto shall be recognized and treated by the Contracting States in the same way as if they had been issued pursuant to this article.

Article 29.—Fiscal charges

1. The Contracting States shall not impose upon refugees duties, charges or taxes, of any description whatsoever, other or higher than those which are or may be levied on their nationals in similar situations.
2. Nothing in the above paragraph shall prevent the application to refugees of the laws and regulations concerning charges in respect of the issue to aliens of administrative documents including identity papers.

Article 30.—Transfer of assets

1. A Contracting State shall, in conformity with its laws and regulations, permit refugees to transfer assets which they have brought into its territory, to another country where they have been admitted for the purposes of resettlement.

2. A Contracting State shall give sympathetic consideration to the application of refugees for permission to transfer assets wherever they may be and which are necessary for their resettlement in another country to which they have been admitted.

Article 31.—Refugees unlawfully in the country of refuge

1. The contracting states shall not impose penalties, on account of their illegal entry or presence, on refugees who, coming directly from a territory where their life or freedom was threatened in the sense of article 1, enter or are present in their territory without authorization, provided they present themselves without delay to the authorities and show good cause for their illegal entry or presence.
2. The Contracting States shall not apply to the movements of such refugees restrictions other than those which are necessary and such restrictions shall only be applied until their status in the country is regularized or they obtain admission into another country. The Contracting States shall allow such refugees a reasonable period and all the necessary facilities to obtain admission into another country.

Article 32.—Expulsion

1. The Contracting States shall not expel a refugee lawfully in their territory save on grounds of national security or public order.
2. The expulsion of such a refugee shall be only in pursuance of a decision reached in accordance with due process of law. Except where compelling reasons of national security otherwise require, the refugee shall be allowed to submit evidence to clear himself, and to appeal to and be represented for the purpose before competent authority or a person or persons specially designated by the competent authority.
3. The Contracting States shall allow such a refugee a reasonable period within which to seek legal admission into another country. The Contracting States reserve the right to apply during that period such internal measures as they may deem necessary.

Article 33.—Prohibition of expulsion or return ("Refoulement")

1. No Contracting State shall expel or return ("refouler") a refugee in any manner whatsoever to the frontiers of territories where his life or freedom would be threatened on account of his race, religion, nationality, membership of a particular social group or political opinion.
2. The benefit of the present provision may not, however, be claimed by a refugee whom there are reasonable grounds for regarding as a dan-

ger to the security of the country in which he is, or who, having been convicted by a final judgement of a particularly serious crime, constitutes a danger to the community of that country.

Article 34.—Naturalization

The Contracting States shall as far as possible facilitate the assimilation and naturalization of refugees. They shall in particular make every effort to expedite naturalization proceedings and to reduce as far as possible the charges and costs of such proceedings.

CHAPTER VI—EXECUTORY AND TRANSITORY PROVISIONS

Article 35.—Co-operation of the national authorities with the United Nations

1. The Contracting States undertake to co-operate with the Office of the United Nations High Commissioner for Refugees, or any other agency of the United Nations which may succeed it, in the exercise of its functions, and shall in particular facilitate its duty of supervising the application of the provisions of this Convention.
2. In order to enable the Office of the High Commissioner or any other agency of the United Nations which may succeed it, to make reports to the competent organs of the United Nations, the Contracting States undertake to provide them in the appropriate form with information and statistical data requested concerning:
   (a) The condition of refugees,
   (b) The implementation of this Convention, and
   (c) Laws, regulations and decrees which are, or may hereafter be, in force relating to refugees.

Article 36.—Information on national legislation

The Contracting States shall communicate to the Secretary-General of the United Nations the laws and regulations which they may adopt to ensure the application of this Convention.

Article 37.—Relation to previous conventions

Without prejudice to article 28, paragraph 2, of this Convention, this Convention replaces, as between Parties to it, the Arrangements of 5 July 1922, 31 May 1924, 12 May 1926, 30 June 1928 and 30 July 1935, the Conventions of 28 October 1933 and 10 February 1938, the Protocol of 14 September 1939, and the Agreement of 15 October 1946.

CHAPTER VII—FINAL CLAUSES

Article 38.—Settlement of disputes

Any dispute between Parties to this Convention relating to its interpretation or application, which cannot be settled by other means, shall be referred to the International Court of Justice at the request of any one of the parties to the dispute.

Article 39.—Signature, ratification and accession

1. This Convention shall be opened for signature at Geneva on 28 July 1951 and shall thereafter be deposited with the Secretary-General of the United Nations. It shall be open for signature at the European Office of the United Nations from 28 July to 31 August 1951 and shall be re-opened for signature at the Headquarters of the United Nations from 17 September 1951 to 31 December 1952.
2. This Convention shall be open for signature on behalf of all States Members of the United Nations, and also on behalf of any other State invited to attend the Conference of Plenipotentiaries on the Status of Refugees and Stateless Persons or to which an invitation to sign will have been addressed by the General Assembly. It shall be ratified and the instruments of ratification shall be deposited with the Secretary-General of the United Nations.
3. This Convention shall be open from 28 July 1951 for accession by the States referred to in paragraph 2 of this article. Accession shall be effected by the deposit of an instrument of accession with the Secretary-General of the United Nations.

Article 40.—Territorial application clause

1. Any state may, at the time of signature, ratification, or accession, declare that this Convention shall extend to all or any of the territories for the international relations of which it is responsible. Such a declaration shall take effect when the Convention enters into force for the State concerned.
2. At any time thereafter any such extension shall be made by notification addressed to the Secretary-General of the United Nations and shall take effect as from the ninetieth day after the day of receipt by the Secretary-

General of the United Nations of this notification, or as from the date of entry into force of the Convention for the State concerned, whichever is the later.

3. With respect to those territories to which this Convention is not extended at the time of signature, ratification or accession, each state concerned shall consider the possibility of taking the necessary steps in order to extend the application of this Convention to such territories, subject, where necessary for constitutional reasons, to the consent of the Governments of such territories.

Article 41.—Federal clause

In the case of a Federal or non-unitary State, the following provisions shall apply:

(a) With respect to those articles of this Convention that come within the legislative jurisdiction of the federal legislative authority, the obligations of the Federal Government shall to this extent be the same as those of parties which are not Federal States;

(b) With respect to those articles of this Convention that come within the legislative jurisdiction of constituent States, provinces, or cantons, which are not, under the constitutional system of the Federation, bound to take legislative action, the Federal Government shall bring such articles with a favourable recommendation to the notice of the appropriate authorities of States, provinces or cantons at the earliest possible moment;

(c) A Federal State Party to this Convention shall, at the request of any other Contracting State transmitted through the Secretary-General of the United Nations, supply a statement of the law and practice of the Federation and its constituent units in regard to any particular provision of the Convention showing the extent to which effect has been given to that provision by legislative or other action.

Article 42.—Reservations

1. At the time of signature, ratification or accession, any State may make reservations to articles of the convention other than to articles 1, 3, 4, 16 (1), 33, 36–46 inclusive.

2. Any State making a reservation in accordance with paragraph 1 of this article may at any time withdraw the reservation by a communication to that effect addressed to the Secretary-General of the United Nations.

Article 43.—Entry into force

1. This Convention shall come into force on the ninetieth day following the day of deposit of the sixth instrument of ratification or accession.
2. For each State ratifying or acceding to the Convention after the deposit of the sixth instrument of ratification or accession, the Convention shall enter into force on the ninetieth day following the date of deposit by such State of its instrument of ratification or accession.

Article 44.—Denunciation

1. Any Contracting State may denounce this Convention at any time by a notification addressed to the Secretary-General of the United Nations.
2. Such denunciation shall take effect for the Contracting State concerned one year from the date upon which it is received by the Secretary-General of the United Nations.
3. Any State which has made a declaration or notification under article 40 may, at any time thereafter, by a notification to the Secretary-General of the United Nations, declare that the Convention shall cease to extend to such territory one year after the date of receipt of the notification by the Secretary-General.

Article 45.—Revision

1. Any Contracting State may request revision of this Convention at any time by a notification addressed to the Secretary-General of the United Nations.
2. The General Assembly of the United Nations shall recommend the steps, if any, to be taken in respect of such request.

Article 46.—Notifications by the Secretary-General of the United Nations

The Secretary-General of the United Nations shall inform all Members of the United Nations and non-member States referred to in article 39:

(a) Of declarations and notifications in accordance with section B of article 1;
(b) Of signatures, ratifications and accessions in accordance with article 39;
(c) Of declarations and notifications in accordance with article 40;
(d) Of reservations and withdrawals in accordance with article 42;
(e) Of the date on which this Convention will come into force in accordance with article 43;

(f) Of denunciations and notifications in accordance with article 44;

(g) Of requests for revision in accordance with article 45.

IN FAITH WHEREOF the undersigned, duly authorized, have signed this convention on behalf of their respective Governments.

DONE at Geneva, this twenty-eighth day of July, one thousand nine hundred and fifty-one, in a single copy, of which the English and French texts are equally authentic and which shall remain deposited in the archives of the United Nations, and certified true copies of which shall be delivered to all Members of the United Nations and to the non-member States referred to in article 39.

About the Editors and Contributors

EDITORS

JOANNE VAN SELM is Senior Policy Analyst at the Migration Policy Institute (Washington, D.C.) and Senior Researcher at the Institute for Migration and Ethnic Studies, University of Amsterdam. She is a member of the Executive Committee of the IASFM and co-editor of the Journal of Refugee Studies (OUP).

KHOTI KAMANGA studied public international Law and European Union Law in Moscow and Amsterdam. He is Senior Lecturer and Head of Department of International Law at the University of Dar es Salaam, Tanzania, where he also serves as Coordinator for the Centre for the Study of Forced Migration (CSFM).

JOHN MORRISON is Head of Global Campaigning at The Body Shop International. He has published two reports on refugee trafficking and smuggling in Europe and has worked on issues of human rights and migration for the United Nations and NGOs. John is a Harkness Fellow, a member of the Amnesty Business Group, and a trustee of the Prisoner of Conscience Appeal Fund.

ANINIA NADIG is the coordinator of the Dutch Working Group on International Refugee Policy, a collective of NGOs in the Netherlands with an interest in international refugee related issues. She was involved in the organization of the

7th IRAP in Johannesburg and will be rapporteur of the 8th IASFM in January 2003.

SANJA ŠPOLJAR VRŽINA is a Senior Research Associate at the Institute for Anthropological Research (Zagreb, Croatia) and Associate Professor of Anthropology at the University of Zagreb. Recently she has undertaken the position of Secretary-General to the Commission on Medical Anthropology and Epidemiology of the International Union of Anthropological and Ethnological Sciences (IUAES) of UNESCO.

LOES VAN WILLIGEN is a Refugee Health Care Consultant in The Netherlands. As a researcher she is involved in various ongoing studies on health issues of refugees and asylum-seekers in her country. Presently she is the President of the IASFM. She also is the Honorary President of the International Society for Health and Human Rights.

CONTRIBUTORS

JEAN ALLAIN is Assistant Professor of Public International Law, American University in Cairo, Egypt.

GEOFFREY CARE is chairman of the Immigration Appeal Tribunal in the United Kingdom. Until his retirement in 1996 he was the Deputy Chief Adjudicator and Acting Chief Adjudicator of the Immigration Appellate Authority. He is also President of the International Association of Refugee Law Judges.

SUPANG CHANTAVANICH, Director of the Institute of Asian Studies at Chulalongkorn University, Bangkok; former Director of the Asian Research Centre for Migration at the Institute of Asian Studies at Chulalongkorn University, Bangkok.

FRANÇOIS CRÉPEAU is Professor of International Law at the University of Montreal, Director of the Revue québécoise de droit international and Chair of the Program Committee for the Eighth Conference of the International Association for the Study of Forced Migration (January 2003, Chiang Mai, Thailand).

JEFF CRISP gained his doctorate in African Studies at the University of Birmingham, United Kingdom, and has worked for UNHCR since 1987. He is currently Head of the Evaluation and Policy Analysis Unit.

EDVARD HAUFF, MD, PhD, is Director of the Psychosocial Centre for Refugees and Professor of Psychiatry at the University of Oslo. He has for several years been involved in capacity building in mental health in low-income countries, especially in Asia. He is Chairperson of the Norwegian International Health Association, and Deputy Secretary General for the World Association for Psychosocial Rehabilitation (WAPR). He also has a part-time psychotherapy practice in Oslo.

GILBERT JAEGER retired from the position of Director of International Protection at UNHCR in 1979. He had been with UNHCR for twenty-seven years. He remains active on issues related to asylum and refugees, and has been chairman, president, and board member of Belgian, American, European, and international charities, societies, and NGOs.

KEMAL KIRIŞÇI is Professor at the Department of Political Science and International Relations at Bogazici University, Istanbul and holds the Jean Monnet Chair in European Integration. He has published widely on Middle Eastern politics, ethnic conflicts, and refugee movements and international migration.

MORTEN KJAERUM is Director of the Danish Human Rights Centre, Copenhagen. He has published widely in Danish and international journals on human rights in general and refugee law in particular. He has participated in Danish official delegations to the UN Human Rights Commission, OSCE, and other international forums.

CARL LEVY is Senior Lecturer in European Politics at Goldsmith College, University of London. He has published widely on comparative European history and politics, and on policymaking and regulations within the EU.

JENNIFER MOORE is Professor of Law at the University of New Mexico School of Law, where she teaches in the international and immigration fields, including courses in Refugee Law and Comparative Human Rights.

COURTNEY MIREILLE O'CONNOR, International Jurist and Operations Policy Advisor, Washington, D.C., provides advice and other services to institutions concerned with human rights and forced migrant protection, violence prevention, peace building, postconflict reconstruction, and gender.

GEORGE OKOTH-OBBO is the Deputy Director of the UNHCR Regional Directorate for southern Africa in Pretoria, South Africa.

ANNEMIEKE RICHTERS is physician and medical anthropologist. She works as a professor in culture, health, and illness at Leiden University Medical Centre, Leiden, The Netherlands.

SUMIT SEN is a consultant in international development. He was previously the Liaison Officer and Head of Office of the UNHCR in Chennai, India. As a Rhodes Scholar in International Law at the London School of Economics, he has written a PhD thesis entitled "International Refugee Law in South Asia," which is in the process of being published.

DALLAL STEVENS is a Lecturer in the School of Law at the University of Warwick, Coventry, United Kingdom. In addition to teaching a course on refugee law and policy at Warwick, she has published widely in the field of refugee and asylum law. She is convener of the Immigration/Refugee Law section of the Society of Legal Scholars (United Kingdom), and is a Trustee to the Immigration Advisory Service.

EFTIHIA VOUTIRA is an Associate Professor in the Anthropology of Forced Migration at the Department of Balkan, Slavic, and Oriental Studies, University of Macedonia, Thessaloniki, Greece, and a Research Associate at the School of Geography, University of Oxford. She is one of the founding members of IASFM.